Teacher-Student Relationships

Crossing into the Emotional, Physical, and Sexual Realms

Ernest J. Zarra III

ROWMAN & LITTLEFIELD EDUCATION
A division of
ROWMAN & LITTLEFIELD PUBLISHERS, INC.
Lanham • New York • Toronto • Plymouth, UK

10/17/14
GB
$27.95

Published by Rowman & Littlefield Education
A division of Rowman & Littlefield Publishers, Inc.
A wholly owned subsidiary of The Rowman & Littlefield Publishing Group, Inc.
4501 Forbes Boulevard, Suite 200, Lanham, Maryland 20706
www.rowman.com

10 Thornbury Road, Plymouth PL6 7PP, United Kingdom

British Library Cataloguing in Publication Information Available

Library of Congress Cataloging-in-Publication Data Available

ISBN 978-1-4758-0236-8 (cloth : alk. paper)—ISBN 978-1-4758-0237-5 (pbk. : alk. paper)—ISBN 978-1-4758-0238-2(electronic)

∞ ™ The paper used in this publication meets the minimum requirements of American National Standard for Information Sciences Permanence of Paper for Printed Library Materials, ANSI/NISO Z39.48-1992.

Printed in the United States of America

To Ernest J. Zarra Jr., my father, the man who demonstrated an unconditional love for his only son

Contents

Figures

Tables

Preface

Throughout the last few decades, there has been a clear and gradual slippage in our nation. This slippage has touched every corner of our society, and few people can say they are unaffected. As with every younger generation of Americans, teenagers are paying little attention to the culture around them. Assembling thousands of teenagers in one location reveals most of the evidence needed to bolster the premise: Today's teenagers are more brazen and bold about sex.

Families, schools, athletics, politics, ministry, and even our military have not escaped this decline in morality. Specifically, attitudes and behaviors have changed significantly in the area of sexuality, and behaviors once deemed off-limits are now emerging as mainstream. Moreover, one particular area where these attitudes and behaviors have changed dramatically is teacher-student relationships.

The cultural shift has blurred lines of authority for the sake of conquest and expediency. There seems less reluctance to start and nurture intimate physical and sexual relationships between teachers and students than any other time in my life. It has been said that what happens in culture always shows up in schools, whether these schools are public or private. This statement is true, and the evidence is overwhelming. Our culture is sex-crazy. Teacher-student sexual relationships have not escaped this craze.

THE REASONS FOR WRITING THIS BOOK

My reasons for writing this book are threefold. First, I hope to begin a national dialogue among administrators, teachers, and communities to explore the reasons why there is an epidemic of teachers and teenage students having sex. The problems need to be brought out into the open and discussed so that something can be done. This topic needs to be taken seriously in all colleges, professional-development meetings, and even town-hall meetings. Certainly, all district and school administrator–parent meetings should address these concerns in schools where teenagers attend.

Many new teachers are not informed as to the nature and characteristics of appropriate and inappropriate relationships with teenage students. However, age proximities are no longer taboo. Teacher-student relationships are not discussed in credential or methods classes. Therefore, I recommend this book to university professors who train teachers and to those students who might have an interest in education as a profession. I also recommend this book to parents and teenagers. Teenagers dialoguing with parents and other trusted stakeholders is a good thing for society.

The second reason I wrote this book is in reaction to the frustration I felt, reading nearly every day that more teachers are arrested for sex crimes against teenage students. All I could think about are the faces of my students and the faces of my own children. My thinking that such stories were media-hyped changed quickly once I began delving into them more deeply.

I found some of these incidents were happening right under my nose—and could have been prevented. However, because they had been personnel issues, as the incidents unfolded the community had been kept at a distance. Therefore, I thought to myself, there have to be suggestions and solutions that can be implemented to save students, families, and teachers from bad choices, arrests, convictions, and eventual devastation accompanying these choices.

The third reason for writing this book is that I love the teaching profession. Teachers and students, as well as families, need information from someone who works with their teenagers in the trenches every day. Working together for the protection of our nations' teenagers is paramount during this age of sexual openness. Like the reader, I am repulsed by the mere thought that trusted educators would somehow consider my own children as sexual conquests. Every teenager is someone's child.

HEIGHTENED AWARENESS

In nearly all fifty states, teachers have been arrested and convicted for sexual crimes with teenagers. Society needs to be aware that teachers and students are connecting emotionally, spending time with each other in private, and developing physical and sexual relationships. We cannot turn a blind eye to this, for the problems associated with such experiences for teenagers project problems into the future for their relationships and may affect their own families and professions for a long time.

This book makes everyone aware of the issue of teacher-student relationships. It does so by focusing down on the question, Why are so many school teachers, administrators, and coaches choosing to become emotionally, physically, and sexually involved with teenage students? In engaging in these illicit relationships, these same adults give up an entire lifetime of achievement, their families, professions, and fortunes for sex with teenagers. My book goes into this in detail and explains how these relationships develop and how they can be avoided in the first place.

My own personal awareness of the issues addressed in the book broadened over the course of nearly three years, as I spent time collecting and analyzing data. I was also fortunate to communicate with colleagues across the nation, electronically and personally. There is a danger associated with writing a book about teacher-student sexual experiences. However, it is not my intention to celebrate stories about sex between teachers and students.

The reader must understand that I examined thousands of accounts of illicit teacher-student relationships, many of which would sicken the average person. I find it necessary to include some of these stories to demonstrate how serious the problem is in schools. The irony is that many of the teachers arrested for sex crimes with their teenage students were presumed average persons.

I stand amazed at how many adults were victimized as teenage students and yet did not report the abuse. The more I speak with people about this book, the more stories I hear. Most are relieved that someone is finally tackling the issue. The accounts contained within the pages of this book will assist in better understanding the various ways relationships develop between teachers and students, as well as the role technology plays in all of these relationships. School leaders will find these accounts especially helpful, as will district administrators and teachers-in-training. I hold back in neither suggestions nor criticisms.

INSPIRATION FOR THE BOOK

This book came about as the result of a lifetime of personal and professional relationships with my students and their families. There is nothing quite like standing in front of thousands of teenagers, over the course of a career, and watching their expressions as I relate my personal and intimate life story with them. These days I cannot help but ask myself how many of these braced, acne-filled, and perfumed teenagers were sexually active with a teacher or coach.

There is nothing quite like the combination of the teenage brain and the teenage heart, working in tandem. There is nothing quite like an appropriate emotional connection with a classroom full of teenagers either, whether through academics or personal illustrations and anecdotes. We are all human, after all.

The truth is, without students I am not a teacher. Every year, my students continue to inspire me. They inspire me to perform better as a teacher, and they drive me to excel. They inspire me as a person. I owe much to parents who trusted—and continue to trust me—with their teenagers. Furthermore, I would not be the person I am were it not for my loving and supportive family and the excellent colleagues and educational professionals who have surrounded me and helped me along in my profession.

STRUCTURE OF THE BOOK

This book is structured in such a way to keep the reader engaged. The chapter sequencing is purposeful and flows thematically. The chapters are informative and provocative as well as user-friendly. To this end, each chapter is written so that it may be taken together with other chapters as a whole or as a stand-alone lecture to a class or for a class group activity. To accomplish the latter, questions are provided for extending discussion and to encourage the reader to review and apply the material presented.

Chapter 1 focuses on differences between several generations and how changes in technology have redefined today's teenage culture. I also address how technology has affected the nature of relationships between generations and subsequent behaviors, and practices.

Next, in chapter 2 I discuss how technological advancements impact our culture and have introduced significant temptations and choices that are particularly problematic for teenagers, though not exclusive to them. These temptations are geared for the teenage brain and play to the emotional centers of the brain; and so in chapter 3 we explore the chemical composition and working of the teenage brain, teenage maturity, and teenage emotions. There is some question as to whether boys and girls are reaching physical puberty more quickly today. If that is the case, what are the implications for their brains and their bodies, which are as yet emotionally and behaviorally unaligned?

Chapter 4 introduces our next area of study, and we begin by digging deeply into the actual relationships that develop between teachers and teenage students, both appropriate and inappropriate. Here I challenge teachers to examine their roles as instructors and mentors, including their proximity to the students with whose care they are entrusted. And this proximity between teachers and teenage students can be confused with the advent of social networking and communication through the digital realm, so we'll explore it in detail in chapter 5. We ask teachers, How social is too social, both with your students and their parents? There is a balance between social relationships and social capital, which we examine at length.

The extent to which a school perpetuates the status quo indicates much about its culture. The types of relationships between teachers and students are part of a school's culture. Teachers relate to students during the school day and after it ends. With this in mind, chapter 6 examines time frames, and teachers are challenged to reflect on any time spent with students, identifying some of the red flags that may pop up throughout the teaching day.

Schools can do a better job training their focus on morality, purpose, and sense of mission. They can also do a better job approaching at-school and after-school teacher-student relationships with common sense. With these in mind, in chapter 7 I suggest a thorough reform of the teacher-candidate interview process, offering my rationale for this paradigm shift. As states begin reforming professional codes of conduct, they struggle to balance teacher rights with student safety, which is made only more difficult by the explosion of communication technologies. And in the mean time, some teachers and teenage students are drawing closer and closer each day.

Technology has become a boon to today's sexual predators. In chapter 8, we examine their tools and tactics, as I make the case that students are not teachers' soul mates. I challenge teachers with a series of questions about and consequences for their choices. And in the course of this chapter I help schools better understand why sexual predators might now exist on their campuses. And we even explore the notion of a teenage sexual predator—a new phenomenon within our culture. And finally, I help schools figure out how to put in place strategies that stop illicit teacher-student relationships even before they start.

Acknowledgments

A book about relationships between teachers and students would lack serious credibility if it did not acknowledge the educators who have touched the author's life. I owe a tremendous debt of gratitude for the teachers and professors who have graced the pathway of my life. There are so many who have made an impact on me both personally and professionally and helped shape my career. One in particular, Dr. Kevin Ryan, a mentor and friend, remains significantly instrumental in continuing to draw attention to the need for character and moral education in schools.

Dr. Tom Lickona is another mentor, one whom I respect deeply for his work in psychology and character education. His passion for teachers and students is contagious. A third person whose work has impacted my life is Eric Jensen, an expert on brain development. His books have been in my classrooms for years. Together, these experts helped shape my own ideas into blogs, articles, social-media posts, and now this book.

I acknowledge both Stanford University and my alma mater, the University of Southern California, for their fine work in education and conferences, particularly their conferences on learning and the brain. Their innovative research, along with journal articles from various disciplines, is an educator's delight—particularly essential when writing about teenagers and their brain development and emotions.

California State University–Bakersfield has been my testing ground for many of the ideas found in this book. I am grateful to Dr. Jacqueline Hughes for her collegiality and friendship these past thirteen years. My university students continue to show that the next generation of teachers is going to be something special.

My family has been a constant source of positive inspiration and motivation. My lovely wife of thirty-six years endures much when the writer's urge surfaces. Yet, through it all, she is my emotional and spiritual support.

Last, and certainly not least, I must acknowledge my colleagues for their genuine excitement over my work. I am humbled at their excellence and acceptance every day. I celebrate the many ways they understand the roles and applications of appropriate relationships with teenagers.

ONE

Boundaries and Barriers to Teacher-Student Relationships

The old gray mare
She ain't what she used to be
Ain't what she used to be
Ain't what she used to be
The old gray mare
She ain't what she used to be
Many long years ago
—Anonymous

AT A GLANCE

The nine major sections in this chapter include (1) the natural course, (2) do teenagers care?, (3) boundaries and barriers, (4) previous generations, (5) a changing culture, (6) disintegration of manners and behaviors, (7) media extremes, (8) developing trust, and (9) crossing over. We close with a chapter summary and discussion questions.

THE NATURAL COURSE

Somewhere around ages twelve or thirteen, something occurs in children. One day what we have been told and even warned about begins to become reality. Children become adolescents—teenagers—marking a universal passage and youthful march toward adulthood. It is the natural course of life.

When children become teenagers, their worldview is naturally myopic. Essentially, to teenagers, the world is all about them. What transpires

1

within their spheres of influence and affection often impact them deeply. Adults perceive this teenage "self-absorption" and conclude that, to teenagers, nothing else in the world matters than their friends and themselves.

In addition to being labeled self-absorbed, teenagers' actions often appear disjointed from their thoughts, which leads to relational conflicts and may generate additional challenges. These challenges then reinforce the stereotypes held about teenagers, as boundaries are created between them and the adults in their lives. Adults must remember that this cycle of self-absorption, misunderstanding, and isolation is part of the natural course of development for most teenagers.

Consider the average adult today trying to win the attention of the average teenager (my parents' generation handled youth *so* differently): Many adults have tried to communicate with teenagers whose ears are stopped up with earphones and earbuds and whatever other music-listening devices. It can be quite frustrating. And so often, when asked a question, the predictable teenage response is a grunt, or perhaps the adult is summarily rebuffed by a gesture.

Today, communicating with teenagers aged eighteen and above—whom sociologists call *the Millennial Generation*—is both expedited and challenged because of technology. And people who do not know a time before cell phones and computers have been given the nickname *Generation Z*. Communication for today's youth is vastly different. This group was born in 1990 and graduated from high school in 2008. "As young teenagers, they were chauffeured from activity to activity . . . while plugged in to the Internet through handheld devices. Even stuck at home they were still totally 'connected' to their peer ecosystem through social media. With parents, teachers, and counselors focused on keeping them safe and scheduled, they have nonetheless been privy to unprecedented information from a painfully young age."[1]

Add Gen Z's technology to age-related issues, natural boundaries, and cultural stereotypes, and average adults think that having significant relationships with teenagers is a lot of work. Nevertheless, this is not always the case, as we shall see. Generations of the past had exclusive technologies, to be sure. However, no one carried around a television or a stereo. The closest thing was a boom box in the 1980s, and that phenomenon quickly fizzled. It was highly impractical. What is both unique and highly interesting about teenagers is that they set specific boundaries with their use of "cultural toys." Developing a healthy and significant relationship with a teenager is accomplished today through an appreciation and understanding of the place technology occupies in their lives—a challenge we must accept.

DO TEENAGERS CARE?

Apathy is defined as "absence or suppression of passion, emotion, or excitement."[2] This lack of passion is accompanied by a "lack of interest in or concern for things that others find moving or exciting."[3] Adults sometimes have difficult times distinguishing between a teenager's willful choice and a biological state. On any given day, a teenager could be completely bored out of her mind. But once something relevant to her culture catches her attention, her brain signals to her that it is time to show some excitement and passion.

An old American anecdote involves a veteran scientist who experimented with a frog. In his first experiment, the scientist wanted to see how the frog would react to changes in water temperatures. To begin his experiment, the curious scientist placed a frog in a deep pot, filled with tap water. He then recorded the frog's movements in the tap water.

Next, the scientist placed the pot on a stove and turned the flame to a low setting. He measured the temperature of the water again and recorded the actions of the frog as the water temperature gradually increased. The frog appeared to move about the water in rapid fashion. Within minutes, the frog's motions slowed and the water was too hot for the frog to survive. The frog eventually died.

The specimen's insides were literally cooked. This result caught the scientist by surprise, for one reason. Surely, he thought, the frog would have tried to save itself before being overcome by the temperature. However, that was not the case. The scientist was surprised the frog made no effort to leap from the pot. In fact, the scientist concluded the frog died because it had become accustomed to the rising temperatures in its gradually changing environment.

The scientist learned two lessons learned from this experimentation: (1) He was not aware what was going on inside the frog while the temperatures were increasing and (2) the frog did not discern the changing environment into which it was placed until it had reached dangerous levels and was then too late.

If we substitute another authority in place of the scientist, the relevance of the message takes on added meaning. Adults are watching teenagers adjust to changes in America. Teenagers' environments affect many of their choices about much of life, including the relationships they develop. Teenagers do not come packaged with the wisdom to comprehend what is good for them. Consequently, many are not ready to deal with the forward thinking necessary to coming to terms with the possibilities of their life-changing choices—especially if emotions and social interactions are in play. Teenagers have apathy toward adult advice while being conflicted by a culture that is full of adult-like pleasures—and their impulses.

BOUNDARIES AND BARRIERS

The following sections in this chapter provide insights into particulars that separate teenagers and their peers from the adults in their lives. I refer to these particulars as *natural boundaries* and *created boundaries*. These two boundary types have direct bearing on the development of relationships with teenagers and are present in and through most of their relationships during the adolescent years. Adults who understand this will find it much easier to come to terms with teenagers' seeming changeability.

There are natural boundaries, and there are created boundaries. Generally, *natural boundaries* occur by virtue of differences in current culture, from generation to generation, age, gender, or some other naturally related occurrence, normally outside of a person's choices. Whereas natural boundaries are not products of one's choice, *created boundaries* are chosen and result in clear, overt separation between adults and teenagers. Examples of created boundaries include education and degrees, athletics, wealth, upbringing, certain virtues, and notoriety. For purposes of this chapter, a *boundary* is defined as *something that limits, draws clear distinctions particular to a generation, a person, relationships, employment, leisure, or other areas of life.*

Boundaries usually affect relationships and communication. For example, if a science teacher instructs from notes assembled in the 1970s, a natural boundary is erected between student and teacher because of the teacher's age. However, along with the age factor is the concern with the curriculum. The "older" curriculum may be a boundary that acts more like a barrier to the learning of the student, which, in turn, may adversely affect a meaningful relationship between teacher and student.

If this same teacher went back for an advanced degree in modern science, then his newer education and information become created boundaries. Boundaries are good things and are essential in education and in families. Boundaries between people are the relationship lines that designate what is appropriate and what is not. These may also be called *moral boundaries*. The two types of boundaries are illustrated in figures 1.1 and 1.2.

Age, or aging, is a natural boundary between people and is beyond anyone's control. By virtue of age, a natural line of separation results between generations. It is no easy task to ask one generation to step outside itself to fall into alignment with another generation. However, this is precisely what teenagers sense happening to them. Those teachers, regardless of age, who find ways to reach across one or both boundaries are those whom the students define as "cool." The cool teachers are in touch with teenage culture, thereby finding acceptance by the teenagers. In this sense, age is irrelevant.

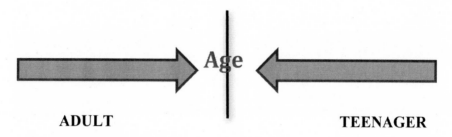

ADULT   **TEENAGER**

Figure 1.1. Natural Boundary

Teachers, who often set and reach many goals in their own lives, are often natural heroes to students. Heroes can transcend boundaries and find acceptance. However, once inside the teen's boundary, the adult has great responsibility. How will teenagers discover how to be healthy adults unless they are shown the process of maturing through appropriate expressions of mature mentors?

PREVIOUS GENERATIONS

Not all parents of today's high school students were born during the baby boom. In fact, most of the parents of my students were born in the 1970s. Therefore, for them the *baby boom* is a historical term. That being said, nearly 60 percent of adults alive today were born during the baby boom—which makes them and me part of the majority age-group demographic.

Baby boomers, born anywhere from 1946 to 1964, can recall a time when culture had clearer lines of authority and boundaries between homes and schools were more clearly defined. In fact, there are distinct memories of authority figures assumed in parents, teachers, coaches, politicians, pastors, and community leaders. When teenagers got into trouble at school, they also found there were consequences at home. Respect for others was drilled into our daily lives, and we were corrected when we forgot to say *please* or *thank you*.

World War II and the Korean War are actual event memories in the minds of many older adults. For some, it was their reality. For others, like me, the wars were recent history. A great number of baby boomers hail veterans as heroes, while celebrating the lives of those labeled by some historians and the media as the greatest generation of Americans.[4] Many of these people today simply refer to life then in the United States as "the good old days." Teenagers do not understand compulsory military service, because it was shelved in the early 1970s. They register for the draft, but there is none. The concept of having to do things for authorities is more of an annoyance to today's youth. Many teenagers of today would

TEACHER CONTENT   **TEACHER CONTENT**

Figure 1.2.   Created Boundary

rather find victory over tyranny through months of near addiction to video gaming and LAN parties than by donning a uniform and taking up arms. Expelling dictators is now accomplished from sofas and bedrooms, on virtual battlefields.[5]

Unidirectional Communications

Every generation seems to have one or more pieces of new technology available to it. Cultural fads come and go. Transistor radios, televisions, record players, telephones, blow dryers, and even automobiles were all introduced as fads. These fads, and others, were billed as options to make our lives easier. And many of these things, which were initially seen as desired luxuries, have come to be viewed as needs. This want-to-need progression continues today.

Now consider communication technologies. The vast numbers of communication-oriented inventions of the past were unidirectional. That is, the technology allowed one-way communication from "them" to us. With few exceptions, like the landline telephone, communication with others was limited. The unidirectional paradigm also pertained to face-to-face verbal communication from parents to youth. Some readers might smile as they remember the family phone and its location in the home or maybe even chuckle remembering the party lines used in many neighborhoods. (FOR THE YOUNGER READER: Ask a baby boomer about party lines.)

Multidirectional Communications

Americans are the inventing sort. Over the course of just a few decades between the late twentieth and early twenty-first centuries, a myriad of changes occurred in technology. These changes gave rise to a new horizon. Communications became multidirectional and instantaneous.

Thanks to nineteenth-century inventors from Alexander Graham Bell to Bill Gates and Carlos Helu—as well as the late Steve Jobs—the world is remarkably connected like never before. Add satellites, the digital world, microwaves, laser technologies, social-media sites—such as Facebook, Google, Yahoo!, and America Online—and billions of people have the capacity, literally, to be connected to one another in seconds. But with every up side to new technologies, there are down sides to consider: not everyone with access to these newer modes of communication will use them in healthy and appropriate ways or use them for the purposes for which they were intended.

Technology brings with it many choices. The ways in which these choices play out, and how the new medium is incorporated into culture, informs society as a whole.

Communication technologies have enabled relationships to be formed in ways that are a natural fit for teenage brains and their emotional impulses. Advertisers and marketers understand this quite well. Companies create applications for cell phones to capture impulses. Each company forms a type of digital communication in an effort to create an ongoing relationship with the app user. However, businesses are not alone in understanding teenagers and their technology.

Purveyors of sex understand this medium as well. This is one of the downsides to the new digital-communications paradigm. Those who encourage inappropriate relationships with our teenagers are also aware of the technological possibilities that can be exploited. There is an old adage that *impulsivity and temptation have the same parent.* Certainly, one would be hard-pressed to find a more visible nexus of impulsivity and temptation than in some teenagers.

The Good Old Days

Once upon a time, a person's reputation and family name were tantamount. Words and actions that reflected poorly on either were not acceptable. Life was much more about family and less about the individual. As many parents would still agree today, "You have to watch what you do and say, because people are always observing you." Along with neighborly omniscience, or gossip, came the reality of the larger community finding out much about our lives. News traveled quickly by word of mouth and by telephone. (And it travels even faster today, for obvious reasons.)

When we were disciplined back then, most people heard about it. In fact, sometimes our teachers were our literal neighbors, which added new meaning to the term *family accountability.* I will never forget the day I saw my father speaking with my social studies teacher, who lived one block from our house. I was never told what was discussed, which is another hallmark of the baby boomers: *not everything that happened in a family was open to conversation and corporate opinion.*

As teenagers, we took risks at our own peril—and often paid the price. Teenagers are no different today, in that there is a certain precociousness and notion of immortality among many of them, despite the risks inherent in their actions. Many teenagers just appear more physically mature today than they did not so long ago. However, emotional maturity is a different story and is sometimes masked by cultural assumptions, applied to physically mature outward appearances.

Today's teenagers do not really properly fathom self-discipline, and technology has something to do with this. Many of them hear the word *discipline* and draw negative conclusions. When a previous generation, back in the good old days, decided to challenge the status quo, it found that being grounded and sent to one's room meant having little or nothing to do. There were consequences for actions. For example, not once were my friends allowed to get away with using swear words at home. Today, the "f-bomb" is fast becoming a common adjective.

As with most memories, the passing years remove the edge off feelings—especially negative feelings—associated with original experiences. Memories are often not accurate records of what occurred exactly. Overall, our parents did the best they could to instill proper boundaries between youth and adults, and one way they succeeded was through applying consequences for improper actions.

Sensory Overload

Today's music and lyrics are so very different from the days of Elvis's pelvis gyrations and from the drug-laced music of Hendrix, Grateful Dead, The Who, and many others. Today, experimentation has gone wild. It does not take long for a parent to discover that many unwholesome things are glorified and celebrated in their teenager's entertainment.

Most teenagers seem desensitized to the abuse of women, descriptions of sexual acts, and blatant pornography. The average teenage entertainment diet consists of sensory overload and heightened emotionality. Teenagers whose minds and bodies are always on the go are less apt to make good decisions in the midst of their excitement. Parents are correct about many things, including the admonishment to "Be careful what you put into your brain, because it is going to come out eventually."

Do parents really want their young people filling their minds with abusive talk about women, preached especially by today's rappers? Luke 6:31–32a has changed in its application. "And just as you want men to treat you, treat them in the same way. And if you love those who love you, what credit is that to you?"[6] Today's interpretation of this passage reads more like "Do unto others before they do unto you." It all comes down to an ethic that centers on self. It is the ethic of "Do as I please," and it is spreading among youth like wildfire.

Now, perhaps I'm mistaken, but the general sense and sentiment among today's teenage students seems to be that personal self-esteem is held in higher esteem than the feelings of others. This may very well be the result of years of meandering through the "self-esteem movement."

Self-gain is given more weight than helping others, unless the helper gets something out of it. In the "good old days," moral lines were formed by life at home with both parents and reinforced largely by values reinforced on television and in the media. Schools supported these values.

Persons who can relate to teenagers, establish boundaries, and develop appropriate relationships are people who actually understand the grander scheme of things. A person who still practices the Golden Rule is one to be admired. Conversely, it is disheartening to confront the news stories about teachers who somehow forgot these natural boundaries and compromised their profession, their morality, and the lives of students with which they were entrusted.

Memories Transcend Generations

The words "When I was your age . . ." transcend generations. The phrase also generates predictable eye rolls from our youth. Teachers use this phrase; parents use it; so do grandparents. Teenagers of all generations despise those words. And yet parents intentionally use them. For this is not only a powerful phrase, aimed at transcending modern culture, but it also implies that longevity of a generation is of great value.

Today's grounded teenagers are sent to bedrooms full of technology and communication devices, so that they can vent with their friends, find empathy with strangers, post nasty and profane statements on social networks about how bad life is for them. Each new generation believes it has a handle on life and that no previous generation can truly understand what the current generation is going through.

Through all of the difficulties faced by our predecessors, the vast majority of them somehow made it into adulthood and became productive. One family member remarked to me that in the post-Depression era "everyone lived similarly, so no one knew what was out of the norm; we were all poor in those days, but few of us knew we were, and even fewer seemed to care. We were far too busy trying to find work and worrying about putting food on the table every day."

It has been said that we can always go back to our youth, but we can't stay! Recently, when visiting many of the neighborhoods of my youth, something interesting happened: Seeing my old house brought back many memories and experiences that together had comprised my youth. It is true that the enormity of the past is perceived differently in the context of the present (which we'll explore in chapter 3).

Today, many students rely on teachers and coaches as their sole memory-making authority figures. Some families today are not traditional and might even be absent a parent. What today's teenagers will one day remember can be affected by the context in which they are living. Therefore, placing trust in those who help make those memories is a serious issue with serious implications for all involved.

Memories are often associated with some very deep emotions that mellow over the years. For example, all of the struggles of one's teenage years, the discipline meted out by fathers, and the hassles caused for mothers, mostly fade into warm memories, and this warm feeling is quite real, to this day. The arguments and the anger that resulted in my discipline and grounding somehow do not seem that atrocious anymore.

Memories have a way of flooding back. This happened to me when my father fell terminally ill. And today his words still ring in my soul. After his passing, I took Dad's remains to the top of the highest mountain in the lower forty-eight and scattered them to the wind. At the top of Mt. Whitney, my relationship with my dad took on new meaning—the kind that surpasses generations. My dad not only instructed me in life, but he continues to inspire me, even after his death. There were stark differences between our generations, but on that day, on that mountaintop, my dad and I were one. In many ways, memories are the results of boundaries of generations and serve as points of intersection of souls! These memories represent the good old days.

Respect

My generation was taught to respect property, to respect one's neighbors as oneself, and to stand up for oneself when wronged. However, standing up to any of the *authorities* of the day would have led to serious consequences. Disrespect of authority was a boundary not to be crossed.

A significant number of Americans today are from the baby-boom generation. According to the Pew Research Center, "On January 1, 2011, the oldest baby boomers . . . turn[ed] sixty-five. Every day for the next nineteen years, about ten thousand more will cross that threshold. By 2030, when all baby boomers will have turned sixty-five, fully 18 percent of the nation's population will be at least that age."[7] There are stark differences between members of the baby-boom generation and the current tech-oriented teenage generation. One of these differences rests in the attitude toward the nation. On holidays, many communities turned out to honor people who sacrificed for America. In the past, parades honoring them were the norm. However, this is not so much the case today. Individual pursuits and self-oriented success is replacing community success. Youth today would rather gain instant notoriety from friends online than wait for an honor to be bestowed by an authority figure some time in the indeterminate future.

When I was young, we were free to publically say a prayer of protection and blessing for the community and nation. Relationships were not *Fifty Shades of Grey*, and sexuality was something to be held as modest and special, and usually reserved for marriage. Teachers reinforced the values of our homes. However, all of this is rapidly changing.

A CHANGING CULTURE

Culture has changed so very much over these past few decades. Today 83 percent of those millennials between eighteen and twenty-nine years of age state that they sleep with their cell phones turned on, and 75 percent of them believe that prior generations had a better work ethic.[8] According to Pew Social Trends, there is less of a generation gap today between millennials and their elders than there existed between the elders and youngsters of the 1960s and1970s.[9] Adults aim at holding onto youth for as long as possible.

One of the more unfortunate things about a young adult in today's America is that he usually respects himself much more highly than he respects others. This is closely related to the fact that we live in a highly litigious society: Courts are full of individuals and small groups seeking to force their way against the majority opinions of culture. Individual freedoms are celebrated in the media to the detriment of the majority. Things are less united by a common good than they are divided by self-interest. One wonders what Alexis de Tocqueville would write about "democracy in America" today.

The fact that we are celebrating the individual's rights over the group appeals to today's teenagers. Culture is shifting from respect of the American ways of the past to a newer understanding of what it means for the individual to be American. This cultural shift sends a mixed message for all Americans, and it reinforces the notions of those seeking their own adult brand of self-expression.

The majority of teachers during the 1960s and 1970s held students' feet to the fire. There was one certainty about classrooms of a few decades ago: Discipline was not absent from the classroom, and most parents believed the teacher's word over that of the students. The same respect was accorded coaches and administrators. Today, distrust is the default position.

Experimentation and Distrust

Decades ago, teenagers were expected to show respect for others, because it was the right thing to do. Then the late 1960s came along, and the media began to report on the excesses of professors and the experimentations of social radicals. America was told by Jerry Rubin at the 1968 Democratic Convention, when he was arrested for nominating a pig for president, to "trust no one over thirty."[10] Harvard professor Timothy Leary proclaimed that young people should "turn on, tune in, and drop out." Leary's book of the same name was originally published as *Politics of Ecstasy*.[11]

Today, children are allowed to act in a boorish, self-centered fashion. In school we hardly hold them accountable for their actions. Generally, when a problem arises in school, parents are very defensive and believe their children's accounts first, over those in authority. Teachers are often blamed for the poor education their children receive. Years ago, children came to school with prerequisite knowledge that offered a much greater chance of success. Today's parents generally believe the government should educate their kids—after all, why do schools exist anyway?

As an educator I am reminded constantly that each year becomes the "good old days" for yet another generation. As we did in my day, students challenge the "good" of the past with their current practices and behaviors. As time goes by, ever-greater edgy teenage behavior finds its way into the classroom. Wondering what is filling my teenage students' minds outside of school—and wondering how susceptible they have become to things once deemed off-limits—occupies a lot of my thought.

Filling Minds

Many adults can recall talks their fathers gave them about the "things" being placed into their minds. Fathers of old were more concerned about entertainment and externals, such as what hair looked like, the person I was becoming. As a youth, I felt that music and hair were more important personal identity issues and that this personification proved that issues about the family were less important than my own.

Baby boomers raised their families "to be seen and not heard." Object lessons were regularly made. In fact, I remember one conversation with my father: He had caught on to the fact that I was into listening to Led Zeppelin and had become increasingly uncomfortable with my shoulder-length hair. To him, I was either a hippie or a girl, and he made it clear he wasn't sure which. Here is an example of a typical conversation between a baby boomer and his father:

DAD: Come here, son. You have to be careful what you fill your mind with and how you look.

ME: Why, dad?

DAD: Because it's not good for you. That's why.

ME: Yeah, but why? Didn't you and mom do things when you were teenagers?

DAD: Look, I am not going to sit here and explain this to you all night. That's just the way it is.

ME: Huh? That's not fair.

DAD: In my house and under my roof you will do things my way. Is that clear, young man?

ME: I know, I know.

DAD: Don't get smart with me, young man.

ME: I'm not.

DAD: Don't backtalk me.

ME: But—

DAD: Go to your room, and stay there until I tell you to come out. But before you go, change the channel.

Parents are not perfect, and maybe "the good old days" weren't quite as good as our memories of them. That said, the baby-boomer generation has much to celebrate. Boomers have contributed so very much to the American way of life. In fact, boomers paved the way for the very things teenagers possess today. And, as ever, today's teenagers want their "stuff," with little appreciation for what it costs to get it, which is the point at which distinct generations lock horns.

Competing Philosophies

Today objects are afforded status once reserved for people. Building social capital between people and groups varies today. These differences are captured in Robert Putnam's meta-analysis of previous and current cultures in his book *Bowling Alone*.[12]

Today's Americans are less involved in civic organizations and community efforts than they once were. However, what it means to be involved has been fairly radically altered with the advent of communication technologies and the ease with which people can now access organizations at national and international levels. Today's philosophy of involvement is quite different from what it was just a decade ago.

Putnam warns that "the very fabric of our connections with each other has plummeted, impoverishing our lives and communities. . . .We're even bowling alone. More Americans are bowling than ever before, but they are not bowling in leagues."[13] Age, suburban life, television, computers, women's roles, and other factors have contributed to this decline. And today's teenagers are becoming captives to themselves.

It's Just Stuff!

We live in a time when so many particulars—including human life—have become someone's legal property. Consider the laws regarding abortion, the arguments surrounding embryonic stem-cell experimentation and usage, the patenting of gene therapies by research companies, and so on. We even see this litigiousness at schools, where people are protective of their grades, their standardized-test scores, and their admission into prestigious universities.

Possessions and attainment have quickly become our identities and our definitions. Take this with the increasing debasement of human life and personhood in underground and illegal subcultures, and even in some areas of science, and we see that life itself has been reduced and commodified, to the extent that our status is little more than a thing.

Child sex trafficking is rampant internationally, and women and men openly sell themselves on the Internet. People smuggling drugs across our borders are described as pack mules. More money can be made illegally than legally. A former student once used to brag about his family members' drug deals and the "boatload" of money that he saw whenever he visited them. He stated boldly that he did not want to work for mere minimum wage when he could be rich. Then, one day, his family members were attacked, and his uncle was murdered. This young student of mine quickly and painfully changed his opinions and began more carefully weighing life versus wealth.

Over time people are desensitized to new ideas—ones that may have even been considered an assault on the culture of the recent past—and eventually adopt them. Today we live in the midst of a disintegrating culture, and this culture is enjoining and ensnaring both teachers and students in American schools.

DISINTEGRATION OF MANNERS AND BEHAVIORS

Ralph Waldo Emerson once wrote, "Good manners are made up of petty sacrifices." I think Emerson was onto something. What is sacrificed by not burping loudly in a restaurant? Who is the loser who allows someone to check out in front of us at the grocery store?

Assemble a large group of people together in one location, and sit back and watch the displays of manners. At times when my awareness is heightened, I ask myself, Are things really this bad? Are we, young and old, really this rude? Raucous behavior at youth and professional sporting events, noise levels and profanity in restaurants, and discourtesies on airplanes diminish us. And people behave this way because they do it for themselves—not others. And manners are lost, because, after all, manners are a matter of respect for others and their property.

We have all witnessed the screaming children, allowed to exercise their lungs in stores. Doors are closed in the faces of the elderly or infirm, and the use of profanity is on the rise. Pejoratives and curses are common adjectives, words of the week. Some parents adore the cuteness of their toddlers' profanity. But we have to recognize that the information and experiences fed to the brain will one day emerge in tandem as an auto-mated entity. The ways we respect and treat others have significant im-plications across all of our relationships, especially now that politeness is becoming a parliamentary dinosaur!

Beatriz Valenzuela, staff writer at the Victorville *Daily Press* in Victor-ville, California, speculated back in 2008 as to whether manners are dead today:

> Many great ideas and inventions arose from the 1960s. There was the artificial heart, the first video game, the height of the civil-rights move-ment, and the beginning of a lot of political change. Another result of the 1960s has been the decline of manners. . . . Prior to that, families ate together at the dinner table. Manners were reinforced all of the time. . . . Even the basics of common courtesy have been lost, according to some Victor Valley residents.[14]
>
> "You don't even hear please and thank you anymore," said Angela Cruz, forty-five, as she waited for her skinny latte from the Starbuck's inside Barnes and Noble. "And I'm not just talking about the kids, although they're another matter. I mean adults. They get in line in front of you, cut you off while driving, and offer nothing in the way of an apology. It's getting really bad." The concern over bad manners has reached such levels that the Web site EtiquetteHell.com gives people a place to document their run-ins with rude people. One woman was horrified by her mother's lack of manners when her mother nearly knocked over a waitress and refused to apologize, since the waitress didn't actually spill anything.[15]

Clearly, incivility isn't just a problem among young people. But where do we place the blame for this decline in manners? And how can we expect the younger generation to emulate good manners if there are no good manners to emulate? If adults do not model appropriate behaviors where will the youth learn what is appropriate decorum and public protocol?

MEDIA EXTREMES

Reality shows are ubiquitous on cable stations, where contestants are brazen about their sexuality and flaunt themselves in a clear celebration of self. Impulsivity comes off as omnipotence and is celebrated as a posi-tive trait. Virtues of the past such as humility, long-suffering patience, persistence, and dedication to morality have taken a backseat to indulgence and hedonism, sarcasm and profanity. And the implications this switch in mores has for schools and teachers are serious.

Schools bear some responsibility to make certain that values like respect and common courtesy are part of their school culture. In their attempts to modernize, schools ought not embrace all of the common elements of general culture. And yet schools are populated by individuals replacing the "old guard," with a heightened sense of self. And where individuals fail to self-police, enforcement of personal standards and codes of conduct are left to large entities, such as governments and bureaucracies. Standards and expectations can be set higher. If we think not, we seriously underestimate our teenagers. (See chapters 6 and 7 for more on this.)

Manners, just character, and morality are best taught when openness and calm exist. Ideally, they should be addressed at home; schools should not have to take sole responsibility for building their students' characters.[16] Schools are tone setters, culture shapers, and boundary definers. Education is one of the best tickets in town for a youth's success. According to celebrated education expert Robert Sylwester, the teenage brain functions well when instruction on behaviors and manners occurs. "Manners are not natural" to the teenager "and therefore must be taught" and modeled.[17] Teachers can assist in the practical development of manners by allowing students to work in groups and then debriefing them afterward. The same strategy that works in the classroom can also work around the dinner table at home—in what educators and parents call "teachable moments." Our culture needs more of these.

DEVELOPING TRUST

There are two basic forms of trust, and both are very important to our discussion. Teachers are usually granted high levels of *implicit trust* by younger students and their parents. Implicit trust, by my definition, is granted to another by virtue of position, authority, ability, education, levels of earned respect from the past, or character or title. Many children trust their parents in the same way as they trust their teachers; it comes with the territory and is often second nature. However, the rewards of this trust are fleeting with teenagers unless earned anew, on a consistent basis. When it comes to teenagers, yesterday's trust is not tomorrow's closer relationship. So those in authority over teenagers usually gain a natural trust for a short time, initially.[18]

Teenagers with teachers who have reputations for being tough, mean, or heavy on the discipline have high implicit trust granted them. However, this trust is probably born of fear. In a healthy relationship, someone has to commit serious actions or violate the integrity or confidence of another for implicit trust to completely collapse. It can be earned back, which leads to another form of trust.

A teacher or coach known to have issues with self-discipline or who is scattered or professionally disorganized or does not follow through on set rules and protocols will find difficulty in creating explicit trust. In the classroom or on the field, teachers must work very differently to gain the trust of students, athletes, and parents. *Explicit trust is earned trust.* Explicit trust is event-oriented, whereas implicit trust is granted the person because of attribute or authority.

A parent who promises time and again to show up at a child's event but time and again fails to do so, dashes the child's confident expectations and, eventually, trust. Trust either is wonderful human capital and sets the tone for appropriate relationships or else is a wedge and roadblock that must be overcome. Consider an example of trust violated.

A thirteen-year-old teenager had an older teenage uncle, whom he idolized. The teenager enjoyed spending time with this uncle. A very close bond developed between the two. When the uncle turned eighteen, he began drawing closer to his high school friends, and the relationship with his nephew grew more and more distant.

One day, the uncle contacted his nephew and promised to take him to a professional baseball game during that afternoon, along with a group of his older friends. This thrilled the nephew. He dressed, put on his baseball cap, and even made a sign to hold up during the game, and he waited for the uncle to arrive.

He waited. And he waited. One hour went by. Two hours went by. Eventually, the time for the first pitch came and went, and the nephew grew increasingly disappointed that he had not heard from the uncle. Despite persistent phone calls to the uncle's home, there were no answers.

The nephew phoned the uncle hours after the game had ended, and the uncle answered the phone, and said, "Oh, I forgot to tell you that you couldn't go. My friends didn't want you to go." After the years of closeness the two had shared, a violation of trust tarnished the relationship. Teenagers can be irreparably harmed when those they hold dear violate their trust.

Teachers and coaches who manipulate their reputations for personal gain, or ruin their professional body of work by cutting corners to win, violate the trust of others. The breaking of trust is the first step toward compromise. Seldom are teenagers mature enough to contemplate the depths of these compromises, which is why adults should be cautious in forming personal relationships with teenagers to begin with.

Some compromises can never be reversed or even amended. Frankly, not every teacher who has an inappropriate relationship with a teenage student is completely untrustworthy, though they cannot be trusted around teenagers. Likewise, not all teachers who have never said or done anything inappropriate are completely trustworthy in all circumstances. However, a good thing to remember is that every inappropriate relationship begins with a violation of the trust. Adults violate trust by choice. Teenagers act on impulses. Combine the two, and the result is wreckage.

CROSSING OVER

The boundaries between teachers and students, many of which are necessary for professionalism, legality, and ethics, are being breached as teachers and students form personal and sexual relationships at and outside school. These relationships are abusive and violate the law and vestiges of American societal and moral codes.

Statistics indicate that sex abuse is a casting a "shadow over U.S. schools."[19] Sexual misconduct between teachers and students is at an all-time high. In July 2011, a female high school physical-education teacher in Ohio was arrested for having sex with five high school boys. Thirty-three-year-old Stacy Schuler initially pleaded not guilty, but later that summer she changed her plea to guilty by reason of insanity for sixteen counts of sexual battery and three counts of offenses involving underage persons. The indictment record showed that Schuler had sexual relations at her Ohio home with the five students on five separate occasions between August and December 2010.[20] And Schuler is only one of thousands of teachers arrested for having sexual relationships with teenage students.

Educational expectations change yearly. Teachers cannot be all things to all students professionally. They certainly should not be the models of interpersonal relationships. The professional naiveté of newer teachers, along with the temptations of power combined with passion and zeal, place a target on their backs. Each day teachers, newer and seasoned professionals, stand against the lines of fire of moral compromise. Age is no longer a boundary for sexual relationships between teachers and teenage students (as we'll discuss further in chapter 4).

The system thrusts humans with raging hormones closely together in work environments. Competitions and "play" conditions force proximities and are sometimes abrasive to moral boundaries. Yet with our culture of diminishing corporate morality, individuals must view their actions through personal lenses. In such proximity, and with lax personal morality, serious temptations can arise. In chapter 2 we will look at some of these concerns and some of their ramifications.

SUMMARY

American educators have long operated on the premise that the nation's public-school system is student centered. This premise has been accepted into all of American culture, where it affects even family structure. Today technology complicates the challenge of communicating with teenagers.

Adults are watching teenagers adjust to changes in America. Teenagers' environments affect many of their life choices, including the relationships they develop. Teenagers do not come packaged with the wisdom to comprehend what is basically good for them, so many of them do not have the forward thinking necessary to grappling with life-changing choices—especially where heightened emotions and social interactions are in play.

There are natural boundaries in relationships, and there are created boundaries. Boundaries usually affect relationships and communication. Boundaries between people are the relationship lines that designate what is appropriate and what is not. These are also referred to as *moral boundaries*.

Teachers must never cross moral boundaries by having sex with teenagers. Such actions are never appropriate.

Baby boomers recall when culture had clearer lines of authority and boundaries between homes and schools were better defined. Today's teenagers do not understand discipline the same way we were raised to understand it, and technology has something to do with this. American culture has changed so very much over these past few decades, and today a young adult's valuing self over others is a sad by-product.

Today objects have a revered status once reserved for people, which deeply impacts a teenager's view of the world. Teenagers learn from adults, and a spirit of rudeness seems to be stretching across generational boundaries.

Virtues of the past such as humility, long-suffering patience, persistence, and dedication to morality have taken a backseat to indulgence and hedonism, sarcasm, and profanity. Teachers and coaches who manipulate their reputations for personal gain, or ruin their professional body of work by cutting corners to win, violate the trust of others. The breaking of trust is the first step toward compromise. Consistency is the key to working with teenagers.

Teachers cannot be all things to all students professionally. Every day, teachers are tested by moral compromise, veteran teachers as well as those facing their first classrooms. Age differences are no longer sufficient barriers against sexual relationships between teachers and teenage students.

DISCUSSION QUESTIONS

1. Are there any boundaries and barriers that should exist between teachers and students?

2. What are some "natural" and "created" boundaries? Explain the differences.

3. What has affected stereotypes and subsequently lessened the boundaries in American culture between adults and teenagers?

4. Do you think today's teenage students are more or less apathetic about education and their future? Explain.

5. In what ways are today's technologies problematic, in terms of relationships between teachers and students, and between parents and teachers?

6. What are two cultural changes brought about by newer communication technologies?

7. To what extent has modern technology detracted from the importance of face-to-face relationships? Is this a good thing or a bad thing?

8. Has technology contributed to the denigration of manners and etiquette in America? If so, in what ways?

9. What differences exist between "explicit" and "implicit" trust?

10. What are three ways modern communication technologies can both add to and detract from the classroom experience?

NOTES

1. Bruce Tulgan, "Column: High-Maintenance Generation Z Heads to Work," *USA Today*, June 26, 2012, accessed July 3, 2012, www.usatoday.com/news/opinion/forum/story/2012-06-27/generation-z-work-millenials-social-media-graduates/55845098/1.

2. Dictionary.com, s.v. "Apathy," accessed June 5, 2012, http://dictionary.reference.com/browse/apathy?s=t.

3. Dictionary.com , s.v. "Apathy."

4. Tom Brokaw, *The Greatest Generation* (New York: Random House Publishers, 1998, 2004).

5. "Symptoms of Video-Game Addiction in Teens," *Video Game Addiction*, accessed August 15, 2012, www.video-game-addiction.org/symptoms-computer-addiction-teens.html.

6. From the New American Standard Bible.

7. D'Vera Cohn and Paul Taylor, "Baby Boomers Approach 65—Glumly," Pew Research Center, December 20, 2010, accessed March 12, 2011, www.pewsocialtrends.org/2010/12/20/baby-boomers-approach-65-glumly/.

8. "Confident, Connected, Open to Change," *Millennials: A Portrait of Generation Next*, Pew Research Center, February 2010, accessed January 2, 2011, www.pewsocialtrends.org/2010/12/20/files/2010/10/millennials-confident-connected-open-to-change.pdf.

9. "Confident, Connected, Open to Change."

10. Dennis Dalrymple, letter to the editor, *New York Times*, August 10, 1988, accessed July 7, 2012, www.nytimes.com/1988/08/10/opinion/l-before-jerry-rubin-603488.html.

11. Timothy Leary, *Turn On, Tune In, Drop Out* (Oakland, Calif.: Ronin Publishing, 1965, 1999), 3.

12. Robert Putnam, *Bowling Alone: The Collapse and Revival of American Community* (New York: Simon & Schuster, 2000), http://bowlingalone.com/.

13. Putnam, *Bowling Alone*, 17. Cf. also http://bowlingalone.com.

14. Victorville is a community of 118,000 residents.

15. Beatriz Valenzuela, "Are Manners Dead?" *Daily Press*, August 7, 2008, accessed May 4, 2012, www.vvdailypress.com/news/manners-7905-1960s-ate.html.

16. Kevin Ryan, "Mining the Values in the Curriculum," *Educational Leadership* 51, no. 3 (November 1993): 16–18.

17. Robert Sylwester, *The Adolescent Brain: Reaching for Autonomy* (San Francisco: Corwin Press, 2007).

18. Dictionary.com, s.v. "Trust," accessed August 2, 2012, http://dictionary.reference.com/browse/trust.

19. Martha Irvine and Robert Tanner, "Sex Abuse a Shadow over U.S. Schools," *Education Week*, October 24, 2007, accessed August 12, 2012, www.edweek.org/ew/articles/2007/10/24/09ap-abuse.h27.html.

20. "Teacher Accused of Sex with 5 Students Pleads Not Guilty by Reason of Insanity," *Huffington Post*, September 12, 2011, accessed September 23, 2011, www.huffingtonpost.com/2011/07/13/teacher-accused-of-sex-wi_n_896982.html.

TWO

Technology, Temptation, and the Teenager

Temptation cannot exist without the concurrence of inclination and opportunity.

—E. H. Chapin, *Living Words*

AT A GLANCE

There are seven major sections in this chapter, which include (1) the nature of the problem today, (2) technological advancements offer additional choices, (3) communication technologies invade the classroom, (4) sexual temptations in today's teen culture, (5) cultural voices affecting relationships, (6) a wake-up call, and (7) scenarios. We close with a chapter summary and discussion questions.

THE NATURE OF THE PROBLEM TODAY

Who can forget the infamous 1990s criminal case of convicted rapist Mary Kay Letourneau and her Seattle elementary-school student Vili Fualaau? The Letourneau case broke just prior to the communication-technologies boom. But sexual predators don't require advanced technologies and social networking to gain access to their prey and will use whatever means are available to them.[1] Letourneau used more-traditional handwritten notes and letters to communicate with her student victim, which eventually proved to be her undoing, as documented in a television biography.

> As a teacher, Letourneau took sixth-grade student Vili Fualaau under her wing and encouraged his artistic talents. He spent time at her

house, and she encouraged a friendship between him and her oldest child, Steve, who was only a year younger than him. In June 1996, however, she began a sexual relationship with the thirteen year old, a relationship that Fualaau would later say he welcomed. The relationship came crashing to a halt in February 1997, when Steve Letourneau found love letters that his wife had written to Fualaau. Later that month, a relative of Steve's reported the affair to officials at Shorewood Elementary. The police were notified, and Letourneau (who at the time was pregnant with Fualaau's child) was arrested and charged with statutory rape.[2]

Letourneau's access to the young student had begun at school, with regular contact in the classroom. Then it grew into spending time together away from school. Teachers who invite their students to their homes on a regular basis, form relationships with them outside of the profession, and communicate with notes and cards are sending signals. In the years since the Letourneau case, communication access points have multiplied exponentially, and predators have found new ways to target victims.

In an article addressing sexual predators' use of technological advancements, journalist Kristen Doerschner writes that "before Internet and cell-phone technology, most predators stayed close to home. The only way they could contact a victim was in person. Now, through such sites as Facebook, predators can look for potential victims who either fit a specific profile or who simply seize upon an opportunity."[3] Letourneau took advantage of the professional platform entrusted to her. She eventually left her family and sought out an elementary-school child as her soul mate. She persisted even after her arrest and imprisonment.

Thanks in large measure to the Letourneau case, more attention focuses on teacher-student relationships. The emergence of new technologies enhances the possibilities of regular contacts between student and teacher outside of the classroom. The simple fact today is that "technology plays [a] role in inappropriate student-teacher relationships."[4]

Is This Happening More Often Today?

Are teacher-student sexual relationships actually occurring more often today, or are they just being reported more often? Are the laws stricter today than in years past, revising what was allowable culturally in past decades to be a crime today?

A vast number of studies are relevant to teacher-student relationships, pertaining to (1) learning outcomes and student-classroom achievement, including high school exit exams and standardized testing,[5] (2) increased literacy scores,[6] (3) teacher stress, (4) self-efficacy, (5) classroom management, and (6) student motivation.[7]

Meta-analyses on teacher-student relationships focus mostly on what we already know: teachers have tremendous impact on student learning and achievement, both positively and negatively. In his article covering twenty years of research on the subject, Theo Wubbels says that "the research examines teaching from an interpersonal perspective using a communicative systems approach and proposes a model to describe teacher-student relationships in terms of teacher behavior."[8]

An older British study asked "whether students' misbehavior had been consistently linked to teachers' reports of stress."[9] The authors speculate as to whether or not "teacher stress, negative affect, and self-efficacy predict the quality of student-teacher relationships."[10] The obvious answer was that teacher stress affected the learning outcomes of students in elementary classrooms.

There is no secret that the training of classroom teachers has changed over the past few decades. What is missing from the training is correlated to what is missing from the bulk of education research: greater attention needs to be focused upon appropriate and inappropriate relationships between teachers and students, teachers and teachers, and teachers and administrators. (Hence this book.) Therefore, additional research and analysis is needed in the following six areas:

1. social and communication technologies
2. determination of outcomes, vis-à-vis learning and class effects
3. adjustments into adulthood
4. impacts of romantic and sexual relationships in defining and expressing eventual student sexual preferences
5. marital stability, longevity, and infidelity
6. whether teenage victims grow up to be adults who continue the cycle of abuse, acting out and victimizing others

Rediscovering the Teacher

Another issue that plagues the American education system is the loss of teacher identity. The *identity* we're discussing pertains to authority and profession and is not a descriptor of personal morality or sexuality. For a long time teachers have been told they are the most important person in the classroom. This is not the case. That said, it could be argued that teachers must focus on themselves more and a little less on the process and results, a focus that does not refer to selfishness but to teacher health and vibrancy.

The teacher needs to be rediscovered as a person in the classroom so as to better serve his or her students. Teacher identity has become muddied over the years. Lines of authority have eroded. Respect levels are down (as we discussed in chapter 1). Credibility has been taken to task. High-stakes accountability and testing have replaced the art of teaching with the tact of test taking and data measuring. Products are replacing processes. Gradually, the stakes have risen higher and higher in education. Material goods are sometimes judged to be more important than people, and test scores increasingly define the teacher and the school. The teacher is often lost in this maze.

No Child Left Behind (NCLB) mandated that all teachers in public schools were to be "highly qualified" by 2014. "The Elementary and Secondary Education Act (ESEA) requires all teachers of core academic subjects to demonstrate ESEA teacher quality compliance. The federal definition of a Highly Qualified Teacher (HQT) is three fold: teachers must hold at least a bachelors' degree, be appropriately licensed by the state, and demonstrate subject matter competency."[11]

Assuming all teachers placed in secondary schools have the equivalent of a major in their content area, the concerns of student achievement persist. There is obviously something else going on in schools that NCLB could ever expect to fix in a decade. Placing less focus on the teacher as a person but more focus on what he or she does might be part of the problem. More laws do not ease previous compliance concerns, and neither do they raise test scores. People working together accomplish these results. However, people working in conditions that are emotionally draining are at greater risk.

These are truly desperate times in our schools. We are focusing on things that are not essential to the healthy relationships among students, teachers, and administrators. How can we expect healthy relationships to develop and be maintained if all the "stuff" of education is often in the way? Relationships that develop without a healthy foundation and clear moral lines are relationships headed for trouble. Some of these relationships begin because of a need for attention (as we will discuss in chapter 4).

TECHNOLOGICAL ADVANCEMENTS OFFER
ADDITIONAL CHOICES

Easy Access

Modern technology allows ordinary people to cross paths quickly and on a regular basis. The same technology allows people to learn more about others and even begin relationships. Commercials abound on cable television, advertising websites that proclaim to have helped people find the loves of their lives or perfect dating partners.

Proximity and location are no longer prohibitions to relationships. If there is communication service available, there are possibilities. People can send text messages to cell phones, post messages online, read and write e-mail, connect with a person on a voice call, or combine all of those into a conference call. We live in an amazing technological age.

Technology goes wherever we go, unlike in the past when we had to go to the hardware itself. Phone booths have become passé and nearly nonexistent. The proliferation of communication technologies has also blurred lines once deemed clearly marked between the professional and the personal. And new technologies have softened some of the edges of traditional American cultural and moral customs. The digital world has brought voices and images to new places and faces around the globe. The American classroom has also been affected by this global technological boom.

Failed Policy

Visiting high schools is quite revealing. Whether in Texas, New Jersey, California, or North Carolina, the story is always the same: Walk the hallways or corridors, walk into a restroom, watch the goings-on during lunch, and there are students everywhere using their cell phones. Some students are smiling as their phones are pressed against their ears. Mostly, they're all texting. The banning of cell phones in schools will not work, because neither adults nor students would respect the ban. [12]

Cell phone technology has brought with it a bevy of choices, and most people choose communication over compliance with law or policy. Several teachers at three large high schools in southern California have given up trying to enforce such bans altogether. Administrators all take the same ineffectual approach to addressing the problem: "Here is the district's cell phone policy, and it is to be supported on campus." It is time to admit that cell phone policies have failed.

These same teachers from the schools I visited stated they use their phones in class for social and educational reasons, knowing their usage is against district policy. School districts all over the nation are revisiting their technology, acceptable-use policies, and generating updated versions. [13] Why is this so important? Because it magnifies what we discussed in chapter 1—that today we live in a self-centered society where the high is self-gratification.

COMMUNICATION TECHNOLOGIES INVADE THE CLASSROOM

Mind-Sets Matter

Students think their cell phones are private property and that they can do whatever they wish with them at school. States like New York have tough bans on student technologies on campus. However, banning cell phones and music devices does very little to change teenage behaviors and mind-sets.[14]

Privacy issues have caused numerous headaches for many parents, teachers, and administrators. Parents often support their children and contact them via text message and phone calls during school hours. And teachers battle this every day: the distractions are annoying and unprofessional. Mixed mind-sets provide a false sense of security for teenagers. "It's my mom," somehow makes the violation of policy and the distraction of education for everyone else an acceptable rationale.

I joke with students about this, replying, "Your mom has a very deep, youthful voice." Even teachers are falling into the trap, thinking their communication by cell phone is completely protected by privacy law while on campus, despite school-district policy and regulation against certain usage. They think they are safe, until they are fired, or arrested—or both—for something they texted or for a voice mail they left.

Cell phone–communications technology has done little to assuage the selfishness and harsh language in our nation's schools. On any given day, profanity is an issue in the classroom, and students get away with using far too much foul language. How is it allowed, you ask? The answer might surprise you.

Profanity is allowed when teachers permit students to use their cell phones to text their friends and post to social-media sites. You would be shocked by what is being texted to students. Students texting students is one concern, but students and teachers texting each other during the school day is another. Some students receive questionable communications from teachers—including photographs. To make matters worse, these digital communications often go unreported.

Ubiquitous and Smart

Recent estimates indicate that approximately four hundred thousand K–6 elementary-age students now have their own cell phones, with more than two hundred thousand children between ages five and nine bringing their cell phones to school with them.[15] Students of all ages can take photographs in restrooms or can violate test security by forwarding photographs sent to them by others. Secret videos have captured everything from sixty-second fights to teacher rants to sex in restrooms. Through cell phones students can plan flash mobs, start fights, bully others, or even start and perpetuate rumors that persist throughout the course of an entire year. They also use their phones to flirt with teachers.

Teachers must be aware of what goes on in classrooms, including what is said, written, and photographed. Students must be told that whatever goes on in the classroom is under the jurisdiction of the teacher and the school. Aside from this setting a good example for students about the appropriate uses of technology, this classroom rule addresses other serious issues that loom large.

Society is becoming more litigious each year. Teachers and schools are rapidly approaching a time when they will be held legally responsible for what technological transmissions occur from within their classrooms and on their campuses. It will no longer be enough to say that there is a policy in place concerning cell phone use. When a major incident occurs, the first question that will be asked will be about the nonenforcement of the district's cell phone policy.

Teachers must be aware that students send sexual comments about them to their friends in the class and that these comments circulate around the school. Also, think about a person who is bullied for his looks, ridiculed for her demeanor, reviled for a sexual reputation, etc. What happens when the bullying victim takes drastic action against the perpetrators or decides to hurt him- or herself or even worse? Society holds schools accountable for so very much because of the murky social, emotional, and legal brew that is a school filled with thousands of teachers and teenagers rubbing shoulders every day.

Let the record show that teachers are not the only school employees that have problems in the area of relationships with teenagers. For example, twenty-three-year-old former youth hockey coach Zachary Meints was arrested and charged in Boulder, Colorado, for sending *thousands* of sexual texts and Facebook messages to minors, asking them for naked photos and encouraging "masturbation races." He pleaded guilty to Internet sex exploitation.[16] Are cases like these just extremes? Unfortunately, today, they are not (and we will explore this in greater depth in chapters 4 and 5).

Cell Phones and Changes in Ethics

With smartphones today, students can photograph tests and compromise security. They can send their photographs to anyone on campus who has a smartphone and a data plan, or they can upload whatever they desire to a social-networking site. In a recent study of U.S. schools, the University of Alabama determined that "cell phones are a tool for cheating."[17]

Although once used for communication and pleasure, students are increasingly using cell phone technology to cheat, usually with the built-in camera. Camera phone sales grew from four thousand in 2002 to 21.4 million in 2004. Today students have stopped hiding cheat sheets and have ceased whispering to their neighbors. Instead, they have started swapping test answers by cell phone via camera and text. Students intent on cheating snap a photo of another student's test paper or take a picture of their own notes to use during the test. States have to try to enforce standardized-test security measures, unlike in the past. Tests are showing up online, even forcing states to stall the release of API scores in order to make certain that nothing has been skewed or that no cheating has taken place.

Not long ago cell phones were just an isolated annoyance, ringing occasionally during class. Today, the issue is keeping students from taking pictures, recording videos, and sending texts during class. One clandestine video can ruin a career or lead to serious allegations that will hang over a person forever. We have seen this time and time again.

That is the bad news. The good news is that, despite the bad news, cell phones can also be used effectively to enhance learning in the classroom, as they now have many features that are similar to the computers we use.

Prensky recommends that teachers stop fighting with students about cell phones and instead use the technology for "their educational advantage."[18] I agree with Prensky (as we'll see in chapter 7). Given smartphones' powerful search capabilities and Internet access, we must ask ourselves whether we are keeping our students from taking advantage of a better education and more rigorous learning by attempting to ban them from schools altogether.

Arousal

Easier access to people through technology brings with it the possibility of elevated emotions and the possibility of an aroused state between those who communicate. To what extent does regular communication stimulate the brain? Adults who spend an inordinate amount of personal time communicating through technology tend to communicate in a relaxed manner that they would never brook in face-to-face communication. Similarly, the use of technology for information and work can help to scale back emotional states in some high school classrooms.

Emotions left to simmer over long periods of time can be catastrophic. Cooling-off periods for emotionally negative experiences become rare in our age of instantaneous and continuous communication, and constant emotional highs even seem attractive. However, the problem with continual emotional highs, as with most things in life that are pleasing, is that the levels become commonplace and then necessary, and additional highs are sought to replace the previous ones.

Online bullying can create such a high-level of emotional stimulation that does not abate quickly. Much has been made recently about student-to-student bullying. Students have taken their lives or harmed themselves after suffering through a continuous negative emotional state brought on by online bullying. However, bullying is not only affecting students. Adults have realized that with certain anonymity they are able to punish people, sullying their reputations and distorting the facts. Parents have been known do this to teachers over unresolved issues involving their children. There is a certain confidence of impunity that accompanies faceless communication. Fortunately, social-networking sites are making it more difficult to remain anonymous. Again, removing the veil of secrecy means more balance and accountability.

Teenagers face an onslaught of stimuli that arouse them emotionally and physically. Video games, social events, communication with friends, and even food all "fire up" the average teenager's brain. Another flashpoint for arousal pertains to sex, which now increasingly infiltrates teenage culture via the cell phone. Technologies on the go mean that stimuli are also on the go, continually affecting teenagers and adults.

Today's Teenagers Have It Made!

When the current generation matures into middle age, one can only wonder whether they will relate to their children the hardships they encountered when teenagers. If so, it might very well read something like this:

> When I was your age, our parents drove us everywhere. We had it rough. We were shuttled from soccer to piano and from piano to ballet. Then we were driven to football practice, baseball games, gymnastics, and cheer. On Wednesday evenings, we were at youth-group meetings. We spent so much time in the car, it wasn't even funny.
>
> We had cell phones, and our parents always wanted to know where we were. So they texted us and left us voice mails all the time. It was a hassle. We had computers and text messaging, so it was time-consuming talking to everyone all the time. We couldn't concentrate half the time, because friends wouldn't leave us alone. Then there was the drama. You do not know how much drama we had in schools in those days. Everyone knew everyone else's business.
>
> Add all of this together with preparing for college and visiting all those schools and getting good grades, and it was a lot of pressure. Then, when I was a senior, having my own car—and a job—was a lot of responsibility. Life was annoying, tiring, and pressure-packed when I was your age. Your generation has no clue what mine had to go through.

Each generation looks back to the previous generation as a point of reference. Access to technology is like playing with toys, which adds to the illusion that most teenagers have it made in this nation. Yet with every new toy comes another set of possible temptations.

SEXUAL TEMPTATIONS IN TODAY'S TEEN CULTURE

Temptations are not evil. But what people do when temptation arises can result in serious problems. I have identified six sexual temptations in today's teenage culture. Each of these allures is a flashpoint for teenagers. While teachers and students are both affected by sexual temptation within the classroom, it is to varying degrees. That is to say, not all teachers and students are tempted to have sex with each other. Absent temptation, there is no reason to initiate emotional, physical, or sexual relationships with teenagers. The teacher who leers at a student or looks down a female's low-cut blouse, for example, may have succumbed to sexual temptation of the mind. Actions that follow are evidence that temptation won.

Table 2.1 lists the six sexual temptations I mentioned, which I explain and analyze immediately following.

Sexual Identity

The first sexual temptation is to convince people there is no longer a standard for "normal" behavior. The term *normal* has been given many definitions over the years and will no doubt continue to evolve with each new generation. Today, a new definition is aligned with sets of desires, particularly regarding sexual expression, and we are told it is hopeless to attempt to secure a change of identity consciousness. Surgeries are becoming more popular for people who feel trapped in a body that is not meant for them. What is normal now is what is normal to the individual's sexual identity. For example, some believe that "homosexuality is not just a sexual orientation but a cultural orientation."[19] To this group, culturally oriented homosexuality is a norm.

As a result, people are known more today by their cultural labels or by their personal feelings about their identities rather than by a corporate label, such as "Americans" or "humans." Everyone seems to have a hyphenation, which tends to focus on differences. Therefore, part of the

---

Table 2.1.   Six Sexual Temptations in Today's Teenage Culture

1. Sexual Identity:
Sexual expression of the past is now sexual identity, defining who we are over what we do.

2. Sexual Expression:
Expression of sexual identity in class draws attention to self.

3. Pornography:
Pornography and sexual experimentation attract teenagers for sexual exploitation.

4. Sexual Boldness:
Teenagers use bold approaches to express sexual identity in language, photographs, and practice.

5. Sexual Language:
Students post specific sexual language on public Internet forums toward teachers and friends.

6. Sexual Fantasy:
Sexual identity combined with technology and youthful imagination may be giving birth to a new cultural phenomenon—*the emerging teenage sexual predator.*

problem today in schools is the notion that one's sexual identity needs to be owned and expressed, over a larger corporate label. Students' identities are now defined by "what" students call themselves. A major problem with this is that teenagers are not mature enough to know the extent of their beliefs or actions or to understand that owning a label may not be such a good thing. Connections with groups and individuals via the Internet help to feed this temptation toward definition and self-expression during the experimental teenage years.

Sexual Expression and the Teenage Student

The second sexual temptation involves students' *expressions* of their sexual identities. These are the actions they take based on their proclaimed identities. Teachers today contend with various expressions of student sexuality. Some students are activism-oriented and boisterous about their sexual relationships. This type of conversation appears in classrooms through texting and digital voice communication. Teachers are threatened that speaking out against sexual expression of one group or another is hateful. Sexual expression on campus has no place, as it interferes with the focus of the school. Schools do not exist for self-expression. They certainly do not exist for any one person's sexuality.

Not all sexual expression should be considered moral or valid. In fact, not all sexual expression is even legal. Pedophilia, bestiality, polyandry, and polygamy are examples. Sexual predators abound worldwide. A sexual predator is generally defined as "a person attempting to initiate or initiating sexual contact with another person in a metaphorically 'predatory' manner. It is most commonly used in reference to pedophiles [who] prey on innocent children but may refer to any other sexually vulnerable group, including the mentally disabled and elderly."[20] The term is pejorative and not morally neutral.

A survey of the fifty states reveals agreement with this basic definition, but there are many additions as states also incorporate specific behaviors as part of the definition. Technology is a central part of all states' definitions as to what constitutes methods used by a sexual predator, since technology is used in drawing in victims. We need to take a few moments to address the growing problems associated with sexual predators in the classroom.

National and state databases of sexual predators are found online, thanks to Megan's Law.[21] The United States Department of Justice's website is an online portal for tracking registered offenders who may also be legally classified as sexual predators.[22] Anywhere that children assemble is a place restricted to sex offenders. Just contacting children via the Internet is enough to weigh against a person classified as a sexual predator.[23]

Sex trafficking of children is an enormous problem, and teenagers do not escape the attention of predators. In some ways, self-expression, political correctness, and technology have been put together by criminal minds and place not only our students at greater risk but also diminish our security as a nation.

The British newspaper the *Derby Telegraph* warns its readers that "any youngster with a mobile phone or Web access is at risk of [sexual] exploitation." In the article Mandy MacDonald, child protective manager for the city of Derby, goes on to say that "it's very easy for someone to manipulate [the] adolescent phase, where the young people are so naive and feel they are invincible. They are very impulsive. They think emotionally rather than reasoning."[24]

Pornography

A third sexual temptation exists because of the easy access today's teenagers and adults have to pornography. Sex has gone mainstream, digitally. It can be brought to immediate attention with the click of a mouse and shared with a simple "send." The Internet allows millions of users daily to securely access pornography through computers, cell phones, and other devices that have online access.

Ogi Ogas and Sai Gaddam, coauthors of *A Billion Wicked Thoughts*, were interviewed by *Forbes* contributing columnist Julie Ruvolo, where they drew the following conclusions: "In 2010, out of the million most popular websites in the world, 42,337 were sex-related sites. That's about 4 percent of sites. From July 2009 to July 2010, about 13 percent of Web searches were for erotic content. You could also look at the number of 'adult sites' that are blocked by various parental filtering software programs—for example, CYBERsitter claims to block 2.5 million adult Web sites."[25]

Sexual predators prey on women and men and pay them to record their actions in permanent retrieval systems. College campuses are especially targeted. Female students are paid a sum of money to perform sex acts, and coed escorts are paid to participate in fraternity and college sex parties. Interest at a younger age in posting sexually suggestive photos correlates to eventual higher-risk behavior during early adulthood. Temptations to both advertise and secure "flesh for sale" have taken hold and place another stone along the path of participation in multiple pornographic settings.

"Female teens are far more likely than male teens to post personal photos or videos of themselves online."[26] This is evident in our schools, both public and private. Some teachers and students send around photos and videos of themselves through real-time communications by video cam and cell phone live streaming and recorded videos.

Sexual experimentation, which now includes "sexting," is viewed by youths as a technorecreational sport. "Seventy-one percent of teen girls and 67 percent of boys who sent or posted sexually suggestive content say they sent it to a boyfriend or girlfriend."[27] Sexual exploitation of students in schools involves minors. Sadly, teenagers are sometimes all-too-willing participants in this exploitation, another indicator of the impulsivity and immaturity that often accompany this age group.

Sexual Boldness

The fourth sexual temptation deals with boldness in flaunting sexuality. Teenagers know sexuality is powerful. Students today are less shy about their approach to adults than in the past. A major reason for this is faceless digital communication.

Many students feel as if they can talk to their teachers about anything and tease them in ways that ought to be reserved for friends. Frankly, teachers are skilled at opening up teenagers to reach into their lives. However, are teachers really any good at knowing how to deal with them once these teens are open to us? Crossing lines and then scaling back afterward sends mixed messages. Teenagers view teachers as buddies in some cases, and with relational impunity.

Students today often refer to their teachers by their last names only. Whatever the motivation, the students feel empowered by limiting the authority of others.[28] Another part of teenage sexual boldness comes from watching adults play at their sexuality and command respect from the elite within the culture for their playfulness. For example, we see this in the rise of the cougar and cub phenomenon, portraying "mature" women as sex-starved and needing to appease their sexual appetites with much younger men.

Programs like *Sex and the City* celebrated the cougar phenomenon weekly, though *Sex and the City* writer Candace Bushnell rejects this notion.[29] However, the "cougar" approach is apparently quite appealing to teenagers and might be a leading cause of young female teachers seeking even younger males as sex partners.[30]

As an example, a local community was stunned to learn that a forty-something parent had had sex with her daughter's eighteen-year-old boyfriend. The teenager, a recent high school graduate, was her victim because she said "it made her feel sexy." This story was related to me by the woman's teenage daughter. The daughter was appalled, but her boyfriend referred to the experience as "cool," and "no big deal." This phenomenon is increasing to alarming levels in our nation.

Television programs and movies celebrate sexual boldness in many ways. One way it is celebrated is playing up relationships that have age differences. Hollywood also uses the coupling of power and fantasy to perpetuate the boldness. Hollywood stars, such as Tom Cruise and Katie

Holmes, as well as Demi Moore and Ashton Kutcher, gain notoriety and headlines for their undying love that spans the age differences, only to be found again in the headlines when they break up a few years later. Charlie Sheen's notorious drug-sex parties were all students seemed to talk about for months. He described his antics as *winning*, a modifier that became quite an annoying fad in some classrooms. Teenagers are susceptible to imitating adults' sexual antics.

If culture makers are to be believed, then everyone is now sexy at all ages. In addition, everyone is pursuing their openness about sexuality and all are boldly advancing personal pleasures as hedonists. Those who shape culture would have us believe that sexuality is now a national preoccupation and national pastime.[31] Teenagers who have bought into this philosophy are left devastated after their attempts to secure the feelings in real-life that are fictionalized on weekly cable programs.

Sexual Language

Fifth, sexual language is a powerful tool, given the uniqueness of teenagers. Sexual empowerment is found in the words and images they use to describe each other. Words can elevate someone's sexual stature, or they can bring someone to ruin in a flash. Recently, a group of male students said they wouldn't mind having sex with a younger female teacher, describing what they would do if they had the chance. After having stepped into the middle of that conversation, one look caused that conversation to change course. In a moment, their passion dissipated, and remorse was expressed. Their sexual empowerment had lost to an authority with a different empowerment.

Many teachers have heard others referred to as "hot" and "sexy." Websites like ratemyteacher.com and ratemyprofessor.com actually allow students and parents to rate "teacher hotness." In terms of the word *hot*, notice the following. Pay close attention to the punctuation:

- HOT = Hands Off Teachers!
- HOT = Hands Off, Teachers!

Descriptions of sexual acts students would enjoy performing on teachers are posted for the world to see on social networking sites. Whether teasing or not, if you think about it, students' comments about sex acts with teachers equate to a form of sexual harassment and possibly even bullying. This is a form of "teasing" and can ruin a person's reputation and even result in the loss of a career. Some students think that all that is required to negate such comments is to follow it with an LOL (laughing out loud) or JK (just kidding). Language is a powerful tool, and using it wisely can lead to wonderful outcomes. Being tempted to use it unwisely may lead only to trouble.

Sexual Fantasy

Finally, there is power in sexual fantasy, which the teenage mind mixes with reality. Fantasy includes words, images, and emotions stirred with idealism and imagination. Technology enhances these fantasies, whether virtually or by personal contact with people. Technology allows deliberate visual and audio fixation and thereby increases the opportunity to dwell on something as if it's real, though actually only fantasy. As an example of this, a male student who thinks his young female math teacher is "hot" and shares this with his friends is likely to get encouraging responses from his peers about things he ought to do with this teacher. What is the reality, and what is the fantasy?

The prolonged mental entertainment of fantasies sometimes allows them to take on lives of their own. Sexual fantasy is not assigned only to teenagers. Adults also use fantasy to manipulate the minds of others, which is why fantasy narratives are so appealing. When sexual fantasy orchestrated by adults reaches into the reality of teenagers, there can be serious problems. Some teenagers actually believe the images painted for them by culture shapers.

Students—especially male students—are well aware of sexual-escort sites and other sex sites such as Ashley Madison's site for married men and women looking to cheat on their spouses. Madison's site is now even commercially advertised on cable television. Literally, anything and everything sexually can be found on the Internet for a price, or even for free, if you think about Craigslist and Backpage.

It does not take an extensive search online to find women willing to engage in sexual activities with younger men, including adult teens. Likewise, adult teenage girls can be found seeking out "daddy figures" on the Internet, teasing supposedly older men. Certain slightly built gay men are known as *twinks* and offer their services to men attracted to boyish young adults. Older, hairy men, known as *bears*, seek out sex with *cubs*, the term for younger men. Women seek males nicknamed *cubs*, or they seek females they call *kittens*, a term for younger lesbian lovers.

Whatever the homosexual or heterosexual temptation, it is easy to find—and so are fantasies. Though many of these relationships begin in the mind as sexual fantasies, in the end the issue here is that the sex is real. And many of these fantasies are enabled today through communication technologies. Teachers would be amazed at how many students have played out the sexual fantasies mentioned above. (We'll discuss this in greater detail in chapter 7.)

So what does it take for a teenager with no sexual experience to move into a very risky behavioral mode? Igra and Irwin "describe that risk-taking behaviors usually display a 'developmental trajectory,' increasing as a teenager grows older. For example, rates of sexuality, reckless vehicle use, and substance use increase with age."[32] Why do teenagers view teachers as conquests? Is there a new teenage phenomenon rising from it all where adults are willing to participate for a forbidden sexual prize? Could it be we are witnessing the birth of a new breed of sexual criminal, *the emerging teenage sexual predator*?

CULTURAL VOICES AFFECTING RELATIONSHIPS

If we are to believe the students we teach, then parents are more concerned about their new personal relationships than they are about making sure their child's homework is finished. Most adults understand that stereotypes involving parent selfishness yield more heat than light. However, beyond the stereotypes lie some genuine cultural voices that have proven effective in damaging the lives of teenagers and adults. We will examine four cultural voices, followed by several cases.

The Voices of Seduction and Immorality

Until recently, a person had to slither through a doorway of a store to purchase pornography. Today, because of the digital revolution, pornography is easily displayed in still and video formats for all to see. Technology has made it easy to publish rumors and lies and to blog hateful messages, vilify everyone, from those participants in teenage online drama to political constituents. The potential for wide readership of anyone's commentary is great today, and a reader can easily choose to access it from home or work.

Certain old-school seductions present themselves in newer ways to each emerging generation. Those of us who have been around for some time understand that there really is nothing new about these seductions, except opportunities, access points, and glitzy digital and cultural packaging. King Solomon, who reigned circa 970 to 931 b.c., uttered words of wisdom so familiar to many readers of the Bible:

> All streams flow into the sea, yet the sea is never full. To the place the streams come from, there they return again. All things are wearisome, more than one can say.
>
> The eye never has enough of seeing, nor the ear its fill of hearing. What has been will be again, what has been done will be done again; there is nothing new under the sun. Is there anything of which one can say, "Look! This is something new"? It was here already, long ago; it was here before our time. No one remembers the former generations, and even those yet to come will not be remembered by those who follow them. [33]

There is really nothing new under the sun, in terms of what humans face, which is the larger general principle addressed by Solomon. Chasing after vanity leaves a person exhausted in the pursuit. Solomon was correct in his assessment of life. He tried it all and came up woefully empty as a person. To the extent that technology speeds up the opportunity to experiment, the results and consequences of the experimentation are borne more quickly, as well.

Just as there was time before the atomic bomb and space travel, there were times before our current communication technologies. Today's teenagers have been sexualized, and their senses are overloaded. Children and women are sometimes reduced to objects of lust, torture, and abuse. Recently, one of the largest busts of child pornography was made. Let the reader beware of the graphic nature found in the summarized text below:

> [Forty-three] men have been arrested over the past two years in a horrific, far-flung child porn network. . . . Authorities have identified more than 140 young victims so far and say there is no end in sight as they pore through hundreds of thousands of images found on the suspects' computers. Photos and online chats found on computers owned by [Robert] Diduca and [Robert] Mikelsons led to more than three dozen other suspects in seven countries. . . . The oldest victim in the Netherlands was four, the youngest just nineteen days old. Massachusetts U.S. Attorney Carmen Ortiz said the demand for photos of sexual assaults of young children, including babies and toddlers, has increased sharply in recent years. Diduca pleaded guilty to child-porn and sexual-exploitation charges and was sentenced to eighteen years in prison. His lawyer said Diduca was sexually abused as a child by a Boy Scout leader. Mikelsons also received an eighteen-year sentence, followed by indefinite psychiatric commitment, after confessing to sexually abusing more than eighty children. The horror did not let up after the Mikelsons case . . . authorities arrested Michael Arnett of Roeland Park, Kan., after finding pornographic photos he allegedly produced. What they found on Arnett's computer was unlike anything some of the investigators had ever come across: long, graphic, online chats about his desire to abduct, kill and eat children.[34]

The Voices of Neutrality

It has been argued that technology is a neutral invention, that molded plastics, thin wires, and circuit boards have no morality. There is agreement. Yet one must always consider the motivation behind an invention and the inventor's original vision for the technology. There is an argument to be made that agenda and purpose are companions to invention.

The moment humans use an invention, it becomes purposeful. We can see this from the example of the child pornography bust, where it was revealed that criminals had used technology for evil, but law enforcement had used the same technology for good. Teenagers need to be made aware of the evil and the good that can come of their use of technology and then be instructed on distinguishing the differences.

In terms of the Internet, the worldwide web only became a reality for the public between 1993 and 1995. However, what we now know as the Internet had its fledgling beginnings during the Cold War period. It was created for a purpose and was initially labeled ARPANET, used by the Department of Defense and other government agencies subsequent to the 1960s. The authors of "Brief History of the Internet" illustrate the importance of this technological advancement. "The Internet has revolutionized the computer and communications world like nothing before. The . . . telegraph, telephone, radio, and computer set the stage for this unprecedented integration of capabilities. The Internet is at once a worldwide broadcasting capability, a mechanism for information dissemination, and a medium for collaboration and interaction between individuals and their computers without regard for geographic location."[35] Today, the Internet is used to gather campaign donations and assist in billing transactions and banking. Stock trading is done online. E-mail is still a significant type of communication in businesses and education. The Internet has revolutionized many areas of communication and research.

Hearkening back to the words of Michael Fullan, one wonders whether scratching a good teacher who uses today's communication technologies wisely and appropriately becomes part of a new paradigm of moral purpose.[36] Who can forget the sights and sounds of the Arab Spring of 2012? We revel in Skype having become *virtually* a household name. Technology has changed our lives. It was just a few decades ago that comic-loving children imagined a world with a Dick Tracy–like watch or a *Get Smart* shoe phone. Cell phones have surpassed the imaginations of the recent past. While many changes in technology have been notably wonderful additions to modern culture, some have not been so kind. Technology can bring out the best and worst of our character.

The Voices of Availability

Social-networking sites provide voices for all seeking an audience. Information sites and search engines take us to worlds of data on nearly any topic in the universe. Emergency notifications and rapid life-saving responses are available in minutes or even seconds. People can be in touch with others in foreign countries right from their automobiles or living rooms. Websites are even set up for people to make quick selections of goods and services.

Some of our teenagers will have sex this year for the first times in their lives. We will no doubt hear about how girls dumped their boyfriends after discovering that they'd used their cell phone cameras to record private acts or to immediately text their friends. Some young women will get pregnant, and their reputations will be denigrated around school campuses. Others will drink, get drunk, or try drugs for the first time in their lives. All of these behaviors are made easier to come by as a result of technology. Groups can assemble quickly and impulsively.

The Voices of the Mob

A *flash mob* is the gathering of hundreds or even thousands of people informed about an event via online technology. Blogger Tina Sieber writes that "flash mobs are an Internet phenomenon of the twenty-first century."[37] The short-lived Occupy Wall Street 2.0 movement of 2012 is an example of the use of technology to organize many people in a short period of time.[38] Technology has been credited with helping to orchestrate the fall of regimes in the Middle East[39] to violent robberies of dozens of pairs of jeans from clothing stores.[40] Over 90 percent of the crimes committed today by teenagers are committed in flash mobs. "Technology hasn't just made it easy to plan and organize events and tempting to take part in. It has allowed the thieves to off-load their loot. A recent survey done by a leading retail-industry group shows that technology has led to a spike in organized crime, mostly as thieves find it easier to sell stolen goods online."[41]

Case Examples

The following headlines reporting cases around the nation represent a small fraction of the overall cases involving sexual relationships between teachers, coaches, administrators, and students.

But how many of these arrests could have been avoided with a commitment and follow-through with professional development and a focus on guidelines consisting of appropriate relationships with students and the ethics of technology use after-hours with students? (We'll examine this question more carefully in chapters 6 and 7.) No one knows the answer to that question.

- Teacher Accused of Having Sex with Student Allegedly Had Toddler Present in Home[42]
- Teacher, Accused of Having Sex with Teen 300 Times[43]
- Female Teachers Having Sex, Inappropriate Relationships with Students[44]
- Female New York Teacher Accused of Having Sex with Student in Motel[45]
- Former Arvada High School Assistant Principal Arrested for Alleged Sexual Relationship[46]
- Head Soccer Coach Accused of Sex with Minor[47]
- Former Teacher Allegedly Had Sex with 16-Year-Old Student in School Closet[48]

- Assistant Cheerleading Coach Arrested for Allegedly Performing Sexual Acts on Student, Age 17[49]
- Former Band Teacher Pleads No Contest to Sex Acts with Child under 14[50]
- Freedom High School Teacher, Notre Dame Standout Charged with Sex with Minor[51]
- Rhonda Eisenberg, Teacher Who Gave Birth to Student's Child, Will Be Fired[52]
- Boxing Coach Arrested on Suspicion of Molesting Teen Boxer[53]
- Woman Accused of Raping Teen with Ex-Husband[54]

Sexual teasing and degrading language, sexual harassment, sexual abuse, and inappropriate relationships between students and teachers seem to be occurring more and more often. There has been a spike in female teachers having sex with teenage students. Inappropriate relationships are sweeping the nation in unprecedented numbers, and America needs to awaken from its moral slumber. (See chapter 4 for a continued discussion on these points.)

A WAKE-UP CALL

As they are lobbied by teenagers for more trust, adults find themselves increasingly more encircled by culture. One of the best things we can do for our teenage students is to wake them up beforehand to the dangers that exist with improper use of technology. What should we do if we find our own teenager is involved in a daily habit of adult or child pornography or has downloaded something criminal?

Appropriate relationships with teenagers begin at home. Teachers and parents should work together to ensure that students make the best and most wholesome choices possible for their lives and not allow the very tools and toys they own to become a source of moral compromise in their lives or the lives of their friends.

SCENARIOS

Read the following real-life scenarios, and answer the following questions. Discuss your answers in small groups. Consider what these cases have in common and what roles communication technologies play in each.

Scenario 1

Imagine that one day a teenage member of your family begins spending significant time devising a plan with others to bully a fellow student. Their plan includes anonymous online tactics.

- Are you concerned? If so, at what level? Or are teenagers just doing what they always do?
- What steps, if any, would you take to end their plan?
- In what ways would your relationship with your teenager be impacted, both positively and negatively?

Scenario 2

One day, after arriving home from your work, you discover one of your teenagers is missing. After phoning the police, you are informed that your daughter was possibly abducted by a registered sex offender. Following a preliminary check of your daughter's computer, police discover that your teenager was entertaining a relationship with a person who had been pretending to be a lovesick teenager. After a time, the man is luckily caught where he had planned to abduct your daughter, and your daughter is returned safely to you.

- What are your feelings about this incident?
- Is there anything you would have done differently with your teenage daughter?
- What discussions would you now have with your teenage daughter about sexuality?
- What role did technology play in all parts of this scenario?

Scenario 3

A male teacher who coaches a team your son plays on begins making advances toward your sixteen-year-old son. You notice something odd between the coach and your son after one of his games. However, you let it go. Two weeks later, you read in the local newspaper that the coach is arrested for allegedly molesting some of his players. You find that your son and the coach were texting sexual comments to each other in the evening hours, and now you must question your son.

- How could you have handled the occurrence of the odd moment differently after one of your son's games?
- In what ways would your communication with your son change?
- What conversations would you have with your son now that the coach has been arrested?
- What would you change if you were the parent in the scenario?

- What assistance would you need if you discovered your son was also a sexual victim of the coach?

SUMMARY

Today we place greater attention on teacher-student relationships. The media pounces on scandals that involve schools. The emergence of new technologies enhances the possibilities of contacts between teachers and students. The simple fact today is that technology plays roles in inappropriate student-teacher relationships.

There is great need for education-research institutions to study and analyze the impacts of teacher-student romantic and sexual relationships. High-stakes accountability and testing have shifted education from the art of teaching to the tact of test taking and data measuring. Material goods are sometimes more important than people, and culture has determined that test scores define the worth of the teacher and the school.

Teachers are humans with real human needs. Modern technology allows ordinary people to cross paths quickly, and on a regular basis. The same technology allows people to learn more about others and even begin relationships. Proximity and location are no longer prohibitions to relationships.

The message is clear that students do not respect school cell phone policies, as a rule. Parents often support their children and contact them via text message and phone calls during school hours. Teachers battle this every day. The distractions are annoying and unprofessional. Even teachers are beginning to think that their cell phone use while on campus won't impact their professional lives.

Cell phone technology has done little to change the course of selfishness and harsh language in our nation's schools. Smartphones enable students to photograph tests and to compromise privacy. Students can send their photographs to anyone on campus who has a smartphone and a data plan, or they can upload whatever they desire to a social-networking site.

Temptations are not evil. But what people do when temptation presents itself could result in serious problems. Six sexual temptations exist in today's teenage culture: (1) to convince people there is no "normal," (2) for students to express their sexual identities, (3) to easily access pornography, (4) to use sexual language empowers words and images, (5) to build up or tear down someone's sexual stature and reputation, and (6) to engage in sexual fantasy. All of these are associated with the use of smartphone technology and computers.

Teachers and students experience sexual temptation within the classroom, but to varying degrees. That is to say, not all teachers and students are tempted to have sex with each other.

Social-networking sites provide voices to all who seek an audience. Information sites and search engines provide us with worlds of data on nearly any topic in the universe. Emergency notifications and rapid life-saving responses are available in mere seconds. People can be in touch with others in foreign countries right from their automobiles or living rooms.

DISCUSSION QUESTIONS

1. In what ways are teenagers tempted today with the use of available technology?
2. Why do you think more teachers are having sexual relationships with their teenage students?
3. What do you think is a good balance for schools, in terms of expectations of relationship levels for teachers and students?
4. Does your district or school have a sensible acceptable-use policy for its teachers and students?
5. What are the six cultural flashpoints of the chapter, and how have they become a part of culture?
6. How would you define a *voice of culture*? Provide three examples of such voices.
7. How would you approach your teenager if you were to discover that he or she has been viewing a great deal of pornography as well as sexting older friends?

NOTES

1. Ernest J. Zarra III, *It Should Never Happen Here* (Grand Rapids, Mich.: Baker Book House, 1997), 13–25.

2. "Mary Kay Letourneau: Biography," Biography.com, accessed May 3, 2012, www.biography.com/people/mary-kay-letourneau-9542379.

3. "Technology Allows Sexual Predators to Operate Differently," *Times Online*, April 17, 2011, accessed April 25, 2011, www.timesonline.com/news/technology-allows-sexual-predators-to-operate-differently/article_05199b28-68b0-11e0-b4a4-001a4bcf6878.html.

4. "Technology Plays Role in Inappropriate Student-Teacher Relationships," *eSchool News*, June 28, 2011, accessed August 2, 2011, www.eschoolnews.com/2011/06/28/technology-plays-role-in-inappropriate-student-teacher-relationships/.

5. Ruby Larson, "Teacher-Student Relationships and Student Achievement" (University of Nebraska–Omaha, 2012), accessed September 1, 2012, http://coe.unomaha.edu/moec/briefs/EDAD9550larson.pdf.

6. A. M. Klem and J. P. Connell, "Relationships Matter: Linking Teacher Support to Student," *Journal of School Health* 74, no. 7 (2004): 262–73.

7. G. P. Montalvo, E. A. Mansfield, and R. B. Miller, "Liking or Disliking the Teacher: Student Motivation, Engagement, and Achievement," *Evaluation and Research in Education* 20, no. 3 (2007): 144–58, accessed May 28, 2011, http://dx.doi.org/10.2167/eri406.0.

8. "Two Decades of Research on Teacher-Student Relationships in Class," *International Journal of Educational Research* 43, nos. 1–2 (2005): 6–24.

9. Isca Salzberger-Wittenberg, Gianna Henry, and Elsie Osborne, "The Emotional Experience of Learning and Teaching," *Journal of Child Psychotherapy* 10 (1984): 125.

10. Salzberger-Wittenberg, Henry, and Osborne, "Emotional Experience of Learning and Teaching," 125–27.

11. "NCLB: The Drive for Education Reforms," *California Department of Education*, accessed June 16, 2012, www.cde.ca.gov/nclb/sr/tq/; see also www.ed.gov/news/press-releases/26-more-states-and-dc-seek-flexibility-nclb-drive-education-reforms-second-round.

12. Lisa Barone, "Banning Social Media Doesn't Work, Education Does," *Social Media*, May 5, 2010, accessed November 4, 2011, http://smallbiztrends.com/2010/05/banning-social-media-doesn%E2%80%99t-work-education-does.html. See also www.webpronews.com and Tom Andreesen and Cal Slemp, "Managing Risk in a Social Media–Driven Society," *Protiviti*, 2001, accessed April 22, 2011, www.protiviti.com/en-US/Documents/Insights/Managing-Risk-in-a-Social-Media-Driven-Society.pdf.

13. Kern High School District, "Kern High School District Technology Plan: July 2010 to June 2013," accessed July 19, 2012, www.khsd.k12.ca.us/Business/PDF/KHSD%20-%20Technology%20Plan-10-13.pdf.

14. Associated Press, "School Cell Phone Ban Causes Uproar," CBS News, February 11, 2009, accessed March 6, 2012, www.cbsnews.com/2100-201_162-1616330.html.

15. "Cell Phones and PDAs Hit K–6," *Education Digest* 70, no. 8 (2005): 52–53. See also S. Campbell, "Perceptions of Mobile Phones in College Classrooms: Ringing, Cheating, and Classroom Policies," *Communication Education* 55, no. 3 (2006): 280–94, accessed December 3, 2011, www.bamaed.ua.edu/edtechcases/case7.html.

16. "Zachary Meints, Youth Hockey Coach That Sent Boys Sexual Texts, Pleads Guilty to Internet Sex Exploitation," *Huffington Post*, May 30, 2012, accessed June 3, 2012, www.huffingtonpost.com/2012/05/30/zachary-meints-former-bou_n_1557128.html.

17. Vivian H. Wright et al., *Technology Education: A Series of Case Studies* (University of Alabama–Tuscaloosa, 2009), accessed December 3, 2011, www.bamaed.ua.edu/edtechcases/.

18. M. Prensky, "What Can You Learn from a Cell Phone? Almost Anything!," *Journal of Online Education*, 2004, accessed December 3, 2011, www.elearningsource.info. L. Etter, "Technology: A Special Report; Putting Tech to the Test. As Students Turn to High-Tech Gadgets to Cheat, Schools Consider Turning to High-Tech Gadgets to Stop Them," *Wall Street Journal*, R17, September 17, 2004. Wright et al., *Technology Education*. V. Gerard, "Updating Policy on Latest Risks for Students with Cell Phones in the School," *Education Digest* 72, no. 4 (2006): 43–45. M. Walker, "High-Tech Cribbing: Camera Phones Facilitate Cheating," *Wall Street Journal*, B1, September 10, 2004.

19. David Halperin, "How to Be Gay: Queer Men Are Different, and We Should Hold On to Our Culture," *Chronicle of Higher Education: The Chronicle Review*, B13–17, September 7, 2012.

20. Fred Cohen and Elizabeth Rahmberg-Walsh, *Sex Offender Registration and Community Notification: A "Megan's Law" SourceBook* (Kingston, N.J.: Civic Research Institute, 2001). TheFreeDictionary.com, s.v. "Sexual predator," accessed July 9, 2012,http://medical-dictionary.thefreedictionary.com/Sexual+Predator.

21. United States Department of Justice (NSOPW), The Dru Sjodin National Sex Offender Website, accessed June 10, 2012, www.nsopw.gov. State of California Department of Justice, Megan's Law Home, accessed June 10, 2012, www.meganslaw.ca.gov/.

22. The Dru Sjodin National Sex Offender Website, www.nsopw.gov. Megan's Law Home, www.meganslaw.ca.gov/.

23. TheFreeDictionary.com, s.v. "Sexual Predator Law," accessed April 30, 2012, http://legal-dictionary.thefreedictionary.com/Sexual-Predator+Law.

24. "Any Youngster with a Mobile Phone or Web Access Is at Risk of Exploitation," *This Is Derbyshire*, July 14, 2012, accessed July 21, 2012, www.thisisderbyshire.co.uk/youngster-mobile-phone-web-access-risk/story-16539284-detail/story.html.

25. Julie Ruvolo, "How Much of the Internet Is Actually for Porn?" *Forbes Magazine*, September 7, 2011, accessed October 6, 2011, www.forbes.com/sites/julieruvolo/2011/09/07/how-much-of-the-internet-is-actually-for-porn/.

26. GuardChild, "Internet Crime and Abuse Statistics," *GuardChild*, accessed June 4, 2011, www.guardchild.com/statistics/.

27. ASK, "Sexting," *ASK: The Alliance for Safe Kids*, accessed June 4, 2011, http://allianceforsafekids.org/resources/tips-for-parents/sexting/.

28. "Rebellious Teenagers," AllPsychologyCareers.com, accessed June 3, 2012, www.allpsychologycareers.com/topics/rebellious-troubled-teenagers.html.

29. Gatecrasher, "*Sex and the City* Author Candace Bushnell Rejects 'Cougar' Tag," *New York Daily News*, August 24, 2009, http://articles.nydailynews.com/2009-08-24/gossip/17931305_1_cougar-candace-bushnell-younger.

30. Amy Oliver, "Sex Education: Why *Are* So Many Female Teachers Having Affairs with Their Teenage Students . . . and Is the 'Cougar Effect' to Blame?" *Mail Online*, May 28, 2011, www.dailymail.co.uk/news/article-1391626/Whats-wrong-female-teachers-America-As-schools-summer-young-teacher-arrested-sex-16-year-old-student--latest-dozens-cases-school-year.html.

31. Sharon Jayson, "More College 'Hookups,' but More Virgins, Too," *USA Today*, March 20, 2011, accessed May 28, 2011, www.usatoday.com/news/health/wellness/dating/story/2011/03/More-hookups-on-campuses-but-more-virgins-too/45556388/1.

32. Vivian Igra and Charles E. Irwin, "Theories on Adolescent Risk-Taking Behavior," in *The Handbook of Adolescent Health Risk Behavior*, ed. Ralph J. DiClemente, William B. Hansen, and Lynn E. Ponton, 35–51 (New York: Plenum Press, 1996), 36.

33. Ecclesiastes 1:7–11 (NASB).

34. Denise Lavoie, "Vast International Child-Porn Network Uncovered," MSNBC, August 4, 2012, accessed August 5, 2012, www.msnbc.msn.com/id/48502531/ns/us_news-crime_and_courts/.

35. Barry M. Leiner et al., "Brief History of the Internet," *Internet Society*, accessed August 5, 2012, www.internetsociety.org/internet/internet-51/history-internet/brief-history-internet/.

36. Michael Fullan, *Change Forces* (New York: Falmer Press, 1993), 10.

37. Tina Sieber, "What a Flash Mob Is and How You Can Participate," MakeUse-Of.com, October 19, 2010, accessed August 5, 2012, www.makeuseof.com/tag/flash-mob-participate-examples/.

38. Jessica Firger, "Occupy 2.0: Protesters Go Hi-Tech," *Wall Street Journal*, March 17, 2012, accessed June 5, 2012, http://online.wsj.com/article/SB10001424052702304459804577285793322092600.html.

39. Carol Huang, "Facebook and Twitter Key to Arab Spring Uprisings: Report," *The National*, June 6, 2011, accessed June 8, 2011, www.thenational.ae/news/uae-news/facebook-and-twitter-key-to-arab-spring-uprisings-report.

40. ViolentFlashMobs.com, accessed June 5, 2012, http://violentflashmobs.com/.

41. Annie Vaughan, "Teenage Flash Mob Robberies on the Rise," Fox News, June 18, 2011, accessed June 18, 2011, www.foxnews.com/us/2011/06/18/top-five-most-brazen-flash-mob-robberies/; see also Ian Urbina, "Mobs Are Born as Word Grows by Text Message," *New York Times*, March 24, 2010, accessed June 8, 2011, www.nytimes.com/2010/03/25/us/25mobs.html.

42. Scott Raynor, *MarionPatch*, April 28, 2012, accessed April 29, 2012, http://marion.patch.com/articles/wisconsin-teacher-who-had-sex-with-marion-teen-had-two-year-old-present.

43. United Press International, "Christine A. McCallum, Teacher, Accused of Having Sex with Teen 300 Times," *Huffington Post*, January 10, 2009, www.huffingtonpost.com/2009/01/10/christine-a-mccallum-teac_n_156867.html (accessed May 3, 2010).

44. Casey L. Holley, *Yahoo! News*, October 26, 2007, accessed May 3, 2010, http://voices.yahoo.com/female-teachers-having-sex-inappropriate-relationships-626615.html.

45. Fox News, August 6, 2011, accessed September 2, 2011, www.foxnews.com/us/2011/08/06/female-new-york-teacher-accused-sex-with-student-in-motel.

46. "Anthony Alvarez, Former Arvada High School Assistant Principal, Arrested for Alleged Sexual Relationship with 15-Year-Old Student," *Huffington Post*, September 6, 2011, accessed September 6, 2011, www.huffingtonpost.com/2011/09/06/anthony-alvarez-former-ar_n_950907.html.

47. Crosby Shaterian, "Miramonte Head Soccer Coach Accused of Sex with Minor," *KERO 23 Bakersfield News*, February 28, 2012, accessed February 28, 2012, www.turnto23.com/news/30554301/detail.html.

48. Laura Hibbard, "Kacy Christine Wilson, Former Teacher, Allegedly Had Sex with 16-Year-Old Student in School Closet," *Huffington Post*, May 8, 2012, accessed May 8, 2012, www.huffingtonpost.com/2012/05/07/kacy-christine-wilson-former-teacher-pulls-student-sex-in-closet_n_1496839.html.

49. Fox News, June 21, 2012, accessed June 21, 2012, www.foxnews.com/us/2012/06/21/assistant-cheerleading-coach-arrested-for-allegedly-performing-sexual-acts-on/.

50. *Bakersfield Californian*, June 1, 2012, accessed June 1, 2012, www.bakersfieldcalifornian.com/local/breaking-news/x84914270/Former-band-teacher-pleads-no-contest-to-sex-acts-with-child-under-14.

51. Jason Bartolone, *TampaPatch*, August 19, 2011, accessed August 19, 2011, http://newtampa.patch.com/articles/teacher-ex-football-standout-charged-with-sex-with-minor.

52. "Rhonda Eisenberg, Teacher Who Gave Birth to Student's Child Will Be Fired School District Says," *Huffington Post*, August 3, 2012, accessed August 3, 2012, www.huffingtonpost.com/2012/08/03/rhonda-eisenberg-teacher-_n_1738724.html.

53. Kathleen Miles, "Anthony Serrano, Boxing Coach, Arrested on Suspicion of Molesting Teen Boxer," *Huffington Post*, July 17, 2012, accessed July 17, 2012, www.huffingtonpost.com/2012/07/17/anthony-serrano-boxing-coach-arrested-photos_n_1680523.html.

54. Mark Barber, "Woman Accused of Raping Teen with Ex-Husband, in Court Next Month," Fox54 News, June 25, 2012, accessed June 25, 2012, www.wfxg.com/story/18818088/woman-accused-of-raping-teen-with-former-husband-in-court-next-month.

THREE

Teenage Brains, Maturity, and Emotions

What happens when children reach puberty earlier and adulthood later? The answer is: a good deal of teenage weirdness. Fortunately, developmental psychologists and neuroscientists are starting to explain the foundations of that weirdness. The crucial new idea is that there are two different neural and psychological systems that interact to turn children into adults.[1]

AT A GLANCE

There are eleven major sections in this chapter: (1) teenage brains, (2) brain differences and their meanings, (3) a little neuroscience for teachers, (4) teenagers and maturity, (5) factors of emotional intelligence, (6) brain chemicals and effects on teenagers, (7) teenagers and emotional memories, (8) humans are social creatures, (9) love and emotional maturity, (10) teenagers and expressions of love, and (11) a few closing thoughts on emotional and physiological differences. At the end of each chapter, there are chapter summaries and discussion questions.

TEENAGE BRAINS

In chapter 1 we specified boundaries and barriers between different generations. Chapter 2 presented some of the temptations that teenagers experience, specifically looking at technology and morality. In chapter 3 you will learn to better understand teenagers as we peer into their brains, levels of maturity, and emotions.

Researchers are uncovering more about the physical and chemical workings in the developing teenage brain in terms of memory transfer and information storage and retrieval. The latest discoveries about student learning are very exciting—literally—as they involve the emotional center of the brain. One of the more recent discoveries is that teenagers have an abundance of synapses—or regions where nerve impulses transmit and receive.

These synapses emit the "excitement-oriented" neurotransmitter called *glutamate*. Synapses encompass the axon terminal of a neuron, where neurotransmitters, such as glutamate, are released. The abundance of these synapses means that teenagers are full of brain excitement. However, by the end of their teenage years, there is usually a decrease in this hyperexcitement in the brain.

Teenage Contexts

Teenagers contextualize their world through their emotions. For example, music they listen to places them within contexts. Regardless of the context—and we all have them—once a long-term memory is written, the music may provide a gateway to reliving the experiences through memory some time in the future. Don Campbell illustrates the impact of music and its use in therapies and healing of brain injuries in his book *The Mozart Effect*.[2] Adult brains use contexts in similar ways.

Teenagers' first major arguments with friends are emotional contexts, and so are first relationships. An event categorizes a period in time and enables the brain to lay down memories of the event, which helps in the formation of emotional intelligence.[3] Events are laid down with the assistance of the amygdalae, the twin emotional centers of the brain. It is there that the contexts of emotions and memories find enrichment in the brain.

A brain with many emotional learning experiences, and with excellent recall of those experiences, is said to be a healthy brain; these are also signs of intelligence.[4] Brains that experience little to no emotion during learning will have less recall. Consider how we teach in high schools and the memories we make with our students. Memories increase tremendously with the engagement of students' amygdalae, the emotional centers of the brain.

Peaks of Maturation

William Hudspeth and Kurt Fischer have discovered that the teenage brain is still "wiring up" and that there are certain growth surges that mark this wiring. The three general periods of brain-growth surges—or "spurts"—occur between the ages of (1) ten and twelve, (2) fourteen and sixteen, and (3) eighteen and twenty—the latter sometimes extending into the mid-twenties.

Hudspeth and Fischer[5] each performed separate studies yet drew similar conclusions. Hudspeth's study involved 561 Swedish subjects, ages one to twenty-one, and identified "three different peaks of brain maturation during adolescence. These peaks generalize into the following age groups: age twelve, age fifteen, and age eighteen and one-half." Hudspeth discovered a very high correlation between his Swedish students and Jean Piaget's "formal-operations thinking processes."[6]

According to Hudspeth, the age peaks are distinguished by maturation within moral judgment and progress in development of social skills. Fischer's Harvard study registered growth peaks similar to Hudspeth's and drew similar conclusions. Fischer placed the peaks within age ranges, which included Hudspeth's peak ages. Fischer ascertained the following age ranges: ten to twelve, fourteen to sixteen, and eighteen to twenty.[7] Table 3.1 summarizes Hudspeth's and Fischer's studies.

BRAIN DIFFERENCES AND THEIR MEANINGS

The latest research in neuroscience has "documented an astonishing array of structural, chemical, and functional variations in the brains of males and females."[8] The older and established views of brain theory assumed that humans were ultimately predisposed to their genetic makeups and would follow predetermined genetic paths as their brains developed. An interesting fact validated by studies is that "some sex differences in the brain arise before a baby draws its first breath."[9] The latest research has led to a more modern view on genetic-predisposition theory.

Epigenetic theory states that certain processes occur outside of genes and affect the traits of genes when they are expressed but do not affect the basic DNA of a person. In other words, "it is now established that

Table 3.1. Stages, Ages, and Characteristics of Brain Development

Stages of Brain Growth	Age Peaks or Age Ranges of Brain Growth	General Characteristics of the Stages and Ages of Brain Growth
Stage 1	10–12 years	Moral reasoning and logic begin to develop; stages coincide with Piaget's Formal Operational-Thinking Processes, including problem solving, classification of data, and an understanding of reversibility.
Stage 2	14–16 years	Ability to relate levels of abstract information. There is also growth in emotions, expressed in actions toward peers.
Stage 3	18–20 years	Ability to understand abstract information increases, and there is evidence of tact and mature emotional responses.

contrasting, persistent, or traumatic environments can and do change the actions of genes."[10] The implications of this research for teachers are highly significant. The environments to which we expose our students' developing brains can literally change lives.

Getting to Know Them

Teachers who understand their students have a distinct advantage in the area of relationships, also. Would teachers develop inappropriate relationships, either emotionally or physically, with a student if they knew what the research indicates about long-lasting trauma on the student? If so, what can we conclude?

Some educators believe teacher-education institutions must begin the process of informing teacher candidates that they will have very important influences over the literal cognitive and emotional health of their students. As an example, Carrion, Garrett, and Menon write about the effects of trauma on youth, addressing a very sensitive but important issue:

> Children who experience maltreatment and development posttraumatic-stress systems (PTSS) may manifest cognitive and behavioral systems and physiological hyperarousal. These systems may interfere with their ability to process information, especially when related to traumatic events. . . . It has been hypothesized that physiological arousal facilitates self-injurious behaviors (SIB) in children with history of interpersonal trauma. In fact . . . youth with PTSS are significantly more likely to have attempted suicide and have suicidal ideation, and adults with PTSS show an association between impulsivity and suicide risk. . . . History of trauma and posttraumatic symptoms have been associated with self-cutting, the most common form of SIB.[11]

Teachers assume great responsibility. Many students look to teachers to assist them, guide them, and provide some sense of healthy grounding to the real world. The truth is that some teachers and students come from similar backgrounds. Some have overcome their pasts, while others have not. Teachers should understand how each student's brain operates and how each will deal with situations from emotional and cognitive vantage points (viz., how a student is wired).

Navigation

Males and females navigate learning quite differently. Many studies suggest that male brains tend to find direction through circumstances by "estimating space and orientation," something referred to in neuroscience as *dead reckoning*. Women, on the other hand, are most likely to navigate their circumstances by monitoring certain landmarks, often through their emotions.[12] Neuroscientists now understand that males and females process the same emotional memories very differently. This means that the phrase *I love you* uttered by a male after a very romantic date processes into his memory quite differently than it is likely processing into the memory of the female.

At the end of the date, the male might remember the way she looked, her smile, and the emotions and feelings he felt when she touched his hand. The female, though, would probably remember his shoes, the color of his shirt, the table and location where they sat, and the emotional sense derived from noticing an elderly couple at an adjacent table who were celebrating their fiftieth wedding anniversary with smiles and laughter. Males and females process emotions differently.

Male and Female Developmental Characteristics

One of the reasons for such differences in emotional memories between males and females is the result of their physical differences. Women possess "significantly larger orbitofrontal amygdalae ratios (OAR) than men do. One can speculate from these findings that women might on average prove [less impulsive and] capable of controlling their emotional reactions."[13]

The amygdalae are the centerpieces of the brain's emotions in humans. There are twin amygdalae, located at the center base of the brain. Neuroscientists have intensified their study via newer technology, such as PET scans (positron-emission tomography), and the results about brain differences have raised some eyebrows. For our purposes we can say that the hippocampus (working memory) works jointly with the amygdalae (basis of emotions) to assist in learning and transfer to the cerebrum (long-term memory storage).[14] The key for educators at every level is teaching so that this transfer takes place more regularly.

Developing Male Brains

Developing male brains have more cortical areas dedicated to spatial-mechanical functioning and use about one-half the brain space that females use for verbal-emotive function.[15] This development is one reason why males desire to move objects through space. Most males will experience words and feelings differently than females.[16]

Male brains have less serotonin than females' have. As a result, males are likely to be more physically impulsive and less likely to sit and show empathy to a friend.[17] Furthermore, developing male brains operate with less blood flow than females' brains and tend to compartmentalize learning.[18]

The male brains configure to renew themselves by recharging and reorienting within what neuroscientists call a *rest state*. This is a reason why teenage males tend to drift off during tasks that are not spatial and are often asleep in the back of the class.[19]

Developing Female Brains

Developing female brains have 25 percent more corpus callosum—the bundle of connecting tissue between brain hemispheres—than do males' brains.[20] This enables "cross-talk" between brain hemispheres. It also increases the ability to multitask and the demonstration of better verbal and emotionally based functions.[21]

Female brains have stronger temporal-lobe connectors than male brains. This means that female brains allow for better sensual, detailed memory storage.[22] Furthermore, females tend to multitask better than males, with fewer issues arising from attention-span concerns. This enables females to be less impulsive than males, in general.[23]

The brains of females have larger hippocampus areas than male brains, leading to an advantage in the language arts. The hippocampus is critical in significance, in terms of working memory, in that it assists in the association and retrieval of long-term memories, based on experiences, and emotions.[24]

A LITTLE NEUROSCIENCE FOR TEACHERS

Thinking Like an Adult

The teenage years are a unique period. Raging emotions, verbal confrontations, boredom, and exhilaration can occur at a moment's notice. Have you ever asked a teenager why he did "something" or why she said "those certain shocking words"? Do you remember their responses? You probably do, but allow me to assist your "memory":

DAD: Why did you do that?

SON: I don't know.

DAD: What were you thinking when you said that?

DAUGHTER: I don't know.

TEACHER: What prompted you to do that?

STUDENT: I'm not sure.

Adults generally believe their teenagers are calculating and knowledgeable about all of their youthful actions. The natural inclination of the adult is application of adult logic, connecting actions and words to motivation and choice. Most adults understand that there are reasons for what people say and do. Consequently, proclaim adults, there must be a series of connections to thoughts and actions.

There is a certain inescapable logic about this "adult thinking." However, adult emotions have experience drawing conclusions. Adult brains are calmer and better wired. Adults draw conclusions based on their experiences, and these conclusions are referred to as *gut-level* or *intuitive* conclusions. Teenagers lack experience for this to be part of their decision making. The frontal lobes of our brains are those areas where impulses are generally controlled. Neuroscientists are telling us that the frontal lobes are not fully developed in young people—especially males—until about twenty to twenty-five years of age. That would explain why some teenage females seem to have their impulses under control somewhat earlier than some males.

There is no standardized age for frontal-lobe maturity. Yet we now know there are different degrees of biological development for female and male teenagers. Teenage behaviors have direct effects on relationships during the teenage years. Emotional "crushes" are examples of relationships exploded into reality by emotions. Teenagers crush on people and things, including teachers. The latter means they could be emotionally susceptible at key points of their high school years.

The implications for teachers and teacher-education institutions are significant. Brain-based learning is nothing new. We all understand that the brain is where learning occurs. Yet what is new is that science and research technology have discovered many physiological aspects as to how the brain learns and that neurogenesis—the making of new brain cells—occurs in us all.[25] Neuroscientist and teacher Judy Willis explains this important discovery:

> For today's students, educators are the lifeline they need to climb for access to the playing fields of twenty-first-century opportunity, open only to those who acquire the necessary skillsets. Teachers who are prepared with knowledge of the workings of the brain will have the optimism, incentive, and motivation to follow the ongoing research and to apply their findings to the classroom.
>
> One example is the research about the brain's neuroplasticity and the opportunities we have as educators to help students literally change their brains—and intelligence. To become a teacher without understanding the implications of brain-changing neuroplasticity is a great loss to teachers and their future students.[26]

An area within the broader discipline of neuroscience is neuroethics. Michael Gazzaniga defines *neuroethics* as "the examination of how we want to deal with the social issues of disease, normality, mortality, life-style, and the philosophy of living informed by our understanding of underlying brain mechanisms."[27] There are amazing connections be-tween emotions and learning. We are also beginning to learn more about teenagers' motivation and what triggers both action and inaction.

Recent research led neuroscientists Jay Giedd[28] and Richard Restak[29] to conclude that "teenagers have the passion and the strength but no brakes." Laurence Steinberg refers to the extremes of teenagers' emotions as "a car with a good accelerator but a weak brake. With powerful im-pulses under poor control, the likely result is a crash. And, perhaps, a crime."[30] Sylwester agrees: "The adolescent brain is very sensitive to pleasure and reward, but the impulse-control systems aren't yet mature. Adolescents are thus vulnerable to exploration with highly rewarding drugs—and alcohol/drugs affect the adolescent brain much more than an adult brain."[31]

David Sousa writes, "Teachers, of course, hope their students will permanently remember what was taught. Therefore, it is intriguing to realize that the two structures in the brain mainly responsible for long-term remembering are located in the *emotional* area of the brain."[32] Teen-agers remember stories and songs so well because their developing brains go way beyond data.

As a result of the work of educators such as David Sousa[33] and Eric Jensen,[34] practitioners have been able to apply brain-based instructional strategies within their classroom. Methods such as Dataworks' Explicit Direct Instruction[35] and the emphasis on common formative assess-ments[36] are results of brain research and outcomes upon student learning and assessment.

Science, education, and data are making a significant impact on edu-cation, in terms of reforming the way teaching and learning take place. However, those who work with high school students know quite well that despite their physical maturity and varying degrees of adult-like behaviors, many of them are still emotionally fragile. Hyperarousal does not always equate to hypermaturity and effective activity, in terms of learning and achievement.

Sadly, a reading of the daily headlines reveals all too often that some teachers exploit teenage fragility. These teachers exploit for personal grat-ification. Evidence of this exploitation occurs at the formation of adult-like romantic and sexual relationships with students. Some students might project that they are ready for such relationships. However, readi-ness by will does not equate to readiness in maturity. Again, impulsivity is the driver of teenage readiness. Nevertheless, how could any teacher, knowing teenage emotions and brain functions, seek to work that to a sexual advantage? It befuddles the adult mind. Most teenagers are emo-tionally immature and do not always catch what is going on before it is too late. Lives become as wreckage. Teachers should beware to tread lightly into the emotional zones of teenage students.[37]

Common Emotions

Several common emotions are hardwired into our brains from very early on. Sylwester posits, "Our six primary emotions are happiness, sadness, surprise, fear, disgust, and anger—and we can add many secondary emotions to that list (such as anticipation, tension, and pride). All [the emotions] are involved in the emotionally important cognitive-arousal systems that must be developed and maintained for our brain to recognize dangers and opportunities. It's a use-it-or-lose-it proposition."[38]

Teachers who connect with teenagers emotionally must take into account their levels of emotional maturity. Teachers who move into inappropriate emotional and physical relationships with teenagers are connecting with students in ways that damage the young person's healthy, emotional growth and long-term emotional stability. Besides being morally wrong and illegal, this damage carries over into adulthood. This is probably why some adults, themselves, connect with teenagers on very personal levels. Drawing close to any teenage student, in an emotional sense, is very delicate.

What educator has not had the privilege of enjoying those moments when a student finally comprehends something with which he or she had struggled? Cognition is terrific! Comprehension and long-term memory are excellent. Brain research is clear that teenage students learn best when their affect is set ablaze.

Take an average teenage male who is not fully capable of exercising self-control intrinsically and who is highly impulsive. Place him in a classroom with a gregarious, young, and attractive female teacher whose smile and personality light up the room. What are the chances the young man is thinking about consequences, in terms of social competency?

A perceptive teacher must be aware at all times of his or her effect upon teens, both individually and across groups. This leads to the next section, as we introduce teenage emotional intelligence and emotional expression. Willis helps us to understand the importance of all of this information in the hands of twenty-first-century teachers:

> The most valuable assets for improving education won't be developed in a neuroimaging laboratory. It will be educators, with the foundational knowledge about the science of learning, who will be prepared to evaluate the validity and potential educational correlations from neuroscience research. . . . Teachers will be . . . frontline professionals who . . . recognize potential applications of . . . research and develop the strategies that bring the benefits of this research to their students.[39]

TEENAGERS AND MATURITY

Emotional Intelligence and Expression

Educators are coming to terms today with understanding that the awkwardness of life as teenagers jades much of their reality and thereby affects emotional recall of life's experiences from that period. Some of the perceptions and emotions attached to memories are accurate, and some are not so accurate. Imagine a teenager whose life is marked by a sexual relationship with a person of respect and authority. The adult years, and subsequent adult relationships, will not escape the effects the past. In fact, there may well be lifelong issues.

Teenage brains are in consistent states of arousal. This means that their brains are three to four times as excited, through the emotional centers in their brains, as adult brains. As a result, teenagers are not often basing their cognitive and emotional perceptions on reality. Jensen agrees:

> Adolescence is a wild ride for everybody. . . . There are fast-moving rapid and dramatic changes in biology, cognition, emotion, and interpersonal relationships. . . . Many areas of the brain are under major construction during adolescence. . . . It's safe to call the teen years a "sensitive period." . . . Larger delayed rewards are valued less than smaller immediate rewards . . . kids seek higher levels of novelty and stimulation to achieve the same feeling of pleasure. Risks, rewards, and fun are driving their brains.[40]

Teenagers are all over the map in terms of their cognitive and emotional makeups, which makes them highly susceptible to the words, actions, and emotions of others. So where does this leave memories and thoughts about the past? Since teenage brains are still developing, one can expect their memories to be somewhat different when they are expressed in adulthood. Memories are malleable, and this means emotions are as unique as the memories prompted by them. The adult brain values its memories. We can never experience the same emotion twice, even as our memories make the effort.

FACTORS OF EMOTIONAL INTELLIGENCE

Emotional Wiring

Teenagers are not ready to deal with the deeper emotions of adult life. This is especially true with males, who reach their apex in brain wiring at about age twenty-five. The physical differences between male and female brains are stark, and researchers have detected general differences with respect to levels of the brain's emotional intelligence. Daniel Goleman illustrates these differences:

> Emotional intelligence has four parts: self-awareness, managing our emotions, empathy, and social skill. There are many tests of emotional intelligence, and most seem to show that women tend to have an edge over men when it comes to these basic skills for a happy and successful life. . . . On the other hand, it's not that simple. For instance, some measures suggest women are on average better than men are at some forms of empathy, and men do better than women do when it comes to managing distressing emotions. . . . Women tend to be better at emotional empathy than men are; in general . . . neuroscientists tell us one key to empathy is a brain region called the insula. . . . Here's where women differ from men. If the other person is upset, or the emotions are disturbing, women's brains tend to stay with those feelings. But men's brains do something else: they sense the feelings for a moment then tune out of the emotions and switch to other brain areas that try to solve the problem that's creating the disturbance.
>
> Thus, women's complaint that men are tuned out emotionally, and men's that women are too emotional—it's a brain difference. . . . The male tune-out works well when there's a need to insulate yourself against distress. . . . And the female tendency to stay tuned in helps enormously to nurture and support others. . . . It's part of the "tend-and-befriend" response to stress.[41]

Emotional Intelligence (EI)

Recent education trends have focused on "emotional intelligence" and its role in learning. According to the theorist Goleman, there are four major factors involved in developing, maintaining, and evidencing emotional intelligence (EI): (1) intrinsic and extrinsic motivation, (2) impulse control, (3) empathy, and (4) social competence.[42] Each factor assists in the development of mature emotional intelligence.[43]

Emotional Intelligence: Intrinsic and Extrinsic Motivation

Intrinsic motivation "emerges from an environment that encourages students to discover and explore areas of personal interest and ability."[44] It comes from the teenagers' own impulses for experiences. How do we determine what motivates teenagers on any given day?

First we must find ways to produce relevance to what we are teaching. Students must see how this teaching fits into their world. Learning that is emotional is fun learning. Fun learning is a motivator in and of itself. The point of emphasis here is that learning which involves the emotional bases of students' brains will also affect their inner being.

Second, most teachers have been challenged by their teenage students, "Why do we have to learn this stuff?" and "When are we ever going to use this in the real world?" The answers to these two questions are as follows. In the first instance, the reply is "brain research shows that you need this in order to continue on into cognitive and emotional maturity."

Grades make things relevant to their world, cognitively, emotionally, and immediately. This is why feedback on students' work is of a high value on their learning curve.[45] Grades contextualize learning. Teachers control the grading and thus become part of the context. Teachers and students develop relationships based on grades and the shared requirements toward earning them. Secondly, student success yields benefits that encourage continuing development of motivation and confidence. Confident students are productive students, from my experience.

Emotional Intelligence: Impulse Control

Teenagers often act without giving themselves any time to think through the details of risks, benefits, and causes and effects. There is usually a very limited logical sequence applied to what is called teen logic. Here is an example:

TEENAGE MALE #1: Dude, I'm bored.

TEENAGE MALE #2: Me too.

TEENAGE MALE #1: Let's cut the rest of our classes and go skating.

TEENAGE MALE #2: Okay, cool. But wait! What if we get caught?

TEENAGE MALE #1: No problem. My mom will give us an excuse.

TEENAGE MALE #2: Sweet! I'll ask one of my friends to go too and see if he can drive us.

TEENAGE MALE #1: Awesome!

TEENAGE MALE #2: Hey, bro! Wanna go skatin' with us? We're gonna go shred, baby!

TEENAGE MALE #3: Dude, aiiiiight. Let's chill.

Just to reiterate in closing, teenagers often do not contemplate their actions ahead of time and act more from emotions and are often unable to separate cognition from these emotions. One reason for this is the chemical makeup in their brains.

Brain Chemicals

Brain chemicals have much to do with the way teenagers form bonds with others. Teenagers are biochemically impassioned. "Five brain chemicals and their influences on teenager students" contains a list of a few basic brain chemicals that influence teenager's lives.[46] The five chemicals in questions are (1) noradrenaline (or epinephrine),[47] (2) dopamine,[48] (3) serotonin,[49] (4) glucose,[50] and (5) cortisol.[51]

The focus in the analysis is the impact the chemicals have on the teenager, as a student in the classroom. The abundance or shortage of these chemicals is indicative of maturity or immaturity. Behavior impulses normally associate with the broader discussion of maturity. This leads neuroscientists, such as Giedd, to conclude that teens are normally full speed ahead in many of their choices, crushes, and connections.[52] A brief analysis of each of the chemicals follows.

BRAIN CHEMICALS AND EFFECTS ON TEENAGERS

Noradrenaline (Norepinephrine)

Students called on in class, or faced with a series of choices in front of their peers, are awash with chemicals. They must choose to either participate or not participate. Either choice involves some degree of stress. If students enjoy working on projects in small groups, one can expect brain chemicals, usually referred to as *adrenalines* (including dopamine), to be at high levels. Teachers who structure their classrooms so that there are never any risks to be taken, or that no pressures are experienced, will find students describing the class and teacher as "boring," "unchallenging," and "impractical." Teaching strategies that press limits of healthy risk-taking provide a host of benefits for students. Assisting students in risk-taking provides excellent groundwork for what most students can expect to experience in their adult lives.

Dopamine

Students that find pleasure in life's experiences and in their relationships with people have good levels of dopamine. Students who seek one emotionally high experience after another are causing regular rushes of dopamine. If asked to settle down in a classroom, these students will find it difficult to learn without excitement built in. The teacher whose classroom includes higher rigors, and displays a deep passion for her students and for learning, will begin to see students finding pleasure in the same.

When something is "fun" to a student, dopamine helps the brain to relate it as enjoyable. Conversely, when there are negative experiences involved, dopamine is also at work, seeking to regulate the pain involved. The classroom environment plays a crucial role in the regulation of dopamine levels in teenagers. The average person usually refers to dopamine as the "adrenaline rush."

Serotonin

Serotonin helps to regulate moods, desire for sleep, and even diges-
tion. Getting students up and about the classroom assists in the creation
of serotonin. In other words, too little serotonin, the student is drowsy.
Physical movement in the classroom by interaction with others is healthy.
Small-group conversations, and anything assisting in the reduction of
states associated with negative anxiety for teenagers, is equally as
healthy.

Glucose

Glucose (blood sugar) and fat work together with cortisol to produce
energy in our bodies. Teenagers whose glucose levels drop—because of
skipping a meal or lack of physical exercise—are going to be hampered
by an eventual lack of energy and motivation. Physical movement and
exertion help to create glucose. So whatever teachers can do to incorporate student movement about the classroom, at pivotal times during the
class period, will help with energy levels and production of glucose and
other chemicals vital to maximizing their classroom time.

Cortisol

Cortisol works together with glucose to provide energy for students.
Glucose also uses stored fat to help the body manage stress. This stress is
not just from pressures put on students by teachers and by life in general.
The stress is also physical. Therefore, athletes and academic competitors
are candidates for increased production of cortisol, working in tandem
with glucose. Teaching students how to manage stress means to instruct
them on balancing their lives, getting plenty of exercise and rest, so that
their brains and bodies are balanced, avoiding an abundance of any one
chemical for prolonged periods. This is precisely why teachers should
recommend their students not be online late into the evening hours or
sleep with their cell phones on. Such behaviors continue the flow of
chemicals at hours when the body and brain need rest.
Let us move into the third of Goleman's areas: empathy.

Emotional Intelligence: Empathy

Empathy is an important emotional expression for teenagers. It de-
rives from emotional intelligence, which occurs in the developing frontal
lobes of teenagers' brains. Empathy allows students to act in ethical ways
and demonstrate altruism, which is why many teenagers care so much
about their friends and others, the nature and animals around them, and
the environment. Fairness is a serious issue for empathetic teenagers,
made all the more obvious when they stand up for their friends in class.

Teachers can help teenagers and their peers in the development of empathy by allowing students to share their thoughts and allow their experiences with empathy to connect with those of others. Sometimes writing is a way for students to express their thoughts. Teachers ought to be aware of the tool they possess in student empathy but avoid using empathy to manipulate students' emotions for an agenda or selfish reasons or to step over the line of propriety with a teenager. Following are two contrasting examples.

First, imagine a teacher with a strong political agenda; he purposefully plays to the emotions of many in the class to win them to his side. This type of manipulation crosses a professional line. Teachers manipulate students in a thousand ways that are healthy and appropriate, and telling the truth in the most unbiased way possible is always a great learning tool for students. Here is a story about empathy from my youth.

> As a fifteen year old, my mode of transportation was a homemade bicycle. Mismatched tires, fabricated handlebars, and a banana seat made up my pride and joy. My friends and I were always making things together, and our bicycles were among our crowning achievements. We rode everywhere on our bicycles, often taking lengthy day trips for fun.
>
> One day, my friends and I went on a long bike ride to see my grandmother. She lived in Towaco, New Jersey, sixteen miles away one way, which meant navigating some very busy roads. Somewhere about halfway into our trip, which began in Bloomfield, New Jersey, we braked to a stop at a four-way highway intersection. As we impatiently straddled our bikes, waiting for the light to change in our favor, a couple of us noticed a small kitten standing in the intersection. We also noticed that it was in the direct path of a turning semi-tractor trailer. Within seconds, all of my friends noticed the kitten and began to yell at the driver to stop. However, it was too late. One of the rear wheels of the truck clipped the kitten's body. "Oh, no!" many of us yelled.
>
> I quickly dropped my bike and ran out into the traffic. One of my friends raised his hands for cars to stop. I scooped up the writhing kitten and cupped her in my palms and then ran to my friends. One of them said, "Put her down; she's almost dead anyway." However, I couldn't put her down. Her bright green eyes were teary. She struggled to breathe. She mustered enough strength to release a couple of high-pitched mews. Within seconds, the tiny kitten shuddered in my hands, went limp, and died. I had never seen anything or anyone die before, and I was at a loss as to what to do. So I laid her partially mangled body against the curb at the intersection and rode off with tears in my eyes.

The fourth and last of Goleman's areas is social competence.

Emotional Intelligence: Social Competence

Social competence is that which allows students to "read" social contexts and then respond appropriately. Teenagers are often socially awkward, particularly when singled out, or in the beginning stages of relationships with persons they care deeply about. They seek to fit in, while removing the need to justify the fit. Teenagers find identity by dressing like each other. Haircuts, taste in music, youthful language, and teenage activities and games are all points of identity for students and demonstrate levels of social competency. Teenagers are attuned to social competence in relation to each other in greater fashion than they are in terms of relationships with adults.

One of the most intriguing things about teenagers is their propensity to think they are the sole inventors of style, music, and language. Since they have such strong emotional connections to shared perceptions and common words, there is the tendency to conclude that no one but them understands the meanings behind their generational uniqueness. Most adults experienced the same kinds of things as teenagers. A certain empowerment grows from the notion that no generation is like our own generation.

For example, texting and technology have increased student attention to emotions. The likelihood increases that text and photos will become memorable. Each text is a novelty. There are some important things to consider about texting, especially if allowed in class. One of these considerations is what texting does to a teenager's emotions and the extent these emotions impact student learning.

TEENAGERS AND EMOTIONAL MEMORIES

Recall the father who made national headlines and became a YouTube viral sensation. His fifteen-minute on-camera reading and recording drew all sorts of attention. Essentially, what the father did was read his fifteen-year-old teenage daughter's profanity-filled Facebook posts, one at a time. He told her not to post comments about the family, and she persisted. Therefore, he took matters to another level.

As the father sat outside on a lawn chair, calmly reading his daughter's posts on camera, he would pause briefly, at times, to provide his own profanity-laced comments. When finished, he took out a pistol and shot several bullets into his daughter's laptop computer, which lay on the ground next to his chair. All of this was broadcast for the world to view. The video went viral, which means millions upon millions of viewers watched it.

Shooting and "killing" a computer, as a point to be made, is something the teenager will never forget. The incident was memorable and certainly touched the emotions. However, what was learned in the process? This is no way to relate to a teenager that her disobedience in posting profanity and angry language on her Facebook page was unacceptable. These are extremes and are never the best methods for modeling appropriate behaviors.

Here is another example of extremism, this time occurring in the classroom. Some years ago a junior-high colleague was teaching a unit on terrorism. My colleague had a friend dress up in black clothing and a mask and come into his classroom to hold his students hostage. There was no weapon involved, only the imaginations of teenagers and words of an impostor. The surprise element resulted in shrieks, and some of the students screamed out of shock and fear.

This incident was also memorable. However, these types of tactics are as inappropriate as they are memorable. That was the conclusion drawn by the principal and many of the parents. Teachers should try to remember the "son or daughter rule." Would it be appropriate for another teacher to do or say to my own teenager what I plan to do or say to this teenager? We must remember that teenagers will remember strong emotional experiences.

HUMANS ARE SOCIAL CREATURES

Humans are social creatures. Our brains connect in ways that allow language, expression, feelings, and various other methods of relationship building to take place.[53] Sylwester concurs: "We're a social species, and so much of our cognitive strength comes from our ability to successfully understand and interact with others. Frontal-lobe areas . . . play key roles in developing and regulating social behavior."[54] Social connections, resulting in social behaviors, are part of the norm for social creatures.

Immordino-Yang and Damasio maintain that humans are "fundamentally emotional and social creatures." However, they add implications to these fundamentals, concluding that

> some in the field of education often fail to consider that the high-level cognitive skills taught in schools, including reasoning, decision making, and processes related to language, reading, and mathematics, do not function as rational, disembodied systems, somehow influenced by but detached from emotion and the body. . . . Any competent teacher recognizes that emotions and feelings affect students' performance and learning, as does the state of the body. . . . We contend . . . that the relationship between learning, emotion, and body state runs deeper than many educators realize and is interwoven with the notion of learning.[55]

In addition to the interpersonal relationships developed in classrooms, there is a much greater focus today on student achievement and success.

Years of classroom experience enable teachers to make the adjustments to focus on greater student outcomes, pertaining to learning that is more rigorous. Ultimately, students who have solid relationships with teachers find education more meaningful.

LOVE AND EMOTIONAL MATURITY

What does the average teenager know about love? If you ask any of them this question, they will respond with "I know a lot." The response "I know a lot" indicates they have limited knowledge and even less understanding. Ask the average teenager another question—such as What are the differences between unconditional love and conditional love?, and Can you provide examples?—and things becomes a little more difficult. What teenagers proclaim to know and what they profess to understand are two different realities. They sometimes confuse knowledge with understanding. They are not alone. In fact, some adults are still making efforts to figure this out, as well, which is another reason why this book is such a necessity for those in my profession.

Teenagers view videos and how-to presentations and observe sex and romance in the media, and sometimes they believe the ideals and feelings demonstrated across culture, and on screen, comprise the depths of love. Many Hollywood movie endings leave us feeling good, which touches teenage girls' emotions especially well. Why is all of this a concern for teachers and their relationships with teenagers? Teenagers are not emotionally mature yet, but adults are supposed to be. Consequently, we must analyze whether teenage emotions generated from their impulsivity can ever be trusted.

Emotions can fool us, and emotions can rule us! There must be a balance struck. Teenagers' emotions fool them into believing there is depth of emotional maturity merely because they feel more deeply and are aware of emotions like never before. This gets back to novelty experiences: newness equates to a near epiphany, which comprises reality for the average teenager. Even empathy can fool teenagers into a sense of caring that may be a bit overblown. It has already been established that what teenagers perceive as their feelings may not be based in reality.

Modern culture bombards all of us with sexual images, often aimed directly at teenagers. However, not all sexual pressures aim at youth. Most everyone wants to be sexually attractive and alluring these days. There are matchmaking sites for adults from ages eighteen to ninety-eight. We are told to be sexy at any age. Clothing and music converge toward sexuality. Advertisers are using sexual imagery in ways that include young children. This is especially problematic and plays into the distortions and perversions of pedophiles.

Have you looked online lately? Pornography seems to be everywhere and easily accessible. Those parents who do not engage in a regular discourse about sexuality with their children should not be surprised if teenagers pick up their knowledge from sources that seek more from them than their visual and auditory attention. Some argue that teenagers are more mature today because of exposure to adult-like materials. This is not true. Advocates of that position are either naïve or have not worked with teenagers long enough to analyze their actions to understand their brain development and the characteristics that comprise a lack of emotional maturity.

Teenagers cannot be any more mature than their brains and bodies allow them to be. They exist in awkward physical and emotional states. Their bodies and brains are not yet in alignment or chronologically developed enough for this maturity to occur. Perception is not reality. Teachers who mistake well-developed teenagers as having arrived at maturity must stop to consider that the outside does not match the inside.

When it comes to love, we must ask ourselves the extent to which teenagers understand their feelings. Are they aware that there are many expressions of love? Compared to the images of "love" crammed into their ocular portals, is there deeper understanding beyond the physical? When the teenage amygdalae, the seat of emotions, are hyperaroused, the feelings of love and expressions that accompany the feelings can be overwhelming. However, the reality is that the feelings are more vast and complicated. There are many types of love and even more expressions of love—and only one of these focuses on sex, directly, yet all forms are involved. Nevertheless, we rarely make this distinction because of the rising tide of sexuality that threatens to drown modern culture.

In every generation of teenagers, including this present generation, young people are learning to be like adults in their actions, but they are still young in their souls. How and what they learn depends a lot on the adults in their lives. As we navigate through this age of sex and communication technologies, it is incumbent on adults and people in positions of authority and respect to draw clear moral and ethical lines right down the middle of our culture.

TEENAGERS AND EXPRESSIONS OF LOVE

Types of Love

Teenagers' music is flooded with songs about love, often defined as casual sex. Videos demonstrating affections and playing up one's sexuality, as well as their emotions and crushes, are enticing. However, what exactly is the extent of teenagers' understanding about love? The Greek language helps us to understand the different concepts and expressions of love. Sometimes deeper conceptual meanings are lost when translating ancient words into English.[56]

First, there is *agape* love—a love characterized by unconditional dedication and lifelong expression, not relegated merely to circumstances. It is love that is present in commitment. Teenagers idealize the forever love, even with their innate impulsivity.

A second type of love is found in the concept of *phileo*, a type of brotherly love—whence the city of Philadelphia derived its name (*phileo* = love; *adelphos* = brother). This is the kind of love that rises in support of a sibling wronged by another. This expression comes across as vicarious love, the very expression that accompanies unity in standing with another against a bully or speaking on behalf of a person experiencing an unfair situation.[57]

A third type of love is characterized by the word *storge*. This is the warm, fuzzy type of love. *Storge* is likely the result of a crush, or the love of a family pet, the giving of hugs, and things such as these. One word comes to mind when *storge* is present. That word is *affection*.[58]

This leaves the last type of love as the physical love, eros, whence we derive the word *erotic*. This type of love excites the mind and body and prepares it for sexual pleasure. This is where the brain's hyperarousal in teenagers sometimes meets with difficulty. Deciphering between strong physical attraction and expressions of love that accompany the emotions and feelings are often misread. Of these four loves, eros is the one that modern culture elevates in alignment with teenage impulsivity.[59] In addition, it seems to motivate many of the inappropriate physical and sexual relationships teachers are having with their students.

Today's culture focuses almost exclusively on erotic forms of love—the kind of love that does not lead to lifelong commitment in most cases. Eros is not necessarily compatible with meetings of minds or shared emotions or intellects. Eros sparks lusts and passions, growing ever so quickly from emotions to fiery sexual pleasures. Relating under the notions of two different types of love can only lead to frustration for teenagers. Yet this is precisely where teenagers are subject to deception and manipulation. Adults are equally susceptible to falling into the "pleasure trap," considering each of the four types of love, and various expressions associated with each form.[60]

A FEW CLOSING THOUGHTS ON EMOTIONAL AND PHYSIOLOGICAL DIFFERENCES

Physical maturity has its own time clock, as does emotional maturity. Culture often reduces love to feelings and pleasures. Culture is also classified as (1) societal pressure by those with a certain sensual postmodern mind-set, (2) power in the hands of people who possess the platform to command media and airwaves, control advertisements, as well as set trends for style and entertainment, and (3) people connecting with other people on levels to motivate them to accept their philosophies, products, or lifestyles. We call these folks *trendsetters*, and they are celebrated in our culture. We also refer to some of these people as *cultural icons*, and *iconoclasts of traditional culture*.[61]

Teenagers do not possess the requisite emotional intelligence and maturity to understand the depths of love. They are also unaware when manipulation and substitution occur, resulting in confusion over one or more of the types of love.[62] Are they aware that their brains seek self-gratification? What we call *emotions* are actually complex body/mind states that associate with four different sets of physiological and psychological processes. This leads us to chapter 4, where we will explore relationships between teachers and teenage students. These processes overlap and complicate the hardwiring of the teenage brain. Teachers and students must be aware of this and refrain from anything inappropriate between them.

SUMMARY

Teenagers have an abundance of synapses, or regions where transmission and reception of impulses occurs. The abundance of these synapses signifies that teenagers are full of brain excitement. Teenagers contextualize their world through their emotions. Sometimes these contexts are environmental and their surroundings settle into their memories. Memories increase tremendously with the engagement of students' amygdalae, the emotional centers of the brain.

The latest research in neuroscience is yielding some astounding data. Studies are showing that some gender differences in the brain arise before a baby is even born. Males and females navigate learning quite differently. Many studies suggest that male brains tend to find direction through circumstances by "estimating space and orientation," something that neuroscientists refer to as *dead reckoning*. Neuroscientists now understand that males and females process the same emotional memories very differently.

Adults generally believe teenagers calculate their youthful actions. Adults draw conclusions based on their experiences, and these conclusions are referred to as *gut-level* or *intuitive* conclusions. Those who work with high school students know quite well that despite their physical maturity and varying degrees of adult-like behaviors, many of them are still emotionally fragile.

Hyperarousal of brains and emotions does not always equate to hypermaturity and effective activity in terms of learning and achievement. Emotions are as unique as the memories prompted by them. For example, the adult brain values its memories. The same emotion is never experienced identically, but our memories make the effort.

Recent education trends have focused on "emotional intelligence" and its role in learning. Goleman sees four major factors involved in developing, maintaining, and evidencing emotional intelligence: (1) intrinsic and extrinsic motivation, (2) impulse control, (3) empathy, and (4) social competence.

Brain chemicals have much to do with the way teenagers form bonds with others. The abundance or shortage of these chemicals is indicative of what adults consider maturity. The five brain chemicals discussed in the chapter are (1) noradrenaline (or epinephrine), (2) dopamine, (3) serotonin, (4) glucose, and (5) cortisol. Each has a specific role in learning for both teenagers and adults.

Humans are social creatures. Our brains connect in ways that allow language, expression, feelings, and various other methods of relationship building. Emotions can fool us, and emotions can rule us! Teenagers' emotions fool them into believing there is depth of emotional maturity merely because they feel more deeply and are aware of emotions like never before. Teenagers cannot be any more mature than their brains and bodies allow them to be. What we call *emotions* are actually complex body/mind states made up of four different sets of physiological and psychological processes.

Today's culture focuses almost exclusively on erotic forms of love—the kind that does not lead to lifelong commitment in most cases. Physical maturity has its own time clock, and so does emotional maturity. Culture often reduces love to feelings and pleasures. Since teenagers do not generally possess the requisite emotional intelligence and maturity to understand the depths of love, they also do not recognize when manipulation occurs.

DISCUSSION QUESTIONS

1. How would you define *teenage maturity*, providing three examples of behaviors to illustrate the definition?
2. Can you briefly explain how hardwired emotions play a role in what teenagers and adults remember?
3. What causes teenagers to be impulsive in their actions? What is taking place in their brains to prompt such impulsivity?
4. What are three reasons neuroscientists have concluded that memories are malleable?
5. Given that male and female brains have characteristic differences in structure and function, can you name and explain two of these differences?

6. What are your opinions on Gardner's and Goleman's research into "multiple intelligences" and "emotional intelligence"? In terms of the developing brains of teenagers, do these intelligences exist, or are they parts of something larger and different?
7. What are the roles of the chemicals in the teenage brain, and how does each affect behaviors?
8. In what ways are emotions unreliable as the foundation of knowledge and truth in the lives of teenagers?
9. How has modern technology assisted in expanding and retracting social interactions in human relationships?
10. Considering the average teenage male and female and the "four loves," how would you describe the teenager's ideas about these loves?

NOTES

1. Alison Gopnik, "What's Wrong with the Teenage Mind?" *Wall Street Journal*, January 2012, accessed February 2, 2012, http://online.wsj.com/article/SB100 01424052970203806504577181351486558984.html.

2. Don Campbell, *The Mozart Effect* (New York: Avon Books, 1997).

3. Daniel Goleman, *Emotional Intelligence* (New York: Bantam Books, 1995).

4. Howard Gardner, *Frames of Mind: Theories of Multiple Intelligences* (New York: Basic Books, 1983, 1993, 2011).

5. K. W. fischer and T. R. Bidell, "Dynamic Development of Psychological Structures in Action and Thought," in *Handbook of Child Psychology*, 5th ed., vol. 1, *Theoretical Models of Human Development*, ed. R. M. Lerner and W. Damron (New York: Wiley, 1997), 467–561.

6. Anita Woolfolk, *Educational Psychology*, 10th ed. (San Francisco: Allyn & Bacon, 2007), 26–36. See also B. Wadsworth, *Piaget's Theory of Cognitive and Affective Development*, 5th ed. (Boston: Allyn & Bacon, 1996), accessed February 19, 2011, www.learningandteaching.info/learning/piaget.html.

7. Damon and Lerner, *Handbook of Child Psychology*.

8. Larry Cahill, "His Brain, Her Brain," *Scientific American*, May (2005): 41. See also Larry Cahill et al., "Sex-Related Hemispheric Lateraliztion of Amygdala Function in Emotionally Influenced Memory: An fMRI Investigation," *Learning and Memory* 11 (2004): 3. Robert Coles, *The Moral Intelligence of Children* (New York: Random House Publishers, 1997). M. K. Demaray and C. K. Malecki, "The Relationship between Perceived Social Support and Maladjustment for Students at Risk," *Psychology in the Schools* 39 (2002): 305–16.

9. Cahill, "His Brain, Her Brain," 42.

10. Eric Jensen, *Enriching the Brain* (San Francisco: Jossey-Bass Publishers, 2006), 10.

11. Victor G. Carrion et al., "Posttraumatic Stress Symptoms and Brain Function during a Response-Inhibition Task: An fMRI Study in Youth," *Depression and Anxiety* 25 (2008): 514–26, accessed June 7, 2012, http://med.stanford.edu/nbc/articles/11Posttraumatic%20stress%20symptoms%20and%20brain%20function%20during%20a%20response-inhibition%20task.pdf.

12. Cahill, "His Brain, Her Brain," 44.

13. Cahill, "His Brain, Her Brain," 44. Bracketed inclusion is mine. See also Deborah Blum, *Sex on the Brain: The Biological Differences between Men and Women* (New York: Viking Press, 1997).

14. David A. Sousa, *How the Brain Learns*, 3rd ed. (Thousand Oaks, Calif.: Corwin Press, 2006), 15–24. Michael Gurian and Kathy Stevens, "With Boys and Girls in

Mind," *Educational Leadership*, November 2004, 62, no. 3:21–26. See also Michael Gurian, Patricia Henley, and Terry Trueman, *Boys and Girls Learn Differently! A Guide for Teachers and Parents* (San Francisco: Jossey-Bass/Wiley Publishers, 2001); Michael Gurian, *The Wonder of Boys: What Parents, Mentors, and Educators Can Do to Shape Boys into Exceptional Men* (New York: Penguin Books, 1996); Michael Gurian, *The Wonder of Girls: Understanding the Hidden Nature of Our Daughters* (New York: Atria Books, 2002).

15. Sousa, *How the Brain Learns.*

16. Blum, *Sex on the Brain.*

17. Shelley Taylor, *The Tending Instinct* (New York: Times Books, 2002).

18. Sousa, *How the Brain Learns.*

19. Gurian et al., *Boys and Girls Learn Differently!*

20. Eric Jensen, *Teaching with the Brain in Mind* (Alexandria, Va.: Association for Supervision and Curriculum Development, 1998, 2005).

21. Jay Giedd in Richard Restak, *The Secret Life of the Brain* (Washington, D.C.: Joseph Henry Press, 2001), accessed January 30, 2010, http://elfnj.org/node/21.

22. Jensen, *Enriching the Brain*, 24, 31.

23. Giedd in Restak, *The Secret Life of the Brain.*

24. Sousa, *How the Brain Learns.* See also Jensen, *Enriching the Brain.*

25. S. McGillivray and A. Castel, "Betting on Memory Leads to Metacognitive Improvement by Younger and Older Adults," *Psychology and Aging* 26, no. 1 (2011): 137–44.

26. Judy Willis, *How Your Child Learns Best: Brain-Friendly Strategies You Can Use to Ignite Your Child's Learning and Increase School Success* (Naperville, Ill.: Sourcebooks, Inc., 2009). See also Judy Willis, *Brain-Friendly Strategies for the Inclusion Classroom* (Alexandria, Va.: Association for Supervision and Curriculum Development, 2007); M. Eisenhart and R. L. DeHaan, "Doctoral Preparation of Scientifically Based Educational Researchers," *Educational Researcher* 34, no. 4 (2005): 3–13; and Judy Willis, "A Neurologist Makes the Case for Teaching Teachers about the Brain," *Edutopia* (July 27, 2012), accessed July 29, 2012, www.edutopia.org/blog/neuroscience-higher-ed-judy-willis.

27. Michael S. Gazzaniga, *The Ethical Brain* (New York: HarperCollins Publishers, 2005), xv.

28. Gopnik, "What's Wrong with the Teenage Mind?" See also "Science on Adolescent Development," accessed February 3, 2012, http://eji.org/eji/files/Science%20on%20Adolescent%20Development_0.pdf .

29. Malcolm Ritter, "Experts Link Teen Brains' Immaturity, Juvenile Crime," *USA Today*, December 2, 2007, accessed June 3, 2011, www.usatoday.com/tech/science/2007-12-02-teenbrains_N.htm.

30. Laurence Steinberg in Ritter, "Experts Link Teen Brains' Immaturity." See also Laurence Steinberg, "Adolescent Development and Juvenile Justice," accessed November 28, 2011, http://eji.org/eji/files/Science%20on%20Adolescent%20 Development_0.pdf.

31. Robert Sylwester, *The Adolescent Brain: Reaching for Autonomy* (San Francisco: Corwin Press, 2007).

32. Sousa, *How the Brain Learns*, 19.

33. Sousa, *How the Brain Learns*, 19.

34. Jensen, *Enriching the Brain.*

35. John Hollingsworth and Silvia Ybarra, *Explicit Direct Instruction* (Thousand Oaks, Calif.: Corwin Press, 2006). See also www.dataworks-ed.com/research.

36. Larry Ainsworth and Donald Viegut, *Common Formative Assessment: How to Connect Standards-Based Instruction and Assessment* (Thousand Oaks, Calif.: Corwin Press, 2006). See also Richard DuFour and Robert Eaker, *Professional Learning Communities at Work* (Bloomington, Ind.: Solution Tree, 1998); and www.solution-tree.com/plc-at-work and www.allthingsplc.info/wordpress/?p=46.

37. Gazzaniga, *The Ethical Brain.*

38. Robert Sylwester, "Present at the Maturation of the Adult Brain," revised 2002 paper presented at Learning and the Brain Conference, Stanford University, February

8, 2008, pp. 1–8. See also Jensen, *Teaching with the Brain in Mind*; www.JensenLearning. com ; Sylwester, *The Adolescent Brain*; and www.brainconnection.com/sylwester/.

39. Judy Willis, "A Neurologist Makes the Case."

40. Jensen, *Enriching the Brain*, 101–2.

41. "Are Women More Emotionally Intelligent than Men?" May 6, 2011, accessed March 6, 2012, http://danielgoleman.info/2011/are-women-more-emotionally-intelligent-than-men/. See also *Daniel Goleman Archives*, accessed March 6, 2012, http:// danielgoleman.info/category/emotional-intelligence/.

42. Daniel Goleman, *Emotional Intelligence: Why It Can Matter More than IQ* (New York: Bantam Books, 1995).

43. Gardner, *Frames of Mind*.

44. Sylwester, *The Adolescent Brain*.

45. Jensen, *Enriching the Brain*.

46. Jensen, *Enriching the Brain*.

47. "Noradrenaline (Norepinephrine): How Does It Work?," accessed July 12, 2012, www.netdoctor.co.uk/heart-and-blood/medicines/noradrenaline.html.

48. "Dopamine: A Sample Neurotransmitter," Addiction Science Research and Education Center, College of Pharmacy, University of Texas, accessed July 16, 2012, www.utexas.edu/research/asrec/dopamine.html.

49. "What Is Serotonin? What Does Serotonin Do?" *Medical News Today* (August 4, 2011), accessed July 16, 2012, www.medicalnewstoday.com/articles/232248.php.

50. Roni Caryn Rabin, "Blood Sugar Control Linked to Memory Decline, Study Says," *New York Times*, December 31, 2008, accessed December 18, 2010, www. nytimes.com/2009/01/01/health/31memory.html. See also Jane B. Gore, Desiree L. Krebs, and Marise B. Parent, "Changes in Blood Glucose and Salivary Cortisol Are Not Necessary for Arousal to Enhance Memory in Young or Older Adults," *Psychoneuroendocrinology* 31, no. 5 (2006): 589–600, accessed August 23, 2012, http://pubget.com/ paper/16530333/Changes_in_blood_glucose_and_salivary_cortisol_are_not_ necessary_for_arousal_to_enhance_memory_in_young_or_older_adults.

51. Web MD, s.v. "Cortisol in Blood," accessed April 6, 2011, www.webmd.com/a-to-z-guides/cortisol-14668.

52. Giedd in Restak, *The Secret Life of the Brain*.

53. G. Rizzolatti, "Mirrors in the Mind," *Scientific American*, October 16, 2006, 54–61.

54. Sylwester, *The Adolescent Brain*.

55. Mary Helen Immordino-Yang and Antonio Damasio, "We Feel, Therefore We Learn: The Relevance of Affective and Social Neuroscience to Education," in *The Jossey-Bass Reader on the Brain and Learning* (San Francisco: Jossey-Bass Publishers, 2007), 183–92.

56. W. E. Vine, *An Expository Dictionary of New Testament Words*, vol. 3 (Old Tappan, N.J.: Fleming H. Revell Company, 1940, 1966), 21–24. See also H. E. Dana and Julius R. Mantey, *A Manual Grammar of the Greek New Testament* (New York: Macmillan Company, 1927, 1962).

57. Vine, *An Expository Dictionary of New Testament Words*.

58. Vine, *An Expository Dictionary of New Testament Words*.

59. Nancy Brown, "Sexuality in the 21st Century and Beyond: Adolescents' Behavior and Beliefs" (Stanford University Palo Alto Medical Foundation, 2005), accessed August 6, 2012, www.pamf.org/teen/abc/sex/ethicalsex.html. See also C. S. Lewis, *The Four Loves* (New York: Harcourt, Brace, Jovanovich Publishers, 1960), passim, 53–163.

60. Lewis, *The Four Loves*. See also Vine, *An Expository Dictionary*, 21–24. And see Dana and Mantey, *A Manual Grammar*.

61. Dictionary.com, s. v. "Trendsetter," accessed August 3, 2012, http://dictionary. reference.com/browse/trendsetter.

62. Goleman, *Emotional Intelligence*.

FOUR

Relationships between Teachers and Teenage Students

In making our choice, we've hurt a lot of people. . . . We [kept] asking ourselves, Do we make everyone else happy, or do we follow our hearts?

— forty-two-year-old James Hooker[1]

Temptation is a woman's weapon and man's excuse.

—H. L. Mencken

AT A GLANCE

There are six major sections in this chapter: (1) balancing risk with proximity, (2) the inappropriate and the illegal, (3) two basic flaws in thinking, (4) technological advancements change relationships, (5) teachers as sex seekers?, and (6) predators gone wild. We close the chapter with a summary and discussion questions.

BALANCING RISK WITH PROXIMITY

Now that chapter 3 has helped us understand a bit more about teenagers' brains and their emotions, we must ask a very serious question. How do educators decide how close is too close, in terms of relationships with their teenage students? Educators face a real dilemma in trying to find a balance between expectations and reality as they weigh the proper distance they ought to keep from teenagers. As we begin, let us stipulate that classroom environments and teenagers' demeanors are always shifting. This means certain moral and ethical positions must reach clear points of definition, or they are subject to shifting as well.

How Close Is Too Close?

We begin with examples found in recent headlines.[2] At the national level, some teachers set poor examples by posting sex-related comments, sexual photographs, or comments or photographs involving alcohol use. In the state of Georgia, Facebook and text messages sparked and fueled a sexual relationship between an eighth-grade teacher and her fourteen-year-old male student.

A fifty-six-year-old Illinois language-arts teacher was found guilty of sexual abuse and assault of a seventeen-year-old female student. Records indicated he and the student exchanged more than seven hundred text messages. Likewise, a thirty-seven-year-old California high school band director pleaded guilty to sexual misconduct with a sixteen-year-old female student. Her Facebook page recorded over 1,200 private messages from the band director. In the state of Pennsylvania a thirty-nine-year-old male high school athletic director was arrested for offering gifts to a former male student in exchange for sex. He was convicted on the charge of "attempted corruption of a minor." Technology played a role in developing and extending the relationship, and in the teacher's eventual conviction.

Teachers are too close to students when their proximity in relationship is the foundation for serious moral and educational compromises. As a result, proximity concerns are evident when teachers' relationships with students (1) distract from the mission of the school, (2) provide emotional confusion for students and teachers, (3) manifest themselves by undercutting or usurping family values of teachers or students, or (4) assume that teachers and students share a very special connection or emotional bond between them. Please read those four statements again. If a teacher's relational proximity violates any one of these, he or she needs to reevaluate how close they are to their students.

Shared Activities

Teachers who genuinely care from a wholesome heart and passion can work wonders with teenagers. According to DeRoche and Williams, students learn best when they know teachers care about them and are passionate about their content areas.[3] Students and teachers are drawing more closely together through joint stakes in performance outcomes. No Child Left Behind, newly adopted National Common Core Standards, and other standardized and localized assessments thrust humans together in high-stakes common causes. Such is the stuff that helps to produce educational character.[4]

Stepping up academic rigors can be a good thing for education, nationally. However, resulting stress levels have begun to take their toll among students, administrators, and teachers alike. Likewise, athletic coaches and academic extracurricular coaches have year-round club teams, meeting often to practice or compete throughout summers. They have to press everyone to compete to win. During the year, coaches and students travel together on weekends for various school-related functions. The pressure of competition, joined with the time spent together elsewhere throughout the normal day, can become problematic.

Coaching obligations, combined with mentoring and tutoring, thrust many teachers and coaches into a very different situation today than previously. High stakes pressures to "race to the top" and win, and to do so year-round, lead to exhaustion. Sometimes this exhaustion dulls a sense of right and wrong.

As educators, administrators, and parents remind us, we live in a student-centered world. Education, proclaim the bureaucrats, is first and foremost about students.[5] Parents are increasingly relying on schools to assist in the rearing of their children. Schools have stepped up the whole child-education approach. "At the core of the 'whole child' concept is the understanding that children grow physically, emotionally, and intellectually; therefore, school should attend to all of these areas of growth."[6] More and more parents are using the schools as places to rely on—and places to blame for things that go awry in their teenagers' lives.

THE INAPPROPRIATE AND THE ILLEGAL

There are many examples of teacher-student relationships in the news these days. There are arrests made in this nation almost every day that involve teachers, coaches, and administrators. The criminal charges range from sexual assault to the rape of a child. Teenagers are not helped at all when colleges do nothing about sex parties or when professors even encourage "love on campus," as Yale English professor William Deresiewicz did in his piece titled "Love on Campus: Why We Should Understand, and Even Encourage, a Certain Sort of Erotic Intensity between Student and Professor."[7]

What the professor seems not to have considered is that the eighteen-year-old senior in high school is barely different from the eighteen-year-old freshman in college. To make matters worse, some teenagers are having sex with their professors in college and there is little outcry. Where are the states' laws restricting these behaviors between persons of authority and their college students?

Teenagers are adults at eighteen, legally. However, what is legal is certainly not always moral. These eighteen-year-olds, off-limits in high school, experience direct erotic exposure as eighteen-year-olds in college. When is an eighteen-year-old not an eighteen-year-old? The easy answer is *At college.*

High school students do not need erotic exposure. Yet this is what is taking place in far too many places of academe. Take, for example, one incident involving a Florida teacher and one of his female students.

A single, male teacher in his mid-twenties developed an after-hours relationship with one of his female high school students, a sixteen-year-old. They had been cell phone texting for months, and an emotionally deep relationship had been established. She said they were in love. Has the reader taken the time to consider how these relationships begin and grow into full-blown physical affairs? How could this kind of relationship possibly have blossomed from the limited time the teacher and student would have spent together at school?

It didn't. Technology and communication from home and in private are the primary enhancements of student-teacher relational bonds. Late-night chats, arrangements to meet, and liaisons during school events grew out of their continued communications, all aided by communication technologies.

The teacher and his teenage student shared texts and photos, chatted on the computer late into the evenings, and teased each other right in class via cell phone—the rest of the class oblivious to what was transpiring. The teacher actually sent the teenager random text messages during classes, just to "make her smile." In this case, the teacher was a private-school educator, released from his position because of "an inappropriate relationship" with a female student. At last check, the two were openly dating now that she has graduated from high school.

The communication impulsivity of today's generation is interesting. Teachers should tread cautiously into this realm. These kinds of problems between teachers and students are no longer rarities, as illustrated by Mikaela Gilbert-Lurie:

> With the advent of technology and online communication, teachers have perhaps never had more opportunities to foster relationships with their students outside of the classroom. Thanks to social networking, teachers can now communicate with their students through e-mails, texts, and instant messages. Oftentimes, behind the safety net of the screen, teachers forget their roles as mentors and figures of authority. Instead, they fall into the trap of talking intimately as if they were romantic interests and thus potential sex objects. With just a screen and some changing language, in the privacy of their own homes, teachers might forget they are talking to confused, acne-plagued, shy teenagers from their classrooms. Perhaps they enjoy the distraction, attention, or compliments they are receiving, becoming too easily seduced. Teachers seem to be finding themselves unable to separate their professions from their personal lives, a risk they should be able to afford.[8]

Examining Gilbert-Lurie's words a little more closely compels us to ask four pertinent questions about the case mentioned earlier: First, what made the communication inappropriate? Second, what part did the initial flirtation play between the two? Third, why would a teacher text a student while in any class? Fourth, did anyone cross any boundaries by communicating with each other from their homes, late into the evening, and without parental knowledge? The answers to these questions are evidenced upon review of the above four-point proximity test to conclude whether teachers have drawn too close to students in relationships.

First, the relationship distracted from the mission of the school. One could argue that the teacher had begun the relationship with the school mission in mind. However, that quickly dissipated. The teacher went beyond the school's mission.

Second, the relationship between the teacher and student was responsible for an emotional confusion in the lives of fellow teachers and students, including their own. The moral lines separating adult and teenager were blurred by first allowing an emotional connection, then by exploring this connection romantically. The teacher's actions crossed moral boundaries.

Third, the relationship between the teacher and student undercut—and even usurped—professional and personal values. To this day, families are still feeling the effects of the actions of the teacher and students. At every turn, the teacher and student were developing and engaging in an inappropriate teacher-student relationship.[9] The fact that the teacher and student kept their communications private, and were not accountable to either of the families in their communications, is a serious breach of the average family's values.

Fourth and finally, the teacher and student shared an inappropriate emotional bond—one that ought not be shared by teachers and their students. At no time should an adult, empowered by licensure and authority, believe that a student is a personal confidante and an aide in solving adult, personal problems. Worse still is the teacher who believes that a romantic relationship with a teenager will somehow fill a void in his or her life.

Remove the technology from the equation, and consider how likely is it that the relationship would have gone beyond what only occurs in the classroom. Gilbert-Lurie and others are right on point in their conclusions: student-teacher personal relationships are never okay![10]

Private schools, please take note. The incident in question nearly tore the school apart, because of side taking, rumormongering, and postings on social media sites. Private schools employ teachers who are just as human as everyone else is. In some cases, religious beliefs and practices are merely a cover for a person's predatory inclinations, and spending time off hours with a potential victim is sometimes justified as ministry.[11]

Another example of inappropriate student-teacher relations involves an Alabama middle-school special-education teacher. The teacher was also the sponsor of the Fellowship of Christian Athletes club at the school. She was charged with having sex with at least eight high school students between the ages of fifteen and nineteen.[12] She was arrested and later convicted of several charges. The community was outraged and wondered how such things could happen at the school.

Parents, please take note of my very important accountability plea: check your teenagers' cell phones periodically for messages that might be problematic. If we are providing them the technology, ought we not monitor what goes on with it? If we ramp up the accountability with the technology our teenagers are using, we might very well save a host of people from legal and emotional heartache. If we do not step in, the possibility of future counseling for victims of abuse becomes a greater concern. Doing nothing may damage appropriate relational commitments, as well as future relationships.

Consider another incident that involved an administrator in a private Christian school in North Carolina. The administrator was accused of, and eventually arrested for, having sexual relations with one of his teenage high school students. What made this story interesting was that the administrator moved his family to California to escape the legal and community attention. The administrator sought to restart his private-school administrative career.

Some months after he was hired in California, he announced he had to return to North Carolina to deal with a case in court that was, in his words, "not really a big issue." Shortly after, word came down that he was guilty; he was dismissed from his post.

This case is quite personal to me, since I was in the running for the administrative position for which he was later hired. Suffice to say that there are reasons why private schools must always do background and criminal checks of those they intend to hire. Placing too much power in one person to do the hiring is not wise. For further information on screening perpetrators, refer to my book *It Should Never Happen Here*[13] and to the "Church Law and Tax Report"[14] for additional safeguards and guidelines for protecting private schools and ministries.

Crossing the Line

Analysis of many cases involving teachers and students who have crossed moral boundaries reveal three common elements that pervade each case. Authors Babchishin, Hanson, and Hermann draw an interesting profile of the "characteristics of online sex offenders," contending that "online offenders were more likely to be Caucasian and were slightly younger than offline offenders. In terms of psychological variables, online offenders had greater victim empathy, greater sexual deviancy, and lower impression management than offline offenders. Both online and offline offenders reported greater rates of childhood physical and sexual abuse than the general population."[15]

Table 4.1 provides three generalized statements that pertain to teachers and students in sexual relationships. Taken in context, any one of these may be a cause for concern. The three statements yield two conclusions regarding teachers who have sexual relationships with teenage students. These are included later in table 4.2. The conclusions draw from an analysis of approximately six hundred cases.

Shared Trait #1: Past Abuse

In many of the cases examined, there has been sexual abuse in a teacher's past and the student is absent one or both parental figures in the home. Teachers and students who are in sexual relationships begin these relationships for a variety of reasons. Psychologists tell us that some students seek attention and even love and affection because of one or more parent missing in their lives. Some adults naturally step into that role for the sake of the student, and communities applaud teachers, counselors, and coaches who go this extra mile. However, in some cases it does not end there, and we must ask why.

Jan Wright says that "when the students are teens, [teachers] walk that fine line between being open enough to get and keep the children's attention and losing their respect as an adult. . . . I have also seen teachers who try to be the students' friend. While this type of teacher might be successful in the short term, teens interact with him/her as they would a friend. Thus, the authority that a teacher must have to structure his knowledge and test the students on how much they know has been lost."[16] Wright's point is well taken. Teachers who demonstrate personal desires to be students' friends are demonstrating something deeper than the actions imply and can affect more than students' learning. Inappropriate relationships affect futures, as well as the present.

Students are intrigued by the novelty and mystery of the unknown. There is no exception when it comes to emotional and sexual possibilities. They may fantasize about the conquest of an older person sexually and

Table 4.1.   Three Shared Traits of Inappropriate Teacher-Student Relationships Involving Sex

Shared Trait #1: *Past Abuse*	In many cases, there has been sexual abuse in a teacher's past, and the student victim is absent one or both parental figures in the home.
Shared Trait #2: *Unclear Moral Compass*	Teachers and students have allowed emotions to assist them in misreading of moral compasses, resulting in some compromise of moral boundaries.
Shared Trait #3: *Stealth Communications*	Teenagers and teachers engage in ongoing communications and meetings after-hours, without parents being informed.

then act out their fantasy if the opportunity arises. Others fall prey to manipulation by adults, given substances like alcohol and drugs to soften their wills, and then the exploitation secures them as victims.

Teachers acting out their sexuality with minors have serious issues, normally stemming back to their childhoods. Many of them were likely victims of child sexual abuse, or other forms of abuse, during their formative years. [17] Mullen and Fleming of the American Academy of Experts in Traumatic Stress write that a history of child sexual abuse has been found to be associated with problems with sexual adjustment in adult life; they went on to describe what they termed *reduced sexual esteem* in both men and women who had reported child sexual abuse. [18]

A subsequent study found that women who reported child sexual abuse involving intercourse were significantly less likely to find their adult sexual relationships very satisfactory. [19] As adults, pressures and circumstances unlock the past, unleashing a fury of consequenses affecting the lives of yet another generation. Adults who find emotional solace in teenagers rather than in their peers are demonstrating that there are unresolved issues that need attention.

Shared Trait #2: Unclear Moral Compass

Teachers and students forming emotional relationships have unclear moral compasses. Most teenage students are not biologically or emotionally mature enough to have worked out clear moral boundaries. As a result, they rely on their families, their peers, and other authority figures to assist them in the process.

As we have discussed in chapter 3, teenagers are operating with high levels of dopamine, the pleasure enhancer in the brain. Teachers must acknowledge and affirm that pleasure should never be used as a sole gauge to one's decision making or moral compass—especially among teenagers and their propensity to experiment.

The extreme chemical production in teenagers' brains means their moral decision making is less a factor in their choices than their impulses toward pleasure. This is quite different from when they were younger children. Wynne and Ryan allude to the difference when they assert that "an important part of education consists of posing to students the question, What is the right thing to do? This is a central question in any society, and asking it should begin early and continue through to graduation." [20] Knowledge of this should not be an opportunity for an adult to take advantage of a teenager for his or her own adult pleasure.

Any teacher lacking a moral compass must never have access to teenagers. Beliefs about issues or the ability to analyze opposing viewpoints—and even hold to unpopular perspectives about life—are not at issue here. At issue are the behavioral components stemming from these beliefs. Therefore, in every teacher's interviews for hiring, there ought to be several What If questions presented to gain an initial gauge of the candidate's beliefs and possible solutions to hypothetical classroom situations. (For more on this, see chapter 7.)

A teacher's moral compass is errant if (1) the teacher has no basis to judge whether individual actions are wrong outside of their own beliefs and if (2) the teacher acts for self and does not demonstrate concern as to whether anyone else thinks their beliefs and actions are moral. Unclear moral compasses will eventually lead to serious concerns. Teenagers need healthy moral mentors to assist them through the murkiness of the teenage years.

One example of a teacher having lost her moral compass is the 2009 case of Christine A. McCallum. McCallum was married at the time she was accused of statutory rape for allegedly having sex three hundred times with a teenage boy, beginning when he was thirteen years old. According to the boy, they had sex on his kitchen floor, while taking showers together, and in various locations throughout both of their houses.[21] However, McCallum is but one of thousands of teachers to have lost their way.

The extreme actions of McCallum are clearly illegal, and there is no debate over whether an adult should be having sexual relations with a thirteen-year-old. Consider what first had to take place for the initiation of the relationship, prior to anything physical occurring. What thinking went into the breaking down of moral boundaries in order for an adult to even consider that sex at any time with a thirteen-year-old was appropriate, let alone three hundred times? What type of thinking could ever justify this sort of conclusion? The answer lies in the way the teacher justifies what is right and wrong and when the shift in values occurred.

It is surely impossible to consider that a teacher could fulfill the mission of the school by having sex with a teenage student. There is no validation of appropriate family values that would justify McCallum's actions. There was an obvious lack of moral clarity, which now has affected a teenager's view of morality, thereby affecting the student's future relationships.

Teachers that exhibit fantasies of relationships with their students, or entertain thoughts of any kind about having sex with teenagers, have no business in the classroom. Likewise, teachers who express obsessive language about students or demonstrate inappropriate behaviors toward these minors have no business being in the profession. This also pertains to teacher's assistants, coaches, administrators, and so on. Yet how do so many of these people pass scrutiny?

Amber Marshall, a twenty-three-year-old teacher's aide in northwest Indiana, confessed in 2005 to multiple sexual relationships with special-education students at Hebron High School. Investigators claimed that Marshall admitted what she did was wrong and knew it was against the law and implied that she chose to do it anyway. Marshall made a specific choice to do what she did. She knew it was wrong and did not care that she was sexually exploiting her charges.[22] In some cases, moral compasses can be off by a few degrees, and, over time, one's actions can arrive at destinations unplanned. In other cases, moral compasses point to "self." In the case of the teacher's aide, the latter appears to be the case.

Shared Trait #3: Stealth Communications

It is inappropriate when teachers and students have ongoing communications and meetings after-hours and when these occur without parents being informed. The computer and cell phone are terrific tools. Most of us, whether adults or teenagers, incorporate these tools into our professional and personal lives each day. When it comes to the development and support of relationships via technology, the ease with which emotional bonds can be created is astounding.

Curiously, text does not bring with it the facial expressions, tone of voice, or humor sometimes intended. Yet those relying on text to nurture a relationship deem these things to be quite genuine. However, there are definite problems associated with beginning and nurturing relationships based on technology. The digital world is easy to misconstrue, emotionally. It can also be a tool for those with devious purposes. Photos, text, articles, websites, chats, streaming, and live video all provide ease of connection.

We draw closer to people when we know more about them and spend time with them. Here is a problem, in terms of stealth communications: Communications occur secretly, which brings with it an aura of indecency. It would be "virtually" and nearly impossible to develop closeness between teacher and student without such outside-of-class, regular communication occurrences. Stealth communications occur for reasons of privacy. Teachers must strive for transparency and exemplify proper use of technology in their relationships with teenagers. The question remains regarding the extent to which teachers should relate online at all with their teenage students.

TWO BASIC FLAWS IN THINKING

Teachers who become involved in sexual relationships with students suffer from flaws in their thinking, which can lead to flawed conclusions. They suffer from the flaw of self-exaltation, the flaw of illogical risk taking, or both.

Flaw 1: Exaltation of Self

Teachers who cross the line and are eventually discovered share some basic shortcomings. The first flaw deals with personal philosophy involving the "exaltation of self." This is convincing oneself that he or she is entitled to pursue the course taken—even if there is knowledge of wrong-doing at the time. They believe in feelings over reason and legality, and they place pleasure over professionalism.

Wrongdoers rationalize by a variety of mental gymnastics, not the least of which is the feeling of empowerment and feeding of sensual desires. Therefore, teachers who decide to have sexual relationships with students (1) *express* self over others, (2) *practice* self-justification of wrong over right, and (3) *demonstrate* either a lack of concern, denial, or an inability to assess the production of present and future traumas upon self and others (that is, they lack the ability to sense consequences or any harms in a predicative fashion). All three of these actions illustrate the exaltation of the self.

Cases are emerging in our court system in which some teachers accused of engaging in sexual relationships with their students are claiming their own victimhood. Again, we find a selfish rationale and defense for the criminal action. Child sexual abuse is a correlating factor for why adults abuse. However, for some teachers focusing on self may mean they will more likely victimize other innocents in the future.

There are also cases where teachers are claiming to be victims of bipolarity in order to explain their hypersexuality as adults. In February 2010 thirty-three-year-old Stacy Schuler was indicted on sixteen counts of sexual battery and several other counts involving minors. Most of the offenses occurred with several high school football players from the Ohio school where she was employed, and the offenses dated back to incidents that occurred in her home over a six-month period in 2010. Schuler and her lawyers changed her plea in her case from not guilty to guilty by reason of insanity.[23]

Another administrator, Anthony Alvarez, engaged in a sexual relationship with a fifteen-year-old female student at Arvada High School in Denver, Colorado. Alvarez's wife overheard her husband using X-rated language to someone on his cell phone. It turned out that Alvarez and the teenager had been posting sexual comments to each other on their Facebook pages.[24] In each of these cases, a common denominator is communication technology. What is it about this technology that leads some to take such self-focused risks?

Flaw 2: Illogical Risk Taking

Why would a person who has worked extremely hard to arrive at life's professional calling and spent thousands of dollars and invested time into state credentialing risk throwing it all away only to have an emotional or sexual relationship with a teenager? Think about the logic applied to justify the wrongdoing and then trusting a teenager to remain quiet.

Figuring out those answers warrants its own book. No one really knows what specifically goes on in a person's mind that would lead him or her to take such chances. Whatever is going on mentally, taking such a risk is illogical to most adults. What is apparent is the lack of logic that accompanies a lost moral compass. The sequence seems to play itself out: a lack of morality results in corresponding actions that are just as lost.

The reality is that some teachers become involved in manipulative romantic and self-centered relationships, seeking sexual pleasures, where these passions come across as larger and as important than any context of life and family. Some adults compartmentalize their behaviors into different moral contexts. In addition, personal ideology might be driving the passion or manipulation or both. Yet the risk of the loss of everything, and most everyone in his life, is less impacted by his desire to gain new sexual experiences. This is most illogical and problematic. One recent example of this is the story of James Hooker and Jordan Powers.

The forty-one-year-old former California teacher dumped his wife and children and moved in with a former student—with whom he'd begun a relationship while he was still her teacher. Their actions shocked the nation. Hooker insisted he had done nothing wrong, waiting to start a sexual relationship with Powers until after she'd turned eighteen and graduated. But this assertion is problematic, as there are indications that the sexual relationship began earlier than Hooker was willing to admit.

While being interviewed by a local newspaper, Hooker proclaimed that "in making our choice, we've hurt a lot of people. . . . We [kept] asking ourselves, Do we make everyone else happy, or do we follow our hearts?"[25] Has anyone asked what prompts a forty-something family man to drop everything, everyone—even his employment—for a sexual relationship with a teenager? In table 4.2 we identify several conclusions we can draw from predators like Hooker who have sexual relationships with their teenage students.

The conclusions demonstrate values in teachers whose actions rest primarily in pleasure. It is the epitome of celebration of self. Teachers in

Table 4.2.   Conclusions regarding Teachers Who Have Sexual Relationships with Teenage Students

Conclusion 1:	Teachers decide to have sexual relationships with teenage students to (1) express self over others, (2) practice self-justification of wrong over right, and (3) demonstrate lack of concern, denial, or an inability to assess the traumas and consequences upon self and others.
Conclusion 2:	Teachers have sexual relationships with teenage students because of manipulative romantic and self-centered passion, as well as novel sexual pleasure. The excitement of the risk is worth the gamble of losing everything.

these situations have lost their sense of serving the community. Rather than seeking the best interests of the students, the teachers become seekers of their own selfish interests and personal pleasures. This is the ultimate in serving self and exemplifies a form of somatic or narcissistic hedonism: "Individuals with narcissistic personality disorder generally believe that the world revolves around them. This condition is characterized by a lack of ability to empathize with others and a desire to keep the focus on self at all times."[26]

TECHNOLOGICAL ADVANCEMENTS CHANGE RELATIONSHIPS

Technology has changed the nature of relationships in many ways—and not just between teenagers and adults. The possibility of constant communication with others is quite alluring. Some would even say this type of communication is addictive. Whatever one's opinion, there is no mistaking the fact that technology has changed the way people relate.

According to Robert Sidelinger, "Internet tools allow people to have more freedom and comfort in their interpersonal interactions. CMC (computer-mediated communication) allows people to use hyperpersonal communication . . . this form of communication occurs when individuals find it easier to express themselves in mediated contexts than in face-to-face situations. CMC offers individuals the freedom to express themselves in positive or negative ways."[27]

With new communication technologies, people develop new strategies and methods to initiate and maintain relationships. As each generation has more and more access to communications technology, we can expect the nature of relationships to change, as well. Today there are long-distance relationships between couples and families made easier by video and live-streaming communications. Our military men and women rely on them for regular communication with their families. Oil company's ocean-platform workers and engineers rely on this technology, as do married couples working in different cities. Relationships are less limited by distance today than in years past.

Since about 2007, in every high school and university class under my care, better than 90 percent of my students surveyed have cell phones that include text plans and Internet access. Prior to 2007, the number of cell phone users dropped to between 50 and 60 percent, and those didn't tend to have text plans or Internet access. I've gathered these numbers from a few years of informal surveys filled out during the first weeks of classes.

Automobile Ownership

Consider also that around 50 percent of my students have either their own automobile or use one of their parents' to drive themselves to and from school each day. Today, it is not uncommon for families to own several trucks as well as an assortment of "recreational toys" and travel vehicles. The nationwide per capita automobile ownership statistics place California (with its population of thirty-eight million people) and Iowa near the top, with more than one car owned for every person in their states.[28]

Entertainment

Today music is accessible by means never before seen. Downloaded applications for cell phones number in the millions. Games, music, videos—you name it—are at our fingertips wherever we go. We access the Internet to make digital purchases. Millions of tunes are instantly available through iPods, iPhones, Droids, or Shuffles. Cell phones are now vaults of entertainment and amusement. Music is downloaded onto computers. Today, if parents ground teenagers to their rooms, they are technologically "play grounded."

The "slow-dance" of private technology and Internet pseudoanonymity has begun to ensnare a generation. Some are worried that this relationship between technology and privacy are laying the groundwork for controversial cultural ideologies and the regular exploration of sexual fantasies. Teenagers are naturally given to ideology and fantasizing. This news is not good for our young people online, as each day more stories about teachers and sexual abusers abound. The frightening news is the description of the many methods of digital contact. Consider the fact that teenagers' issues *outside* of school almost always make their way to the attention of others *at* school.

Nationally, vast numbers of students claim that while they are online requests for sex and sexual imagery appear repeatedly. No one is certain whether these requests are from adults or classmates. However, we do know that anonymity makes these types of encounters so very easy. They are easy to initiate and just as easy to respond to.

Keeping Our Guards Up

There are many examples of student-to-student and adult-to-student communication crossing all sorts of boundaries. Take, for example, one incident in a Florida public school: A single, male teacher in his twenties developed an after-hours relationship with several of his female high school students. His smile was said to melt the hearts of teenage girls, and several had crushes on him.

The teacher and students had been texting each other for months. During this time, a deep attraction emerged between the teacher and one of the girls. He crossed a professional line with a seventeen-year-old student and began spending private time with her after hours.

To make matters worse, the two of them would appear at games together, only to disappear for several minutes at a time. Parents noticed this and notified administrators. It turned out that the teacher was warned but allowed to stay on the job as long as he changed his behavior. The teacher promised and revised his communication methods. Administrators believed him.

During one evening school event, the teacher and student were caught alone in one of the classrooms on campus. The girl stated that nothing inappropriate had occurred and that they had just been talking. Suspicions arose when it was learned that the classroom lights had been turned off and the door locked. Cell phone messages and erratic personal behaviors after hours continued to indicate something was going on between the two, contrary to the student's denial. The teacher was subsequently placed on administrative leave, and the teenager entered a counseling program to dismantle the emotional bond that had developed between her and the teacher.

TEACHERS AS SEX SEEKERS?

Could it be that teachers and students are having sex today because of a casual, recreational, and consensual desire to explore each other sexually? Are they having sex because they are so desperately in love that they cannot help themselves? Do teachers begin their careers seeking sexual conquests?

Education these days is replete with pressures to perform and meet high standards. Relationships are not exempt from similar pressures. Making condoms available for students to use, to avoid pregnancy by teachers, is unthinkable. Yet on high school campuses all over this nation, condoms are available for students. Consider the case in Arkansas where a high school teacher was initially convicted to thirty years in prison for engaging in a sexual relationship with an eighteen-year-old student. In the end, however, this case evidenced a state heading in the wrong direction.

In March 2012, the Arkansas Supreme Court struck down the state's law that banned sexual contact between teachers and students. The court held that people (students) who are eighteen years of age or older have right to engage in sexual relationships. So long as they are consensual, these relationships in Arkansas are constitutional.

The court took the side of thirty-eight-year-old David Paschal, an Elkins High School history and psychology teacher. Paschal admitted to having a nearly six-month sexual relationship with one of his eighteen-year-old students. Attorneys for the state argued that the law, which was subsequently overturned by this case, was set in place to protect students from sexual advances from people who are in authority. However, the court found that a sexual relationship between consensual adults was not a crime in Arkansas—regardless of the authority and boundaries between teacher and student.

Writing for the minority opinion, Justice Robert Brown stated that the decision to decriminalize sexual relations between teachers and students would cause disruption in high schools. Teachers could now have sexual relationships with their eighteen-year-old students, and nothing could prevent them from doing so. Here we see our student-centered world now colliding with the world of adult pleasure seekers. This is further evidence of a collapsed morality.

Paschal's overturned conviction does not mean that he can return to his job in the classroom. It simply means that he has a right to a sexual relationship with consenting eighteen-year-old students. Now that he is no longer teaching, it makes little difference. What would happen if states used their ages of consent, versus the age of adulthood, for decriminalization of teacher-student sex? Then we would have near chaos. Currently an estimated twenty-five states do not have laws banning teacher-student sex, while some states make it a felony.[29] Our nation needs clear guidelines and enforceable laws that protect students from predators in states that do not ban teacher-student sex.

Simply put, we must assume that some adults who merely seek sex from teenagers, and form relationships to satisfy these desires, should not be around children. What is more uncharted sexual territory than to be a child's first sexual partner or to teach them to be sexual and how to please an adult? If this was not the case, why was it such a major issue in Paschal's case as to when exactly the student turned eighteen? Some predators make it appear as if they are waiting for legality before they make their move. Others do not wait at all.

Some adults just enjoy teasing about sexual things, and leave it at that. Still others boldly proclaim to have as their goal a lifelong commitment with a teenager and insist that sex is a by-product of the commitment. The Internet is replete with such proclamations. But make no mistake. All such cases involve sex to one degree or another—whether in the present or the future. Sexual relationships are inevitable once the connection passes the point of no return. And technology is right there as a support mechanism.

The Pleasure Factor

What teenagers find interesting and pleasurable may not be what adults find pleasurable. For teenagers, sexual pleasure may be tied to fun and social events, because they feel very sexy spending time with people they enjoy. Performing sex acts with adults may fill a void in their life because of how deeply personal and "soulish" the act of sex can be. Giving sex to an older adult could also be akin to playing out a fantasy of desirability, in terms of idealism, or fantasy concocted by exposure to peers and culture. The problem with this is that teenage fantasy interest becomes teenage fantasy realized by willing adult participants. In terms of adults, there are other factors driving these pleasures and may differ between men and women.

Sex as Novelty

In personal discussions with teenagers and their families, it is quite clear that for the male adult seeking sex, once the sex novelty is diminished, so too may be any proclaimed commitment. A teenage conquest may be as much a novelty for an adult as the older person with authority is a novel conquest for the teenager. Adult women seeking sex from teenagers are more inclined to want long-term commitments because their emotional connection through sex is somewhat different from men's. The Letourneau case is a prime example of this type of connection.[30]

Essentially, accounting for the differences of brains, some give sex for acceptance, while others provide acceptance for sex. So we need to ask what possible connection teachers and students could have and where this connection could go in terms of developing a relationship. More than one-half of high school students have not had sex. So, of those forming the relationships in question, it is difficult to know whether the sexual bond created is the result of a person becoming sexually active for the first time or the result of a deeper personal connection.

The likelihood that the teacher has been sexually active is high. Could it be that some of our students are losing their virginity to their teachers and experiencing sexual pleasure for the first time? Is this not the epitome of the teacher-student fantasy relationship? If so, the power derived from knowing this is predatory and probably provides an emotional boost to the adult's ego.[31]

PREDATORS GONE WILD

Stop and Think!

Robert Coles, Harvard psychiatrist and Pulitzer Prize winner, writes:

> many of the options available to the young come at them not from within (the pressure of instinct, desire, fueling a search for expression) but from without (social and cultural possibilities from a consumerist

society ever ready to pester, entice, and seduce an audience and "age group"). Young people . . . take in values from that world, from the music they hear, the movies and television they see, from the fashion, advertising, and magazine industries as they influence what gets worn, what gets said, how hair is cut or colored, what hobbies are pursued.[32]

Teenagers are ripe for manipulation by people who are good at gaining their attention and affection. Advertisers can be predator types, seeking to make victims of consumers. Social media is a type of emotional fuel for teenagers and their connections. Online sexual predators seek certain types of teenagers.[33]

Studies indicate positive correlations between homes with a single parent and a teenager seeking attention from others. Some evidence also suggests a correlation between adults who were sexually abused as children and a greater risk for committing similar crimes upon others, repeating a vicious cycle of abuse. That said, the reader must take care so as to not project a simple cause-and-effect relationship between past abuse and future abusive behaviors.[34]

Sexual predators desire sexual pleasure through physical contact. They will go to great lengths to secure this contact. Sexual predators do not seek long-term commitments and are not practitioners of lifelong sacrificial love. When teenagers succumb to adults' lusts and passions, their lives are forever changed. The effects are deleterious to present and future generations. The predator moves from one victim to another in conquest. However, do teenagers really know they are being victimized?

Not all teachers who have sex with students are predators in the strict definition of the word. After all, a four- or five-year age difference between teacher and student can cause all sorts of emotional confusion. Make no mistake about it. While teacher-student sex may not be enough to define a person as a sexual predator, it is enough in nearly all states to define the teacher's actions as criminal, even requiring the perpetrators to register as sex offenders.

Students who engage in sexual relationships with their teachers and coaches must come to understand the ramifications of their actions. They are being victimized by participation and will continue to be victimized by the many devastating aftereffects. According to Cathy Spatz Widom, in an earlier report for the U.S. Department of Justice, through the National Institute for Justice, "compared to victims of childhood physical abuse and neglect, victims of childhood sexual abuse are at greater risk of being arrested for one type of sex crime: prostitution."[35]

We need to remember that there might be something missing in the lives of teenagers or the adults who take advantage of them. Again, this is one of the reasons why teachers can be extremely important influences for good in students' lives. Let us also remember that some crimes committed have nothing to do with the perpetrator's past or attempt to blame it on the past. Whatever the case, these relationships with minors are still criminal, and students need protection from those who would manipulate them into a sexual relationship.[36]

So, what is it that causes what we're calling a "hyperemotional sexual relationship" between a teenager and a teacher? Aside from the common denominator of academics, the answer is the same with all close relationships: the key is spending time together. How this time is spent in a digital age looks very different from even a decade ago. In terms of the relationships in question, time alone and time after hours are two of the more critical opportunities for the development of inappropriate relationships between teachers and students.

SUMMARY

Teachers are too close to students when their proximity is the foundation for serious moral and educational compromises. Proximity compromises occur when teachers' relationships with students (1) distract from the mission of the school, (2) provide emotional confusion for students and teachers, (3) manifest themselves by undercutting or usurping family values of teachers or students, and (4) assume that teachers and students share a very special connection or emotional bond.

Technology and communication from home and in private are the primary enhancements for today's relational bonds. There are three shared traits of inappropriate teacher-student relationships: (1) past abuse, (2) unclear moral compass, and (3) stealth communications. Teachers acting out their sexuality with minors have serious issues, normally stemming from their childhoods. Many of them were likely victims of child sexual abuse, or another form of abuse, during their formative years.

Teachers and students in emotional relationships have unclear moral compasses. Most teenage students are not biologically or emotionally mature enough to have worked out clear moral boundaries. Teachers who lack moral clarity are never to be given daily access to teenagers. A teacher's moral compass is compromised if (1) the teacher has no basis on which to judge whether individual actions are wrong outside of their own beliefs and (2) the teacher acts for self and does not demonstrate concern as to whether anyone else thinks their beliefs and actions are moral.

Teachers that become involved in sexual relationships with students suffer from two flaws in their thinking. The first deals with personal philosophy involving the "exaltation of self," subsequently convincing oneself that he or she is entitled to pursue the course chosen. Flaw number two is illogical risk taking. The risk of losing everything for sex with a teenager is illogical. It is also illogical to think a teenage student would stay quiet about such experiences with a teacher.

Technology has changed the nature of relationships in many ways. The possibility of constant communication with others is quite alluring. As each generation has more and more access to communication technologies, we can expect the nature of relationships to continue to change. Teachers who cross into personal relationships with students usually incorporate sex, and technology is right there as a support mechanism.

Not all teachers who have sex with students are predators in the strict definition of the word. After all, a four- or five-year age difference between teacher and student can cause all sorts of emotional confusion. While teacher-student sex may not be enough to define a person as a sexual predator, it is enough in nearly all states to define the teacher's actions as criminal, even requiring the perpetrators to register as a sex offender.

DISCUSSION QUESTIONS

1. What are three factors you would use in determining whether teacher-student relationships are appropriate or not?
2. What is the mission of your school, and how would taking a risk to violate proximity between teachers and students distract from the mission?
3. Can you recall any incidents on a local or national level that illustrate the need for a serious discussion regarding teachers and their relationships with teenage students?
4. Why do you think there are more problems being reported, more arrests being made, that involve teachers and teenage students having sexual relationships?
5. How important are moral compasses for teachers, students, and parents?
6. What personal and professional factors would lead a teacher to risk everything for a romantic connection and sexual relationship with a teenage student?
7. As a teacher, or a parent, what is a good rule of thumb to consider in dealing with teenagers and their friends?
8. What are some factors that are always present when teachers and students engage in inappropriate relationships?
9. If your principal asked you to give a two-minute speech making a case for your faculty and staff to discuss appropriate and inappropriate relationships on campus and off, what would you say?
10. What part do communication technologies play in appropriate and inappropriate relationships between teachers and students?

NOTES

1. Gene Byrd, "Teacher Leaves Family for Student: 41-Year-Old James Hooker's Girlfriend Is 18-Year-Old Jordan Powers," *The National Ledger*, March 2, 2012, accessed March 12, 2012, www.nationalledger.com/lifestyle-home-family/teacher-leaves-family-for-student-154061.shtml.

2. Jennifer Preston, "Rules to Stop Pupil and Teacher from Getting Too Social Online," *New York Times*, December 17, 2011, accessed December 20, 2011, www.nytimes.com/2011/12/18/business/media/rules-to-limit-how-teachers-and-students-interact-online.html.

3. Edward F. DeRoche and Mary M. Williams, *Character Education: A Guide for School Administrators* (Lanham, Md.: Scarecrow Press, 2001), 68–69.

4. Ernest J. Zarra III, "Pinning Down Character Education," *Kappa Delta Pi Record* 36, no. 4 (Summer 2000): 154–57.

5. Richard J. Stiggins et al., *Classroom Assessment for Student Learning: Doing It Right, Using It Well* (New York: Allyn & Bacon, 2009), accessed April 4, 2011, www.pbs.org/teacherline/courses/inst325/docs/inst325_stiggins.pdf.

6. The Whole Child, *Making the Case for Educating the Whole Child* (Alexandria, Va.: Association for Supervision and Curriculum Development, 2011), accessed March 11, 2011, www.wholechildeducation.org/assets/content/mx-resources/WholeChild-MakingTheCase.pdf. See also The Whole Child, "About," Association for Supervision and Curriculum Development, accessed March 11, 2011, www.wholechildeducation.org/about; and Center for Inspired Teaching, "Inspired Teacher," January 18, 2010, accessed March 11, 2011, http://archive.constantcontact.com/fs028/1101676672567/archive/1102949261977.html.

7. In *American Scholar* 76, no. 3 (Summer 2007): 36–46, http://theamericanscholar.org/love-on-campus/.

8. In "Why Student-Teacher Relationships Are Never OK," *Huffington Post*, April 19, 2012, accessed April 19, 2012, www.huffingtonpost.com/mikaela-raphael/why-studentteacher-relati_b_1435275.html. See also Purplmama, "Inappropriate Student-Teacher Relationships, Part One," *Hub Pages*, accessed April 19, 2012, http://purplmama.hubpages.com/hub/Student-Teacher-Relationships-Part-One.

9. K. Boccella, "Inappropriate Student-Teacher Relationships in Lititz," *Philadelphia Inquirer*, May 24, 2009, http://articles.philly.com/2009-05-24/news/24985279_1_warwick-girls-school-board-president-student. See also Purplmama, "Inappropriate Student-Teacher Relationships."

10. Gilbert-Lurie, "Why Student-Teacher Relationships Are Never OK."

11. Ernest J. Zarra III, *It Should Never Happen Here: A Guide to Minimizing the Risk of Child Abuse in Ministry* (Grand Rapids, Mich.: Baker Book House, 1997).

12. Paul Thompson, "Teacher Accused of Having Sex with Eight Pupils on School Baseball Team Faces 20 Years in Jail," *Mail Online*, June 25, 2008, accessed July 23, 2011, www.dailymail.co.uk/news/article-1028816/Teacher-accused-having-sex-pupils-school-baseball-team-faces-20-years-jail.html. See also "Teacher Arrested for Having Sex with Eight Students," *Birmingham News*, June 20, 2008, accessed July 23, 2011, http://privateofficernews.wordpress.com/2008/06/20/teacher-arrested-for-having-sex-with-8-students-wwwprivateofficercom/.

13. Zarra, *It Should Never Happen Here*.

14. *Christianity Today*, "Reducing the Risk," accessed August 14, 2010, www.reducingtherisk.com/.

15. Kelly Babchishin, R. Karl Hanson, and Chantal Hermann, "The Characteristics of Online Sex Offenders: A Meta-Analysis," *Sexual Abuse: A Journal of Research and Treatment* 23, no. 1 (March 2011): 92–123.

16. In "Teacher-Student Relationships: How They Differ Based on Student Age," *Yahoo! Voices*, June 24, 2009, accessed July 13, 2011, http://voices.yahoo.com/teacher-student-relationships-they-differ-based-3534927.html.

17. AACAP, "Child Sexual Abuse," *Facts for Families: American Academy of Child and Adolescent Psychiatry* 9 (March 2011), accessed October 12, 2012, http://aacap.org/page. ww?name=Child+Sexual+Abuse&section=Facts+for+Families.

18. Paul E. Mullen and Jillian Fleming, "Long-Term Effects of Child Sex Abuse," American Academy of Experts in Traumatic Stress, accessed August 25, 2012, www. aaets.org/article176.htm .

19. D. Finkelhor, "The Trauma of Child Sexual Abuse: Two Models," *Journal of Interpersonal Violence* 2 (1987): 348–66. J. Herman, *Trauma and Recovery* (New York: Basic Books, 1982). See also Mullen and Fleming, "Long-Term Effects of Child Sex Abuse."

20. Edward A. Wynne and Kevin Ryan, "Curriculum as a Moral Educator," *American Educator* (Spring 1993): 21. See also Kevin Ryan and Karen Bohlin, "Values, Views, or Virtues," *Education Week* 18, no. 25:72. Kevin Ryan and Karen Bohlin, *Building Character in Schools* (San Francisco: Jossey-Bass Publishers, 1998).

21. "Charge: 'Obsessed' Teacher Raped Student," United Press International, January 9, 2009, accessed July 16, 2012, www.upi.com/Top_News/2009/01/09/Charge_ Obsessed_teacher_raped_student/UPI-18641231550223/.

22. "Teacher's Aide Admits Sexual Intercourse with Student Was Wrong," About.com: *Crime and Punishment*, n.d., accessed June 12, 2012, http://crime.about. com/od/sex/ig/female_pedophiles/Amber-Marshall.htm.

23. Ed Richter, "Female Gym Teacher Accused of Sex Acts with Football Players," *Dayton Daily News*, February 8, 2011, accessed February 15, 2011, www. daytondailynews.com/news/news/crime-law/female-gym-teacher-accused-of-sex-acts-with-foot-1/nMnx9/.

24. "Anthony Alvarez, Former Arvada High School Assistant Principal, Arrested for Alleged Sexual Relationship with 15-Year-Old Student," *Huffington Post*, September 6, 2011, accessed November 5, 2011, www.huffingtonpost.com/2011/09/06/ anthony-alvarez-former-ar_n_950907.html.

25. Byrd, "Teacher Leaves Family for Student."

26. *Psychology Today*, s.v. "Narcissistic Personality Disorder," accessed August 5, 2012, www.psychologytoday.com/conditions/narcissistic-personality-disorder.

27. In *Human Communication: A Publication of the Pacific and Asian Communication Association* 11, no. 3 (2008): 341–56.

28. U.S. Department of Transportation: Federal Highway Administration, "Highway Finance Data and Information: Our Nation's Highways 2008," accessed August 23, 2012, www.fhwa.dot.gov/policyinformation/pubs/pl08021/fig3_2.cfm.

29. "Arkansas Court Rules Teachers Can Have Sexual Relationship with Of-Age Students," CBS News and Associated Press, March 30, 2012, accessed April 20, 2012, http://stlouis.cbslocal.com/2012/03/30/ark-court-rules-teachers-can-have-sexual-relationship-with-of-age-students/.

30. M. Ott, "Media May Prompt Teen Sex," *Perspectives on Sexual and Reproductive Health: WebMD Medical News*, no. 38 (June 2006): 84–89. Lisa Habib, "Why Do Teens Have Sex? For Intimacy, Social Status, Study Says," *WebMD*, June 14, 2006, accessed January 30, 2011, www.foxnews.com/story/0,2933,199540,00.html.

31. Sabrina Weill, *The Real Truth about Teens and Sex* (New York: Perigee Books/ Penguin, 2005). See also Sabrina Weill, "The Real Truth about Teens and Sex," CBS News, accessed August 15, 2012, www.cbsnews.com/2100-500186_162-831562.html.

32. In *The Moral Intelligence of Children* (New York: Random House Publishers, 1997), 164.

33. Abbie Alford, "Social Media Fueling Teacher and Student Relationships," Fox News, May 23, 2012, accessed June 4, 2012, www.fox23.com/mostpopular/story/Social-media-fueling-teacher-student-sexual/pol.

34. Alex Brown, "Experts Explain the Beginnings of Inappropriate Student-Teacher Relationships," WIBC News, May 11, 2012, accessed May 15, 2012, www.wibc.com/ news/story.aspx?ID=1702145.

35. In "Victims of Childhood Sexual Abuse: Later Criminal Consequences," *National Institute of Justice: U.S. Department of Justice* (March 1995): 2, accessed June 4, 2011, www.cj.msu.edu/~outreach/mvaa/Child%20Protection/ Victims%20of%20Childhood%2 0Sexual%20Abuse%20Later%20Criminal%20Consequences.pdf.

36. Zarra, *It Should Never Happen Here.*

FIVE

Social Networking and Relationships in a Digital World

MAN: Hello there!
WOMAN: Hi
MAN: Wanna go out for lunch some time?
WOMAN: Sure. When?
MAN: I don't know. Here's my number. Text me.
WOMAN: I don't think so.
MAN: Why not?
WOMAN: I never have text on a first date.

—Ernie Zarra

AT A GLANCE

The eight major sections in this chapter include: (1) basic definitions, (2) technology and increased risk, (3) how social is too social?, (4) time to talk text, (5) after-hours accessibility, (6) principles for appropriate after-hours communications and relationships, (7) working with parents to build relationships through educational capital, and (8) teacher-parent after-hours relationships. We close the chapter with a summary and discussion questions.

BASIC DEFINITIONS

Two of the more commonly used terms that refer to technology are *social networking* and *social technology*. The general term *social networking* most commonly refers to the actions of using technology to connect with other people on several social levels. The term *social network* pertains to the actual components of the technology. Humans often use technology for social purposes and "depend on social interaction for their constitution."[1] Facebook, Friendster, Friendburst, Pinterest, and MySpace are examples of online social-networking communities. There are also video communities such as YouTube, GodTube, Vimeo, and still others, along with sites like Twitter and LinkedIn, not to mention the millions of online gaming sites.

All social-networking communities operate on the fundamental premise that their mission is to connect people with ease, as seamlessly as possible. The social sites are successful at accomplishing their mission. Our foci in this chapter are the social connections made through communication technologies, as these affect teacher-student relationships.[2]

TECHNOLOGY AND INCREASED RISK

Teachers and students live under enormous pressures to demonstrate successful outcomes of their teaching and their learning. Technology is supposed to assist with classroom instruction, data and record keeping, and measurement of student and school outcomes. Additional pressures are added by local communities, which seek excellence for students in academics, athletics, and activities. The media hop on almost any story that deals with schools. And nothing gets a community's attention like scandal.

Everyone who has access to technology could now look up just how well, or poorly, their children's schools are performing. The communication gap between many schools and their stakeholders has closed precipitously, in large part due to changes in ways we all communicate.

Consider the 1990s: Few students had cell phones on school campuses, and personal computers were gaining in popularity. A parent would phone or maybe e-mail a teacher to see how a student was performing. Many pieces of school literature were mailed home via the post office. Today, a teacher would be hard-pressed to find a student without a cell phone. Why should this be an added concern for schools?

Emphasis on the larger educational-technology components for the classroom is diminishing, while the more social components are culturally on the increase. This might become a wonderful thing for education, if used appropriately. Smartphones are mini-computers and contain a world of power for teachers as educational tools. However, their use in class comes with certain associated risks.

"My Cell Phone Is My Life!"

Students proclaim these words even as their cell phones are removed from circulation for a day. What is it about technology that sends the message that it is actually part of their identity? The easy answer is because the cell phone is their immediate gratification and mode of socialization with many others simultaneously. It is equivalent to having a built-in audience at one's disposal. The possessiveness that people exhibit over their cell phones is evidence of relational intimacy.

Teachers will chuckle at this section. Students use all kinds of reasons to exit the classroom for social-contact time. Many need to use the restroom, where they hide in stalls to text or make phone calls. In the recent past, students would hide in the stall and smoke. Now they hide there for social connections.

How many teachers have asked students to end a phone call only to have the student reply, "It's my mom"? Students are somehow under new mandates to check in with voice mail, to see whether mom left a very important message that must be heard right away.

Some students also use the cell phones to invade others' privacy. If there are other students in the restroom, one could test out the phone's camera and video-recording functions and immediately upload the file to a social-networking site. Student privacy has been violated before. In addition, students also have recorded teachers after baiting them in class.

Through correspondence with teachers from around the nation, and some international correspondence, there is the feeling that cell phone–policy enforcement is a losing battle: Phones are too personalized these days and too much a part of teenagers' lives. And it doesn't end there, as adults feel the same way; and knowing my profession as I do, we teachers are probably some of the worst violators.[3]

Students inform their parents almost instantly about things that occur on campus. Whether a student wins an election, wants to go home for the day, or is upset over personal circumstances, they have instant encouragement and empathy. Quickly, friends are informed, photos snapped, and videos recorded clandestinely and sent to parents and friends. Students post to their social-media sites while sitting in school. Then there are grades. Technology can provide quick access to academic progress and student attendance.

If a student is in tears over a grade, he finds a way within seconds to text his parents, who are within minutes either on the phone or sending an e-mail to a number of addresses. In reality, can the students be held to any serious account for the very culture that engulfs them? If education is student-centered, why should their technology use be any different?

One interesting thing about this is that most school campuses across the nation have policies that cell phones are not to be on or used throughout the school day. If there are policies in print, it is my experience that the policies are not enforced with any regularity. The reason is not a lack of concern but that cell phone–usage policies at school have become lost causes. Just a few years back, here in my home state of California, it was legal to drive a car while talking on a cell phone. Now in many states cell usage must be hands-free. Laws written after permission is granted are difficult to enforce. This difficulty spills over into our schools every day. However, have we truly considered the power of the smartphone these days?[4]

Here are three interesting facts to consider:

1. The Pew Research Center has determined that teenagers exchange an average of sixty text messages a day.[5]
2. In some states, like Minnesota, there are suicide hotlines set up for troubled teenagers and others who are desperate and need someone to text. The number of text messages is equivalent to the number of actual phone calls received prior to the text hotline.[6]
3. An estimated 75 percent of high school–aged teenagers have cell phones. Girls tend to text more, with fourteen- to seventeen-year-olds sending more than one hundred texts a day. According to Pew, teenagers talk to their friends by text message. However, they are much more likely to use voice contact with their parents, via cell phone.[7]

Teaching on Eggshells

Many teachers recall when it was acceptable for students to be personally challenged to become more responsible and to work harder. Remember the extrinsic motivational ploys practiced by some of those high school teachers back in the day? Parents today are less supportive of teachers and schools than they are of their teenagers. Some students claim teachers are picking on them when they confront their work-ethic issues.

Others think they are being bullied by teachers who are "mean" and then proceed to rate the same teacher on Facebook or ratemyteacher.com or Tweet a pejorative under an anonymous moniker. The rise of communication technologies are elevating both opportunities and concerns for schools. Social networking in the digital realm is as exciting as it is concerning.

There is the tendency today for parents to go over the teacher's head to the principal or even above the principal to the district office. Technology and e-mail links mean board presidents and superintendents' offices are a mere click away. Impulsive vents and angry diatribes are received every day by colleagues across this nation. Parents seems to suffer from a "confrontation without confronting" mentality today, which can be hazardous to reputations. Because if I do not have to see the person to whom a letter is written, then it is much easier to say what is felt, even if what is felt is unduly harsh.

The pressures at schools often find their ways into the instantaneous communication world that exists at home in the evenings. Technology has extended school for some but keeps others connected all day if they so desire. The social networking that occurs from home can become problematic for even the more seasoned online veterans. Some teachers are part of this network and enjoy it. Others find nothing but potential drama and avoid it. Here is an example of online social-media drama, offering a few reasons why some teachers choose to avoid social networking altogether.

Interest begins with an innocent set of exchanges on Facebook. Married and single teachers begin "friending" current and past students and open their personal lives to them while away from work. Teachers "liking" students. Students "liking" teachers. It is a genuine approach, and one that students applaud as authentic.

However, what starts out as innocent turns into what some misconstrue as teasing and flirtatious remarks. Photos are posted and comments made. Copies of photos are circulated, and some are changed through digital photography–software programs and then reposted. Students follow posts closely, copy some exchanges, and pass them around. Like wildfire, rumors of on-campus affairs between teachers, students, and administrators are spread around to the hundreds involved in their online community.

Some parents, who are part of the network of online friends, take it upon themselves to copy and paste some of the posts and chats and forward them to the school-district officials. Some teachers are reprimanded and asked to delete their online profiles. One refuses, claiming nothing inappropriate had ever occurred, while the others comply.

HOW SOCIAL IS TOO SOCIAL?

The online world is full of emotions and imaginations—a world where many cyberspace answers are multiple choice. In this world, there are few incorrect responses. Hara Estroff Marano explains how this closeness to others in this new world can ensnare the unaware:

> An extraordinary number of people spend an extraordinary amount of time online connecting with other people. They reveal their deepest, darkest secrets to folks who may be strangers, and they often find these relationships so compelling they seem more emotionally real and alive than the marriages they are actually in. Indeed, online relationships can be unusually seductive. They are readily accessible, they move very quickly, and under the cloak of anonymity they make it easy for people to reveal a great deal about themselves.
>
> Putting themselves into words, getting replies while they're still in the emotional state of the original message, relying heavily on imagination to fill in the blanks about the recipient, people communicating online are drawn into such rapid self-disclosure that attachments form quite literally with the speed of light.[8]

There are obviously many concerns surrounding the digital, online world. The fact that more teachers and students spend significant time getting to know the other has prompted some attention. School districts are asking themselves how social is too social for their teachers and administrators. What policy guidelines exist pertaining to schools and districts that cover employee use of social media during contractual hours? How about after-hours communications?

If a teacher posts a rude comment to a social-networking site, who is liable for the offensive statements? What about material that appears in joke form? Are there any district-level expectations that extend beyond the contractual day if a person online is a teacher or administrator from a particular school?

What happens when students become emotionally and sexually involved with teachers? Recent reviews of large high school–district websites indicate that there is some movement toward establishing general policy guidelines concerning employees and their use of district-provided communication technologies. These pertain to the contract day, and since unions are involved it is difficult to hold teachers to anything that occurs on their own time.

No one knows what actual constraints will be placed upon individual administrators, teachers, counselors, and coaches. However, in a performance-based environment such as schools, which are also highly social environments, school-district employees should sit up and take notice. Advocating for and taking the high road is often best in such environments. Steering clear of anything that smacks of inappropriateness is the high road, and one that is best for students and teachers in the end.

This is the direction that the Los Angeles Unified School District took in February 2012 as it released its first-ever social-media policy. The preference of the LAUSD is that there be no interaction between teachers and students on Facebook, except through professional accounts, which is distinct from any student and teacher personal account, page, or website. The Kern High School District in Kern County, California, has adopted a similar policy, as have the New York City public schools.[9] (For further discussion on this topic, see chapter 7.)

TIME TO TALK TEXT

There is usually a vibration or a catchy tone to indicate an incoming message. Suddenly, thumbs are ablaze, touching letters on a digital screen, or pressing keys on a mini qwerty keypad. Responses must be instantaneous, or else the existence of the teenager has lessened in significance. But adults, too, are quickly becoming entrenched in this immediacy and the instantaneous world of cell phone texting.

Instant gratification, complete with quickly thought-out strings of one-liners, Twitter's 140 characters, Pinterest "pinning," and Instagram's photos have now taken their digital places next to reflection and the spoken word. As gratifying as immediate contacts are to the psyche, there are some cautions that arise with them. The chances of texting something that could be misconstrued or inappropriate rise in proportion to one's automatic impulsivity. Rapid communication of ideas in one-liners and images is just drama waiting to happen in the high-hormone, high-tech world of communication technologies.

Inappropriate Texting

Tables 5.1 and 5.2 provide examples of inappropriate and appropriate text-message exchanges between a married high school teacher and one of his sixteen-year-old female students.

Upon Closer Examination

At first glance, this exchange might seem quite innocent. But this is hardly the case. First, what is the student doing with the married teacher's cell phone number? Second, why is the teacher complimenting a student on her physical appearance, hours after school at that? To the student, it appears that she is on his mind, which plays into the fantasy and idealism of the teenager. Third, he did not correct the flirtatious language offered in reply to his initial flirtation. He actually gave her an open door to reply as she did. Last, he told the student it was no problem for her to refer to him as "mr sexy tchr man" and that he would see her "2morw." This is validation of her communication and a validation for the "cool" teacher.

Stating that one would see a student on the following day is innocent enough. However, coupled within the context of the rest of the brief text messages, this crosses the boundary of joviality and humor into flirtation. The ease at which this is communicated should bring all teachers and parents to full attention. Teachers must remember their calling and position away from the classroom.

Table 5.1.   Inappropriate Text Message

Teenage Student: Wassup

Teacher: Hey J. Not much. Hey you looked nice in class today.

Teenage Student: hehehe, thanks mr sexy tchr man

Teacher: lol np, c ya 2morw

Teenage Student: kk

Technology makes it easier to stay in touch with others and makes it easy to say things that are not appropriate, including leading to the development of sexual relationships. Thirty-nine-year-old Oregon charter-school director Michael Bremont discovered this to be the case. He began texting a sixteen-year-old female student after hours, which then led to flirtation. Over time, Bremont went too far, and a close sexual relationship developed. He was arrested for sodomy, attempted rape, and sexual abuse.[10]

Appropriate Texting

The teacher ought to always be thinking, "If I write this or that, who else is going to read it and how will this message be used by others"? The technologically enabled privacy of one's communications with others provides a false sense of security—one that sometimes bypasses our moral stop signs. Schools need to address this pseudoprivacy with their faculties and staff. Meanwhile, let us examine how the same text message communication could have been shaped into an appropriate message, in table 5.2, following.

Upon Closer Examination

Notice the difference between the two text-message communications. The first is focused on the personal, while the second is an extension of the classroom. One is flirtatious, while the other is informational or about business. It may appear trite to have to inform teachers about appropriate and inappropriate text messages with their students. However, in addition to teachers and students reading this chapter, one may assume that parents and coaches will benefit from these sample text messages. There are obviously times when communicating with students after hours is appropriate. After all, we live in the age of technology. Nevertheless, we must keep some very important things in mind as we do.

Table 5.2. Appropriate Text Message

Teenage Student: Wassup doc?

Teacher: Hey J. Not much. What do you need?

Teenage Student: Just wanted u to know the food is ready 2 go for the class party

Teacher: Cool. I knew I could count on you. Say hi to ur parents for me.

Teenage Student: OK. Bye

Teacher: Laterz.

AFTER-HOURS ACCESSIBILITY

Schools and communities have real-time access to student progress, attendance data, work missed, and grades. Applications are now available for students to access their own grades and academic portfolios. Students pressure themselves to participate in a variety of exhausting extracurricular activities, not to mention applying to numerous colleges and for numerous scholarships. Teachers aren't immune from the hectic pace and are now on call throughout the day when parents want to know why their teenager earned a poor score on a common formative assessment, or are missing homework in one class or another. Accessibility and communication do not end even on weekends.

Beware!

The physical presence of an adult with a teenager is no longer necessary for abuse to occur. The anonymity so easy to achieve online and the ease with which "fakes" can step into our lives should elicit serious concern. And this concern should be heightened any time our children are involved. If a teacher is posting online anonymously, that could be a cause of concern—especially if they are communicating with minors!

Shock waves ripple across the nation when Americans hear of the horrific incidents of bullying that take place in schools. Social media often escalates these incidents. Relationships, appropriate and not, can occur anywhere and for various reasons. I am under no conspiracy-based illusions that all teachers who flirt with students are sexual predators. However, it can be argued that all teacher-student sexual relationships have flirtation and sex talk recorded in some technology's database somewhere. It is merely the nature of the beast, if you will. This is the reason law-enforcement officials issue warrants at the point of arrest to seize cell phones, cell phone records, and other kinds of computer technology.

Teacher-Student Online-Communication Test

Teachers can avoid many of the Internet's thorniest issues with teenagers and younger children if they choose to apply the Teacher-Student Online-Communication Test (see table 5.3).

Illustration of the larger point is found in a confrontation I had with a local journalist. The journalist insisted that society makes much too much out of issues concerning sex. He had written an article in support of a friend who'd been arrested for soliciting a prostitute for sex while on vacation in San Francisco. His friend had "hooked up" via the Internet with a supposed female escort, who turned out to be a law-enforcement officer. The journalist argued that prostitution should be legal and that women who choose that as careers should have every right to do so.

Table 5.3.   Teacher-Student Online-Communication Test

Teachers at all levels . . .

We must always remember that we are dealing with other persons' children.

Therefore . . .

We must walk in the shoes of the parents, asking ourselves whether our behaviors with students would be appropriate and acceptable to us if the situation were different, involving a colleague and one of our own children.

The look on the journalist's face was priceless when I asked whether he had any children and specifically any daughters in his family. He responded that he did and that he had one daughter. Furthermore, I asked whether it would be acceptable to him if his daughter came home one day to announce she'd discovered her life's calling and that she was a sex professional or prostitute-in-training. There was silence.

There is a basic moral lesson to be gleaned from this anecdote. When it comes to our own children, we are less likely to support someone else's immorality. This has also become a concern for parents whose children spend significant time online, exposed to other people's immorality. Do we really want our children, regardless the age, exposed and possibly exploited by using communication technologies, especially in this age of permanent digital storage and retrieval? Too bad more teachers don't stop to consider this basic moral. Their passions and lusts carry them away into criminal behavior.

Something I've stated in an earlier chapter bears repeating: Teachers, coaches, or administrators should never tolerate language from students that implies anything of a sexual nature. Sensual teasing, or what most consider flirtation, should also be off-limits. Sexual relationships between teachers have points of beginning in body language and verbal communication and later grow from immoral to immoral and criminal. They always grow into "after-hours communications" for without AHC there's little likelihood of being able to foster an intimate relationship.

PRINCIPLES FOR APPROPRIATE AFTER-HOURS COMMUNICATIONS AND RELATIONSHIPS

Teachers who either find they are required to communicate with their teenage students after school hours or who have an extended interest in staying in touch with students—including at-risk students—could use some guidelines for appropriate behavior. When done correctly, such communication can be a positive and impacting extension of the class-room, as well as a reinforcement of professional and respectful boundaries. Table 5.4 includes six principles for the teachers who communicate with students after hours through technology and for the relationships they develop as a result.

These principles assist in the balance and focus of appropriate after-hours communications with students. These guidelines should be printed, or blown up to poster size, laminated, and posted on every teacher's classroom wall. Parents could also post these by magnet on refrigerators, right next to their teenagers' academic and activity schedules.

Teachers as Buddies

Adults should carefully consider the environments in which they choose to hang out with teenagers, especially those where control or respect are diminished. For example, a coach or teacher can maintain control of the environment after basketball practice in the gym or talking informally about school, homework, or the next game. Other controlled environments are the classrooms, at lunch, or after school, where doors are unlocked and traffic can enter rooms at any time.

However, spending time with a teenage student one-on-one, grabbing a coffee at a local shop, or enjoying a hamburger with current students, as you would with friends, is riskier. There is nothing inherently wrong with such meetings. However, risk increases each time a teacher moves outside the academic or activity regimen. The addition of privately communicating as friends raises the risk even more. However, what exactly is the risk? That camaraderie could replace professionalism and conversation could become personal, possibly violating the trust the parents place in the teacher.

Teachers should make every effort to be friendly with students and parents. However, there are lines of distinction between being friendly and becoming a friend. The teacher's and student's risk for inappropriate behavior becomes greater when the latter occurs. Any situations that diminish reputations and rational and moral decision making are to be avoided. On a personal note, teachers, take extra caution when transporting students from school events. Transportation raises a set of concerns in and of itself.

Considerations for Teachers as Buddies

Teachers and students who draw closer than they should run the risk of rumor and reputational damage. Because of this, teachers are instructed to never use phrases such as "I like you" or to make up private pet names when dealing one-on-one with students. Sexual terms and

Table 5.4. Six Principles for Appropriate After-Hours Communications and Relationships between Teachers and Teenage Students

Principle 1: Brevity Is Best
• Keep message exchanges with students brief and to the point.

Principle 2: Flirts Are Potential Hurts
• Avoid any flirtatious communication.

Principle 3: Shun "Forward" Thinking
• Never forward any personal photographs or post anyone else's photographs to a student's cell phone or social-networking page.

Principle 4: Permissions Have Conditions
• Do not upload anything to do with a current student's social-media page to any teacher or parent social-media site without parental consent. If the data or photos in question are of a school function or activity, the teacher should get parental consent in writing.
• Often, high schools have forms for students and parents to sign granting permission for students to both access the Internet and appear online in photograph, if they represent the school in athletics or activities.
• Be professional in deciding what to post online.

Principle 5: Seeing Is Believing
• Err on the side of "more information to parents is best." Always CC—or carbon copy—the text message or e-mail communication you have with the student to the student's parents, unless the parent waives this action.
• If a parent will not allow access to his or her cell phone number through texting, then it is probably best not to allow his or her teenager access to yours.
• This same forwarding rule applies to e-mail as well. If parents do not have e-mail, a computer, or a cell phone but the teenager does have access to these, it is incumbent upon the teacher to lay out the ground rules to inform the parent.
• Teachers can serve parents in many ways: one is to provide some education about the technology their teenagers are using most every day.

Principle 6: Arm's Length Means a Leg Up
• Beware of the number of messages sent to students and teachers.
• Remember, the closer one gets to another human being, the greater the chances of relating on personal levels.
• Teachers should beware how close they get to their students, emotionally.
• Do periodic proximity checks: If you notice students drawing closer to you than you would like, parents should be informed. Some students do stalk their teachers for attention. Share these signs of closeness with administrators and student's counselors.
• Minute usage and numbers contacted are records that are easily discovered. Check the minutes used and texts messages you send to particular numbers.
• Make certain there is a balance so as to avoid any notion of impropriety. Doing so might very well open the lines of communication and head off any possibility of a problem at the point of origin.

teasing about gender are always inappropriate. If we learn anything from the cases we've covered in this book, it is teachers should never engage in flirtation with students. Teachers must be above reproach and never lead students on sensually or emotionally. Ignoring this is most likely where boundaries are first overstepped. Among the common denominators in teacher-student sexual relationships is the use of inappropriate language.

Social Networking

A highly recommended professional and personal social-media ethic is for teachers to have no current teenage students on any of their personal social-media pages. Students are welcome on professional pages that are associated with the school and district, but the risk is greater when they are given access to personal adult friends and family. A good general rule is that any student asking to be part of a teacher's personal network must first be a former student and have graduated from high school.

If friends have current students on their pages, a teacher must carefully consider the readership prior to posting on that friend's pages. Taking the high road in deference to the trust given by the community, parents, and employer is the better way to go. There are no formal agreements to sign, but unimpeachable conduct just helps to avoid the conflict-of-interest issues as a professional.

Whatever a current student needs to discuss can be posted on a professional page or even wait until the next morning. Besides, making oneself available twenty-four hours a day, seven days a week via work e-mail is a trade-off. Teachers should not "need" to communicate socially with students or through a website outside of the work server. Learning from others' mistakes means that we teachers should simply not place ourselves in risky situations when it comes to our students. All it takes is one misunderstanding for an allegation of impropriety to work against a teacher's credibility and reputation.

I'm Sexy, and I Show It!

There is a group-feel among online users that sometimes anonymity equals impunity. For many teenagers, there is a sense of power that accompanies the "I will live forever" youthful attitude. The sense of power that comes with technology feeds many egos, and teenagers are not exempt from this frenzy. Sometimes a computer makes us feel sexy, powerful, and even important. A computer can enhance a person's "cool factor" with its slick digital presentation.

Programs that doctor photos or remove image flaws bring out the best in us. We not only can feel powerful and make an immediate impact by using today's technology, but we also feel beautiful and handsome. When you think about it, don't we select only the best photos of ourselves to show to others? Why else would teenagers, or anyone else, post sexually alluring and powerfully provocative photos and video of themselves all over a social network for all the world to see? The reality is that we all want others to like and admire us.

Elias Aboujaoude, the clinical assistant professor in psychiatry and behavioral sciences at Stanford University, confirms that "although studies show that more than 160 million Americans are regular Internet users, little research has been conducted on problematic Internet use. . . . A 2002 study in the journal *Cyber Psychology & Behavior* found that 60 percent of companies surveyed had disciplined, and more than 30 percent had terminated, employees for inappropriate Internet use."[11]

Some colleagues envision a time when such discipline is meted out to those in education, both during and after the school day. There can be little doubt that with today's smartphones teachers and students upload data to social-media sites while "on the clock." Absence of district and school policy could bring legal trouble. The existence of policy and subsequent violation could bring disciplinary action.[12]

More Research Needed

The literature also validates what we already know to be the case in education. Most education research on teacher-student relationships pertains to learning outcomes, enhanced literacy scores, high school exit-exam scores, teacher stress, self-efficacy, and standardized testing. Meta-analyses conclude that teachers have tremendous impact on student learning, both positively and negatively. But where are the numerous studies that analyze the reasons for current teacher-student relationships?

Wubbels has made some inroads by examining the teacher behaviors in these relationships. He concludes, "Two Decades of Research on Teacher-Student Relationships in Class" focuses on "teaching from an interpersonal perspective using a communicative systems approach and propos[ing] a model to describe teacher-student relationships in terms of teacher behavior."[13] In a British study Salzberger-Wittenberg et al. asked "whether students' misbehavior had been consistently linked . . . to teachers' reports of stress." The authors speculated as to whether or not "teacher stress, negative affect, and self-efficacy predict the quality of student-teacher relationships."[14]

There is much work to do. As our nation faces budget crisis after budget crisis, the students still show up for school. Families expect the best possible education for their teenagers—and for all of their children, for that matter. These same families also trust all the education professionals to maintain appropriate decorum with their children, and this includes the relationships that are developed across the educational spectrum of the school. Would we demand any less for our own children? In what ways can teachers and parents work together to ensure the best possible education and the best possible relational outcomes?

WORKING WITH PARENTS TO BUILD RELATIONSHIPS THROUGH EDUCATIONAL CAPITAL

Educational capital can be defined as *the educational and school-related benefits derived from developing and maintaining relationships with parents, students, and colleagues*. In keeping with this definition, booster clubs provide every bit as much educational capital as parent board members, classroom guest speakers, or assistant coaches.

In this age of high-stakes testing and teacher accountability under NCLB, teachers are required to be highly qualified in their field. Such terminology means teachers have yet another hat to wear—ensuring and policing expertise. Parents are also required to wear many hats, and societally we are at a nexus wherein schools and teachers must rely on parents more than in the past few years.

Education as Capital

Consider an Albuquerque, New Mexico, kindergarten teacher who went beyond state mandates in teaching Navajo children to count to one hundred. She has touched a family.[15] Schools assist in the strengthening of the family by providing excellent education for the students. However, the tasks are not often easy to accomplish. If we wanted "easy," why are we in education in the first place? Valenzuela writes, "In secondary schools, teachers have more students and therefore often know them less well. Secondary teachers place more emphasis on teaching subject matter, and some tend to place less emphasis on serving as coach, mentor, counselor, or cultural mediator. The lack of opportunity to develop personal relationships and the variety of teacher and student personalities create alienation. Students want to be listened to and respected as human beings with wants, desires, fears, and emotions."[16]

Most American parents care about the education their teenagers are getting. Making certain that students are challenged and pressed to achieve near or at their potential is one of many teacher responsibilities. Whether within the major metropolitan areas or sleepy country towns, healthy teacher-student relationships are essential.[17]

Civic Involvement as Capital

Civic involvement is another wonderful way for families to support each other and make a difference in communities. Teenagers who are either required or encouraged to fulfill service hours in the community begin to learn to extend themselves and develop empathy. Families who perform service together find a sense of purpose and mission outside of academics.

Many parents already do this with organized sports, but competition in sports is not the same as service. In service, no one is concerned with competition and winning. Service is all about giving—giving of one's time and talent, money and skill, with little thought of return. Even the founders of our nation referred to this enlightened self-interest.[18]

Nearly two decades have passed since the publication of a provocative article by Harvard scholar Robert Putnam.[19] "Bowling Alone: America's Declining Social Capital" was subsequently expanded into a best-selling book, and later the original version of the article also appeared in the appendix section of the *California History–Social Science–Curriculum Framework* with the framework reauthorization of the late 1990s.

In the original article Putnam concluded that "there is striking evidence . . . that the vibrancy of American civil society has notably declined over the past several decades."[20] Putnam's conclusion holds particular relevance for us baby boomers.

We are well schooled in the merits of competition and the pursuit of material wealth. Groups like the Rotary Club, Demolay, Job's Daughters, Lion's Club, Kiwanis, Police Athletic League, and even the Boy Scouts and Girl Scouts have seen numbers drop over the years. Putnam concludes that the national trend of little civic involvement is a major concern for our culture. Parents must be aware that competition through sports, video games, and computers are not replacements for face-to-face involvement. Sports are great to help with character development—for both athletes and their parents. In service, everyone wins.

Since French aristocrat Alexis de Tocqueville noted it during the 1800s, America has been experimenting with democracy, in efforts to refine her identity as a nation. Citizens have sought to work out the details of a connection between a common good, classical republican democracy, and rugged individuality. Almost prophetic to today, Tocqueville writes, "When the taste for physical gratifications among them has grown more rapidly than their education . . . the time will come when men are carried away and lose all self-restraint."[21]

How do we fit into the larger context of American civil society? Is our historical legacy all but gone because of so much diversity and population plurality? How can the family reassert itself and begin to instill a spirit of involvement and community participation? Families need unifying goals to remain focused. Schools can assist with these goals by welcoming families into an active school community. Teenagers, whose focal points are service-oriented and family-supported, are less likely to fall prey to those whose motives are quite otherwise.

A Community Social Contract

First, there must be an agreement that civic participation has some merit or virtue in today's culture. Second, families and schools must decide that serving the community is as important as serving oneself. Third, opportunities must be made available for students of all ages to serve others. Fourth and finally, there must also be a real connection made to historical context, and we all must see our civic participation and ourselves as part of a larger national purpose.

In the high schools of Newport Beach, California, students are required to perform fifty hours of service activities from their first year until graduation. Service can never be only about the number of hours one intends to serve. The quality of the hours, the actual service performed, and life's applications derived from the service exceed any time requirement. Padding one's résumé should not be what service is about, because service is not a competitive sport.

When performing service, students learn much about giving back to a community and see a larger world that exists away from their very busy, individual lives. Exposure to a sphere outside of students' comfort zones pays huge dividends and is worth it all in the end. The hearts of the younger generation are longing to make a difference and just need opportunities—and often extrinsic motivation helps them to find places to plug in.

Consider the following questions in order to begin a community discourse on civic involvement:

- How is civic involvement defined today for a local community?
- What parts do schools and families play in defining civic involvement and its appropriate activities?
- Whom do we contact to find opportunities to serve the community?
- Are there openings for civic involvement that incorporate technology?
- What roles do community members play in passing along the expectation of civic involvement to recent immigrants?

Professional Development as Capital

After thinking about professional development, as well as leading my own sessions on the subject over the years, I came to an interesting conclusion: as educators we could transfer to students and colleagues what we learn regarding our relationships into a working model toward developing appropriate relationships with parents. Table 5.5 contains a series of questions derived from a blend of professional-development sessions and conversations with educational leaders.

These questions appear for consideration as an educational community thinks through how best to transfer educational capital toward working relational capital with parents. These questions and subsequent dialogue would be wonderful assets for a special parent meeting.

Communication as Capital

Parent relationships are vital in developing overall educational capital. The maintenance of parent relationships should be held to a high level of priority. Parents entrust their teenagers into the care of the schools each day, and, in so doing, they risk much. They risk that their teenagers will fall through the cracks and not receive the proper education for college readiness and admission. They risk an institution or a cultural philosophy undermining their rearing and family philosophy. They also risk that someone or something might harm their children in some way. Maintaining solid relationships with parents is equally as es-

Table 5.5. Questions to Consider in Translating Educational Capital into Teacher-Parent Relational Capital

Teacher-Parent Capital

Are the students' home lives good enough for most children to achieve their academic goals?

In what ways can teachers and parents join together in support of the education of the students in question?

What system can teachers and parents devise to hold students accountable for their own progress and eventual success?

Is there an effective process that allows teachers and parents to remain in regular communication so that the collaboration can occur on behalf of the student?

In what ways are teachers demonstrating concern about teenagers' grades, as well as working together to foster studying and writing skills and to match life's rigors with choices for success?

Are parents aware that their teenagers are "wired to admire" and look up to them for direction and guidance?

What is the overall plan used by teachers and parents to enable teenagers to engage in higher-level learning at home?

How can teachers and parents turn normal teenage pessimism into bright optimism so that each day begins and ends on positive notes?

Are there any helpful strategies to engage teenagers in conversation so that they relate how much learning occurred at school?

In what ways can teachers and parents work together to develop a reasonable pace for teenagers to balance school and home life? How would you rate your home life with teenagers: frenetic and crazy, manageable and cool, or lethargic and apathetic?

What strategies exist for teachers and parents to cope with the extreme emotions that sometimes accompany the rearing of teenagers?

How can teachers and parents motivate students to choose success for school and other areas of their lives?

In what ways can teachers and parents work together to learn to gauge the nature and depth of the relationships with their teenage students and children?

sential. Communication with parents is equally as essential. We would expect nothing less if we were the parents.

Teacher-Parent Networks as Capital

Teachers and parents have unique relationships, in that they both share a responsibility to mold lives in the best ways they can. It just makes sense to work together for the benefit of the teenagers. Assuring that parents and their involvement are valued—just as their children are valued—signals the environment of a considerate and appropriate working relationship.

Communication is the key to working relationships. Therefore, in these working relationships, keeping parents in the communications loop is essential. This can be done on appropriate relational levels, and here is where technology can be a terrific tool. Table 5.6 illustrates two self-explanatory, appropriate relational levels for teachers and parents as they network to build overall educational capital.[22]

TEACHER-PARENT AFTER-HOURS RELATIONSHIPS

Building Relational Capital with Parents

Together, teachers and parents can affect substantive change, as they forge appropriate and positive relationships. In building capital with parents, teachers must take extra care to remain as professional as possible. On the one hand, relationships between teachers and students should be developed with care. Likewise, the development of relationships between

Table 5.6. Two Levels of Teacher-Parent-Networking Relationships

Level 1: Professional-Academic Relationships

- Students are the focal point.
- Data and complete information about academic progress and achievement are characteristics of this level.
- This represents the academic, classroom side of the relationship.
- In an ideal educational world, this is a relationship that all teachers should have with parents.

Level 2: Interpersonal Activity–Based Relationships

- Includes non-school-related activities and usually occurs away from the school site.
- Also includes academics in terms of competitions, athletic events, booster-club fund-raisers, school-site councils, church, civic involvement, and political participation.
- Interpersonal relationships exist when teachers and parents work together in areas that are not strictly tied to academics at the school.

teachers and student's parents should be developed with no less concern. With the latter in mind, three questions are presented and analyzed for the readers to consider.

1. Should teachers and parents date and subsequently form personal relationships?
2. What are the chances of special privileges being granted to "favorite" students or players?
3. Is it all right for teachers to befriend parents on social-networking sites, like Facebook and Twitter, and talk freely about life and work?

Should Teachers and Parents Date and Form Personal Relationships?

Americans consider themselves quite sophisticated, and the mere notion that a teacher would suggest moderation of adult relationships is deemed preposterous by some. I remember suggesting this to a colleague, who was seeing the parent of one of his students. He scoffed and said, "What I do on my on time and with whom is my business." I agreed. However, I also told him that what he does on his own time must be examined closely, since what he deemed personal was now spilling into some of his colleagues' classrooms and onto the Internet.

Teachers who live in communities where schools are more neighborhood-oriented are more likely to cross paths with students and parents from their schools. Whether at a mall, movie theater, church, or sporting event, it is a fact that people's paths cross within communities. Sometimes teachers and parents work together on events that are political or perhaps a fund-raiser for a charity. People network over a variety of causes and concerns.

Teachers must be aware that their reputations are not only present in the minds of the students but are also realities for their parents. Conflicts occur regularly on high school campuses. Therefore, teachers must seek to minimize these conflicts. What if one such conflict arises because of a relationship a teacher has with one of his or her student's parents?

For example, a teacher sees one of her students in the evenings because she is romantically involved with the student's father. This teacher is too close to a conflict of interest—adult relationship or not. The implications are many if there is a falling out in the relationship. Campus spirit is affected. The classrooms are affected. The spreading of rumors distracts from the focus on the school, which ought to be education.

Perhaps the student is still in the class of his parent's former paramour. Removing the student from the class would only serve to upset his schedule and continuity with his friends. However the situation is handled, there is the likelihood of a major drama. Whatever happens between teachers and parents always spins into the lives of the students at school.

What Are the Chances of Special Privileges Being Granted to "Favorite" Students or Players?

There are students and athletes with whom teachers have certain affinities, interests, or shared responsibilities or maybe with whom personalities click. Humans are social creatures. Parents find that they might have a closer relationship with one of their children than with the others in the family. When it comes to teachers and coaches, caution needs to be applied in these cases to avoid conflicts of interest. No one needs an allegation of special treatment of one student over another or unfair treatment of one player over another.

Is It All Right for Teachers to Befriend Parents on Social-Networking Sites, Like Facebook and Twitter, and Talk Freely about Life and Work?

This question is asked a lot. Answers to this question vary. If daily news headlines are accurate, then there are serious issues for teachers and parents to consider when interacting on social-networking sites. The very first rule to remember is this: *Never post anything on any social-networking sites that you do not mind being seen by your friends, your friends of friends, your family, and even strangers.* What we post becomes quite permanent somewhere, even if deleted from the page.

People download and save so much from the Internet that the exercise of restraint in what we post online is most prudent, even while joking, embellishing fictional accounts that are analogous, or similar to the account of real people. Teachers need to be careful of those who practice the "gotcha" mentality. Likewise, teachers and parents should always remind themselves that the freedom of expression is not absolute and that people can sue others for whatever appears offensive.

Today, most parents and teachers have access to each other on school-related academic Internet sites. However, there are instances where socializing online may be appropriate. Appropriate use of social technology respects the two levels of relationships established earlier in this chapter. The benefits for teenagers are many, including instruction in the proper use of social technology. They can learn how adults can relate without the gossip, backbiting, and even bullying that occurs on some other sites.

As a reminder to teachers and parents, when posting on social-networking sites avoid making statements about students, programs, teachers, and achievement. Post affirming and positive things, and create a friendly environment for others to post the same. Also, never create anonymous or "fake" profiles to dig for information on someone. Those antics only lead to trouble. Who can forget the 2008 case of Lori Drew, a mother who assisted others in the creation of a fake teenage boy's MySpace page?

The sole purpose of Drew's MySpace page was to form a romantic bond with a teenage girl at her daughter's school and then dump her for everyone to see the falling-out. The victim, Megan Meier, was prone to depression and after the incident committed suicide, having been told by Drew and others, "The world would be a better place without you." Remember to keep it positive, cordial, jovial, and lighthearted.[23]

Teachers and parents must understand that actions online, for more than social reasons, may have implications long after the computer is powered down for the evening.

The last thing any of us needs before retiring for the night is either for our brain to chemically charge up with negative emotions or to read headlines that related to something we wrote, even in jest.

SUMMARY

The general term *social networking* refers to using technology to connect with other people. The term *social network* pertains to the actual components of the technology. Technology increases access points for all education stakeholders and continues to enable that certain instantaneous communication becomes the norm.

Cell phones are teenagers' lives! The cell phone is their immediate gratification and mode of socialization with many others, simultaneously. It is equivalent to having a built-in audience at one's disposal.

In most secondary schools, cell phone–policy enforcement is a losing battle. Other nations also struggle with cell phone–policy enforcement. There is no turning back: phones are too personalized these days and too much a part of teenagers' lives to be removed.

There are obviously many concerns surrounding the online world. School districts are questioning how social is too social for their teachers and administrators. Teachers must remember their calling and position away from the classroom. The physical presence of an adult with a teenager is no longer necessary for abuse to occur. We are shocked by the horrific incidents of bullying that take place in schools and across the digital world. Parents and teenagers are sometimes caught up in social frenzy, often due to the creation of their own drama. Social media often play roles in these phenomena.

Sexual relationships between teachers have origins in body language and verbal communication. They always grow into after-hours communications, because such communication is a prerequisite for intimate relationships.

There are six principles for appropriate after-hours communications and relationships between teachers and teenage students: (1) brevity is best, (2) flirts are potential hurts, (3) shun "forward" thinking, (4) permissions have conditions, (5) seeing is believing, and (6) arm's length means a leg up.

Most American parents care about the education their teenagers receive. Community social contracts are important. First, there must be an agreement that civic participation has some merit or virtue in today's culture. Second, families and schools must decide that serving the community is as important as serving oneself. Third, opportunities must exist for students of all ages to serve others. Fourth, there must also be a real connection made to historical context, and we all must view civic participation as part of a larger national purpose.

Teachers and their teenage students' parents forming personal relationships run the risk of conflicts of interest. The implications are many if there is a falling out in the relationship. Campus spirit is affected. The classroom is affected. The spreading of rumors distracts from the educational focus on the school.

Relationships in the digital realm are as real as relationships that are in the flesh. Teachers and parents must understand that actions online, for more than social reasons, may have implications long after the computer is shut down for the evening.

DISCUSSION QUESTIONS

1. How are social networking, a social network, and social technology different?
2. What are five ways that social networking can positively enhance relationships between teachers and teenagers?
3. Why are teenagers in high schools so attached to their cell phones?
4. Considering the power of information and connection possibilities that exist with smartphones today, what are four ways teachers can harness this power for use in the classroom?
5. How social is too social for teachers, in relation to students and parents?
6. What are your district's policies about teachers and students using technology on campus?
7. If your district superintendent asked you to present to the board your best case as to why there should be an easing of on-campus cell phone restrictions, would you comply? What would you include in your presentation?
8. Are there any restrictions on communication between teachers and students during off hours? If not, should there be?
9. What is the necessity for the teacher-student online communication test?

10. What are the six principles for appropriate after-hours communications and relationships between students and teachers, and are these principles practical for your campus? Why, or why not?
11. What are two good ways to develop educational capital with parents?
12. What questions are important to consider in translating educational capital into teacher-parent relational capital?
13. What are two important characteristics to keep in mind during the development of appropriate parent-teacher relationships?

NOTES

1. Maarten Derksen and Anne Beaulieu, "Social Technology," *The Sage Handbook of the Philosophy of Social Sciences* 201:705, accessed July 24, 2012, www.virtualknowledgestudio.nl/documents/_annebeaulieu/5579-Jarvie-Chap37.pdf.

2. Ferris Jabr, "Insights: The New Rules of Social Networking," *Psychology Today*, (November/December 2008): 15–16.

3. Katherine Bindley, "Teachers Texting Students: Should Schools Ban or Encourage?" *Huffington Post*, April 17, 2012, accessed May 3, 2012, www.huffingtonpost.com/2012/04/16/teachers-texting-students_n_1427418.html.

4. "Educator's Guide to Digital Risk," *Center for Safe and Responsible Internet Use* (November 2011), accessed March 20, 2011, www.embracingdigitalyouth.org/reports-issue-briefs/issue-briefs/educators-guide/.

5. "Teens, Smartphones, and Texting," Pew Internet and American Life Project, March 19, 2012, accessed March 20, 2012, http://pewresearch.org/pubs/2223/teens-cellphones-texting-phone-calls.

6. Jana Hollingsworth, "Teen Callers Turn to Texting on Minnesota Suicide Hotline," *Education Week*, February 8, 2012, accessed September 2, 2012, www.edweek.org/ew/articles/2012/02/08/20tech-wire.h31.html.

7. "Teens, Smartphones, and Texting."

8. In "Cyberspace: Love Online," *Psychology Today*, December 28, 2011, accessed December 29, 2011, www.psychologytoday.com/articles/200412/cyberspace-love-online. See also Aaron Ben-Ze'Ev, *Love Online: Emotions on the Internet* (New York: Cambridge University Press, 2004).

9. Yoav Gonen, "Less than Friends: Teachers Told, 'Stay Offline with Students,'" *New York Post*, March 22, 2012, accessed April 13, 2012, www.nypost.com/p/news/local/less_than_friends_ADEVxfo6cGZfn5zRUKxjGK#ixzz25KSOJfzE.

10. "Oregon Sex Abuse Case Highlights Teacher-Student Texting," Associated Press, March 21, 2012, accessed April 13, 2012, www.kval.com/news/local/Oregon-sex-abuse-case-highlights-texting-between-teachers-students-143563016.html.

11. Michelle Brandt, "Internet Addiction: Too Much of a Good Thing?" *Stanford News*, October 18, 2006, accessed April 13, 2012, http://news.stanford.edu/news/2006/october18/med-internet-101806.html.

12. Brandt, "Internet Addiction."

13. Theo Wubbels, "Two Decades of Research on Teacher-Student Relationships in Class," *International Journal of Educational Research* 43, nos. 1–2 (2005): 6–24.

14. Isca Salzberger-Wittenberg, Gianna Henry, and Elsie Osborne, "The Emotional Experience of Learning and Teaching," *Journal of Child Psychotherapy* 10 (1984): 125–27.

15. Dianne Anderson, "Teacher Goes Above and Beyond," KRQE, February 3, 2012, accessed April 13, 2012, www.kasa.com/dpps/news/education/teacher-goes-above-and-beyond_4062848.

16. A. Valenzuela, *Subtractive Schooling: U.S.–Mexican Youth and the Politics of Caring* (Albany, N.Y.: State University of New York, 1999). See also D. E. Campbell, "Building

Positive Relationships," Education.com, accessed July 16, 2012, www.education.com/reference/article/building-positive-relationships-students/.

17. Yvette Jackson and Valerie Strauss, "Why Relationship-Building Is Vital in Schools," *Washington Post*, May 28, 2011, accessed June 19, 2011,www.washingtonpost.com/blogs/answer-sheet/post/why-relationship-building-is-vital-in-schools/2011/05/26/AG7KVODH_blog.html. See also Campbell, "Building Positive Relationships."

18. Alexis de Tocqueville, *Democracy in America*, vol. 2 (London: Saunders and Otley, 1840), chap. 13, accessed June 4, 2012, www.gutenberg.org/files/816/816-h/816-h.htm.

19. Robert D. Putnam, "Bowling Alone: America's Declining Social Capital," *Journal of Democracy* 6, no. 1 (January 1995): 65–78, accessed June 4, 2012, http://muse.jhu.edu/login?auth=0&type=summary&url=/journals/journal_of_democracy/v006/6.1putnam.html.

20. Putnam, "Bowling Alone."

21. Tocqueville, *Democracy in America*.

22. Denise Witmer, "High School Survival Guide for Parents," About.com, accessed July 6, 2012, http://parentingteens.about.com/od/highschool/u/highschool.htm. See also "The Parent's Guide to High School," Education.com, accessed July 6, 2012, www.education.com/grade/high-school/; "Back to School," Parents for Public Schools San Francisco, accessed July 6, 2012, www.ppssf.org/; Parents for Public Schools, accessed July 6, 2012, http://parents4publicschools.org/.

23. "Parents: Cyber-Bullying Led to Teen's Suicide," *Good Morning America*, November 19, 2011, accessed November 19, 2011, http://abcnews.go.com/GMA/story?id=3882520&page=1; see also www.meganmeierfoundation.org/megansStory.php.

SIX

School Culture and Relationships

If concerns for making a difference remain at the one-to-one and class-room level, it cannot be done. An additional component is required. Making a difference must be explicitly recast in broader social and moral terms.

—Michael Fullan[1]

AT A GLANCE

There are nine major sections in this chapter: (1) navigating the high-stakes environment, (2) three tiers of appropriate relationships between teachers and students, (3) students, schools, and schedules, (4) typical high school day, (5) relationships under pressure, (6) rethinking teacher availability, (7) the good-old-boy network, (8) tough talk to education professionals, and (9) five suggestions for building relationships that produce a healthy school culture. The chapter closes with a summary and discussion questions.

NAVIGATING THE HIGH-STAKES ENVIRONMENT

Schools and local communities cannot escape the high-stakes environment that is our twenty-first-century reality. Test scores speak volumes about the success of a school and are calling cards for families, students, and even athletes. The media publishes test scores, and these publications draw immediate comparisons as well as criticisms. There is no secret that American public schools are dealing with a number of serious concerns. All government agencies can do is provide the impetus for change through policies of reform; it is up to Americans to change who we are as a society and how we do things, including our education system. While test scores do not tell the entire story of a school community, we live in an environment where numbers matter.

Consider that in this day of information overload, reducing our concerns to terms like *proficient, basic,* or *below basic* seems like an oversimplification of a set of more complex concerns. This type of evaluation occurs all the time—and not only in education but across other sociocultural environments as well. Everyone loves to be associated with exciting, positive, growth-focused, and winning environments. The opposite is true with poor educational environments.

High test scores translate to excellent education; at least this is the conclusion of parents. However, excellent schools are more than high test scores. Successful schools have successful teachers who have knowledge of their students inside and outside the classroom and express appropriate interest in their personal lives outside school.[2] This means teachers have appropriate relationships with their students, both in the formal sense and in the informal, that benefit the educational community.[3] To reiterate, the reality is that we live in a time when numbers mean so very much. There is a delicate balance required between policy and people.

Families committed to schools have the right to expect much in return. I have never heard a parent say he was committed to a particular school because his son or daughter tested well each spring on standardized assessments. Parents want more than that—they desire the best overall educational program for their children. Carol Cummings writes, "We teach children, not subjects."[4] Schools assist families in achievement and preparation for both now and for the future, and they must be positive environments where academic achievement and personal relationships can flourish.[5]

Busier Is Not Necessarily Better

As if schools and families aren't under enough pressure, along come the national Common Core Standards Assessments. One local journalist wrote, "The new Common Core Standards strive to make students critical thinkers, not just memorizers. They're an attempt to catch up U.S. education levels to those of other countries and tackle business leaders' long-held belief that graduates lack problem-solving skills."[6]

Busier teachers mean busier students. Busier students mean busier families. Is busier much better in the end? There is great curiosity that comes with the addition of newer tests and different data to examine. Educators hope that the Common Core will make schools more rigorous places of learning and therefore more effective. But what will the change mean for educators, parents, and students in terms of working relationships? Changes and pressures only make things more difficult for already stressed families.

People and Relationships Come First

Appropriate and professional relationships with people form the bedrock of good learning. Therefore, these must occupy a top priority in secondary schools. However, is this possible in the real world or just my fantasy? My experience leads me to conclude that excellent schools both provide content mastery and practice appropriate and balanced relationships.

Secondary teachers know there is more to graduating better students than taking them through added rigors. Students need to be better people, resilient, full of character, respectful, with a sense of belonging, capable of handling the many pressures of a busy world.[7] Establishing a new school culture takes time. The ability to think at higher levels has to begin early in the elementary years.

High-stakes accountability measures do not favor people; they favor previous years' results from people. Therefore, the criticisms of the education profession are sometimes valid. Any school culture operates best when there are guidelines to follow and people know how they fit into the academic culture. Relationships play a large part in determining how students fit within the larger context of education. As a result, in terms of teachers and students, three basic tiers address appropriate relationships. These appropriate relationships can be formed individually or in plurality. The three tiers are (1) intraschool academic relationships, (2) intraschool extracurricular relationships, and (3) interpersonal non-school-related relationships (see table 6.1).

THREE TIERS OF APPROPRIATE RELATIONSHIPS BETWEEN TEACHERS AND STUDENTS

Below, figure 6.1 illustrates the three different relational tiers often enjoyed between teachers and their students.

Tier 1: Intraschool Academic Relationships

Tier-1 intraschool academic relationships are first-tier relationships and are defined as teacher-student relationships that are tied to the academic institution, whether in classes, through counseling, or in fine arts or any other academic areas related to school. Tier-1 relationships are basic relationships that occur in the classroom or within normal school-hour functions and that are also in alignment with the professional mission of the school. Intrapersonal relationships are significantly different from *inter*personal relationships (which materialize in tier 3), yet they work together.

Table 6.1.   Three Tiers of Teacher-Student Relationships and Their Selected Characteristics

Tier 1 Intraschool Academic Relationships	Tier 2 Intraschool Extracurricular Relationships	Tier 3 Interpersonal Non-school-related Relationships
• Class-time banter • Questions and answers at desk, after class • Lunch-time tutoring • Intervention with students • Small-group collaboration • Teacher assistants in classroom • Daily classroom procedures	• Coaching athletics • Coaching and working with academic and competitive teams • Organizing and overseeing students at tournaments • Usually activity-based and extensions of the classroom • Often includes mentoring, character-building, teamwork, and skills that might not be tied to classroom academics • May involve parents and families • Can include tier-1 relationships	• Usually occur away from school day and outside teacher's contractual hours • Do not usually involve school academics or competitions • Few, if any, professional responsibilities • Can be blended with both tier-1 and tier-2 relationships • Moral reputations come into play • Communications are more informal • Expectations in the community usually exceed individual obligations of work

Tier 2: Intraschool Extracurricular Relationships

Tier-2 intraschool extracurricular relationships are developed through extracurricular involvement. Coaching, athletics, working with academic competitive teams, and organizing and overseeing students at tournaments fall under this definition. These relationships are often extensions of the classroom and involve fewer students and smaller groups. However, tier-2 relationships bring with them the addition of mentoring, character building and teamwork, and physical or honed skills not necessarily tied to the classroom academics. These relationships can also involve parents and families and are significant to developing annual school pride.

Tier 3: Interpersonal Non-School-Related Relationships

Tier-3 interpersonal non-school-related relationships are different from relationships in tiers one and two in that they are usually interpersonal, occur away from the school day, and do not usually involve school academics or competitions. Therefore, there are fewer professional responsibilities associated with tier-3 relationships. Ideally, the three tiers work together as seamlessly as they can, providing a healthy blend of

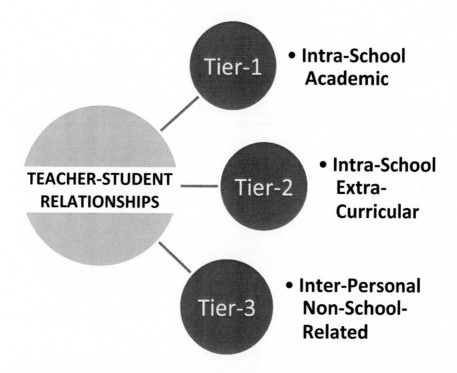

Figure 6.1. Three Tiers of Teacher-Student Relationships

intra- and interpersonal relating. Depending on the circumstances that arise between teachers, coaches, students, and players, tier-3 relationships can sometimes be very powerful and serve to reinforce other relationships.

Beyond the Classroom and Always On Duty

School culture naturally spills over into the surrounding community. Relationships that develop at school are different than those that develop outside of school, but they are all relationships, nonetheless.[8] Teachers in American high schools who think that after the final school bell rings they are no longer teachers need to read this next section very closely. Union members, take note, as well.

Teachers are never really off duty, even after their contractual hours are fulfilled. If relationships are as vital to the soul of education as many believe they are, this premise is certainly sensible. "Teachers must go beyond the scripts they are handed to learn about what students are and what they care about."[9] It is unpopular to maintain the position that teachers are still on duty after meeting their contractual obligations. Merely suggesting to teachers that they are accountable to local communities and for upholding the reputations of schools is met with strange looks and emotional responses of varying degrees.

In many ways, every person associated with the school is an extension of the school. In this sense, teachers are still "on duty," as it were, to parents and students wherever they are seen in the community. Teachers are, as Herman and Marlowe refer to us, "servant leaders," who make caring about students and what can be expected from them their primary concern.[10] Even after graduation from high school, former students refer to teachers—even those long retired—as "my old high school English teacher" or "my former high school soccer coach." Here is something that most high school teachers might know instinctually but that bears direct notation: the largest predictor as to whether students will graduate from high school is whether they have formed any meaningful relationships with their teachers, parents, and friends.[11] Educators must always be mindful that these relationships are appropriate at every turn, for their success or failure impacts lives well into the future.

Parents are still parents, and our students are still our students— whether they've left school or still sit in our classrooms. There is a certain pride in maintaining this identity long after graduation. Any teacher who works with high school seniors, or befriends current or former students on social-networking sites, knows this feeling well. Our title lives on well after hours, into the retirement years and beyond.

This reminds me of the time a teacher friend and I were out for a Saturday run. We had finished exercising and were walking through the parking lot in front of our favorite coffee shop when across the way we heard, "Hey, Dr. Zarra!" It was one of my high school seniors. His father was with him and looked at his son, asking, "Who's that?" I sobered when he replied, "That's my teacher." From that point on I concluded that I am always a teacher, on duty at all times; this is our students' reality.

And the media also seems to think this is true. Think about any time a teacher is arrested: whether they are at school, on vacation, or out in the community, the person arrested is boldly labeled "teacher" in the headlines.

STUDENTS, SCHOOLS, AND SCHEDULES

Student-Centered Schools

In chapter 1 we briefly discussed students' being at the center of the education system and that today's students feel a sense of empowerment and entitlement. In student-centered high schools, the pupils are the recipients of a lot of micromanagement, in terms of decisions made about their academic scheduling and things like off-campus work schedules, athletics, and a host of extracurricular activities.

This model does not empower students as decision makers. Rather, it encourages students to passively receive and respond. Graduation rates, apathy, lower achievement levels in classrooms, and the college remediation of content taught in high school all buttress this conclusion. Students are at the front and center of all of education, yet they graduate from school and are not ready to deal with college or with many adult decisions that unfold subsequently.

In student-centered education it is assumed that students are making sound decisions about classes, work schedules, athletics, and which teachers to take and which to avoid. In the actual world outside of school, it is implied that students make all of their own decisions for themselves. If high schools are responsible for preparing students for life, then ought they actually allow students to be the center of all of their decision making?

Student-centered education also implies that schools expect students to be able to make autonomous decisions about various areas of their lives, including (1) academics, (2) work schedules, (3) athletics involvement, and (4) school activities and balance all of these with relationships with (5) family, (6) friends, and (7) teachers, counselors, and coaches. But are students really capable of making these difficult decisions, given what we now understand about their brain development?

Student-Focused Schools

Rather than a student-centered model for education, I argue that a student-*focused* paradigm would be best. Student-centeredness suggests a sense entitlement and identity and reflects a culture that will be difficult to change even with public schools' addition of the Common Core Standards. Changing to a *focus* on students may be difficult, but making the shift could not be timelier.

The term *student-focused* addresses school mission and student-to-school relationships and incorporates collaborators and vested professionals who seek the best for students. That said, ultimately students are empowered to make their own decisions, with assistance from their families and educational professionals.

Focus brings attention. We do our students disservice by feeding their egos, letting them think that the schools exist for them and their needs. But in reality, the center of a school's attention is not the individual; not everything that goes on at schools has students at the center, nor should it. Focusing on education, and allowing a reemergence of teacher focus, will begin to reshape the culture of our high schools. Schools should be places of learning, not pedestals for teenage icons. Under this new model, students will know we care about them as people when we care about good and healthy decisions for their futures. This is a critical point to remember when developing relationships with students.

So a better education model trains the focus on the students, who receive the attention and specific care of others. This model is based on collaborative reciprocity and aspects of all three tiers of healthy student-teacher relationships.

Instead of hearing my former student say "That's Dr. Zarra—he was my teacher," I'd rather hear "That Dr. Zarra really pushed me to think and guided me into owning my decisions. I am glad he cared enough to think about my future when I didn't want to." Stipek refers to this as "holding students accountable while providing the support they need to succeed."[12] She would argue that this support goes well beyond a relationship that begins and ends with each ring of the classroom bell.

TYPICAL HIGH SCHOOL DAY

Relational Time Frames

Based on a student-focused educational model, high school *relational time frames* are defined as ratios of time that teachers and students could maximize in terms of developing relationships in a thirteen-hour, normal day, which begins with the regularly scheduled first class and ends with evenings at home (see figure 6.2).

Time Frame 1: Relational Time Frame

First, there is the regular academic day consisting of classes and normal contractual duties. This activity represents the bulk of the student's day at school. The model includes this time frame at the bottom, indicating it is the foundation of the school day.

Every school has a schedule unique to its community and district. Many factors go into formulating a schedule. Everyone adjusts to the schedule over time. However, teachers are usually on duty before and after school, fulfilling contractual duties. Most high school teachers in the nation "work" between seven and eight hours a day under this academic time frame.

Time Frame 2: Relational Time Frame

A second relational time frame for many teachers is the time spent coaching or overseeing competitions. This time frame usually runs from directly after the last academic period of the regular day through early evening, several times a week. This time frame is normally two to three hours per day after school and often extends into weekends. Students also are employed during this time frame. Consequently, they may drift

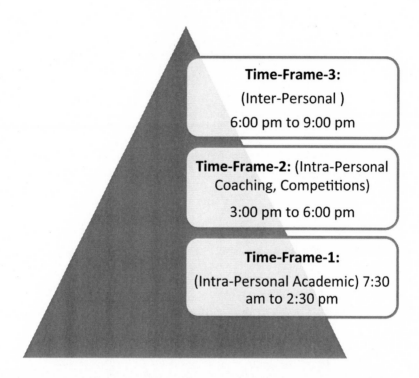

Figure 6.2.   Pyramid of Relationship Time Frames within the Average High School Day

into the third time frame. Time frame 2 represents the second level of the pyramid model, as it connects to the normal day, as well as after hours.

Time Frame 3: Relational Time Frame

The third relational time frame is set aside for study and homework and usually occupies two to three hours nightly. Student might also have part-time work during these hours. At this time the student can choose to be in a variety of places—at home, at work, or elsewhere. During this time frame, teachers and students are usually on personal time, and thus relationships developed during this time frame can vary.

The Real World

High school class sizes vary. Athletic and academic competitive teams are made up of only a select number of the school's students. This is likewise the case for academic competitive groups. Therefore, we cannot assume that one teacher has dedicated his or her time to any one student all day, every day. However, we can assume that teachers who make themselves available outside the classroom do assume other relationship-building roles.

For the sake of a normal schedule, teachers would see the vast majority of their students about one hour per day, in tier 1—typically the classroom. Many students are probably not involved in any official school extracurriculars, so they rarely spend tier-2 time with their teachers. However, every student has the opportunity at some point nightly to communicate with his or her teacher, assuming all parties have access to the requisite technology. So we must ask how it is possible for teachers and students to begin to develop inappropriate relationships from within the three relational time frames presented and what the markers are for such relationships.

Some Red Flags

Teachers and students spending more time with each other benefits both. As long as boundaries are established and the relationships are appropriate to the roles and tasks at hand, all should be well. Consider a scenario involving a teacher and a student who share the same class period one hour per day: What then is the likelihood that an interpersonal relationship would occur based on a mere sixty-minute meeting in a classroom? It's most likely not enough time for an acquaintance to become a friendship, let alone to deepen into a more serious relationship.

Since we can say that time spent together more or less equals relationship depth, there have to be other access points for a teacher and a student to deepen their relationship. Consequently, we guard against these access points, which we'll think of as red flags.

Dismissing all other issues, and things being somewhat equal, there are some key relational elements to investigate. These investigations occur best in the context of three specific questions: (1) Do any teachers spend more time than the average amount per student, per day? (2) Do any teachers and students spend a questionable amount of one-to-one, face-to-face meeting time for apparently social reasons? (3) Do any teachers consume questionable amounts of time communicating with one or more students via technology, from home in the evenings or on the weekends or even while still at school?

Answering yes to any one of these questions might raise concerns. It is normal for teachers and students to spend time with each other throughout the course of a normal day. There are exceptional days where students and teachers talk after class, and even after school. Exceptions are not the concern. But professionalism requires that teachers be aware of the time they spend with students. A properly calibrated moral compass helps teachers modify the amount of time spent with a student and the reasons for meeting, as needed.

RELATIONSHIPS UNDER PRESSURE

Teachers are not the only members in the education network who face scrutiny today. Parents are also under the cultural microscope. Families are under extreme pressure to rear children in a teenage-centered world while understanding that such centrism diminishes their authority as parents. Two-parent households have a difficult-enough time managing this task, but single parents and blended families have added pressures when making certain their children find proper direction in life. And so families naturally look to schools for assistance. Relationships between schools and families have served our nation well for many years. But times are changing, and expectations and roles have shifted, as we discussed in chapter 1.

In the past, many mothers stayed home and oversaw the running of the household. Their children were always sent to school with a lunch, and someone was at home when school let out. This was the case all the way through my high school experience. But today's families view this as a relic of the "old days." Contemporary economic pressures and needs have pressed families into severe debt, and students often cannot fend for their own meals and return to an empty home in the afternoon. And what have all of our busyness and our high-pressured lifestyles done to our abilities to relate on human levels? Once again, we do not have far to look to find the role technology plays in today's culture.

Technology has made dealing with issues easier and more impersonal. People can write things in an e-mail that they would never dare say to a person face-to-face. Distance and anonymity are sometimes used to say hurtful things. Unfortunately, teachers are too often on the end of this impersonalized mean-spiritedness as they scramble to wear many hats to meet many obligations, opening themselves up to criticism from many quarters.

Sharing Many Hats

Like it or not, schools are now involved in family social support. Along with educating students, high schools in particular have become mini college campuses: Psychologists, speech therapists, nurses, academic counselors, emotional-counseling service providers, minority-community liaisons, interpreters for those not proficient in English, aides for special needs students, and other professionals populate bustling high school campuses. There are even full-time police and security working on campuses daily.

Schools and families work together to focus on the education of students and offset the stresses felt by all involved. Families of high school students rely on relationships with teachers, counselors, and coaches for everything from emotional support to child-rearing advice. Such relationality is now part of school culture, which today has become as much about activities and athletics as it has been about academics.

Teachers Are Not the Students' Parents

It is not the job of a teacher to parent students—unless, of course, the teacher is fortunate enough to have their own children in their class or is hosting a foreign-exchange student for the academic year. Teachers definitely wear a lot of hats, which is why they ought to join forces with the equally busy parents in order to forge relationships that positively impact their students' lives—and possibly share their burdens and daily stresses. That said, the larger truth is that teachers are not students' parents and ought never be expected to assume such a role.

The number of activities and events in which today's secondary students involve themselves is breathtaking. Teachers also share in the regimen of school work, after-school athletics practices, weekend tournaments, and organizational meetings. Then add planning for things like rallies, formal dances, and proms, and it makes for a very busy school year for a teacher. Parents are right there, sometimes even offering a paper bag for shared hyperventilation.

Coaches wonder how overscheduled and overburdened students could possibly manage their academics and family obligations *in addition to* their responsibilities to their sports teams. Coaches see grades drop, students become ineligible to participate in extracurriculars, and hear parental disappointment that their teenager could not bear up under all the pressure. But stepping away from the vortex of high school activity, a clearer perspective is possible. Parents, too, will eventually be able to look back on their teenagers' high school years and be thankful that teachers helped them through.

But times are changing, and resources are stretched ever thinner. Some states are facing potential shortages of teachers. And in some states student enrollment in teacher-credentialing programs is down by about a third, which means overworked teachers see no relief in near sight. [13]

RETHINKING TEACHER AVAILABILITY

Teachers are under contract, and their unions and faculty associations balk at contract changes suggested by administrators, parents, politicians, and bureaucrats. But power plays against schools for political purposes do not help students and place an unwelcome focus on teachers. We noticed this recently with the nearly two-week 2012 Chicago teachers' strike. How does focusing on a contract, a union, help teachers focus more on their students? It doesn't. But suffice to say, this is the reality of teacher labor-negotiations today and often results in diminished student learning.

Teachers have different views on their availability to families and students after hours. The rare teacher makes themselves available in the evenings or on the weekends, when they are under no obligation to do so. But some teachers are rethinking their availability beyond the school day for a variety of reasons. Some are simply unwilling to give extra time, especially in places where furloughs and pay cuts are becoming commonplace. Others make the choice for far more troubling reasons: the explosion of allegations of inappropriate teacher-student relationships is affecting the entire profession.

Outside the Norm

Let's say that on a Friday a parent has questions about his underperforming student. And let's say that that teacher was somehow unable to get back to the parent until the following week, or even later. What is the likelihood that the issue would blow up out of proportion over the passing of a few days? But what about the flip side, where the agitated parent has a chance to calm down over the weekend and decides to deal with the issue differently? Waiting to respond is a calming strategy that works for teachers in many circumstances.

Sometimes teachers purposely do not return communication with parents. One math colleague never opened his work e-mail, saying he wanted to talk to parents on the phone only. Placing such a high value on relationships with the parents and students might then change the education paradigm: for if education is student-centered, does the centrism end daily at 3:00 p.m.?

What I am about to suggest will be unpopular for some. Educators would do well to consider our parents as our customers: They make huge deposits every day, at great risk, when dropping their children off at our schools, entrusting them to our care and saftey. To extend the metaphor, in many ways, parents are entrepreneurs hoping for a great return on their investment—an excellent education paving a good professional and personal road for their child. With today's ubiquitous technologically enabled communication, how many of us are available on weekends, holidays, and vacations? Do we take the time to recognize and communicate and relate with parents and students while we are out and about in public?

Now, I can already hear some teachers insisting, "I don't get paid to do that," or "That's not my job." And I agree with both of those statements. Yet educating is a commitment, teaching is our job, and humans bridge the gap between both. I also add that there are teachers who refuse to go near anything that feels like a relationship with their students for fear of being accused of inappropriate behavior; or they are simply not interested in knowing any teenagers outside of the classroom. Having relationships after the school day is also not the teacher's job. I understand this. But I argue the following: if my child has a need, or if my family is in a crisis, I hope every teacher and counselor would come alongside my family and me to offer assistance.

Finding the best time frame in which to assist is often the concern. Teachers are busy people, and if they feel they are somehow required to form relationships, give up their own precious family time, choose between personal fitness and work, and take additional credentialling classes in the process, they might not be long for the profession. All of this is a probable explanation for the decrease in teacher-education applicantions.

A teacher's relationship with the parents is about finding solutions for the student's performance issues and can enrich the entire school community. These relationships help in the production of education capital, which we discussed in chapter 4. And relationships without capital are weak, at best.

On a Personal Note

I once observed a teacher sitting on a concrete planter, just talking with a female student. He gave up his lunch to soothe this sixteen-year-old girl, who had been sitting alone, crying. It turned out that the young woman had a secret concern and was afraid to share it with her parents. Her relationship with them, at the time, was very strained. But the teacher's kind attention made it possible for the student to deal with her circumstances. Another colleague once received an evening phone call at home from a student's mom and was able to help her work through some serious issues she had with her son.

These are the kinds of things that occur at schools all across this nation because of healthy teacher-student bonds. As we discussed in chapter 5, such relationships help to build educational capital with families, and going the extra mile results in huge dividends for schools. In forming relationships with students, teachers also form relationships with their families. Coaches especially know this to be true, as most of their relationships are extensions of the school, outside the normal academic day.

Again, my own personal experience has taught me that my classroom instructional time makes a difference after hours. Back in 1999, a student phoned me at home. I happened to be in, so I answered, asking with whom I was speaking. A younger male voice said, "You know who I am. You were my teacher a few years ago." "Oh, all right," I said, moving the conversational pleasantries right along, when I was abruptly interrupted. "Zarra," the caller said, "I have a gun to my head, and I going to kill myself tonight. Before I do, I wanted to talk to someone I thought cared about me and my life." Stunned, I somehow managed to calmly say,

"May I ask your name, please?" He declined to tell me. To his credit, he did offer that he was high from smoking marijuana. In short order, I was able to get law-enforcement on another line to help me, all while continuing to talk with the young man. Luckily, in the end things worked out all right.

I could have chosen several courses of action when I received my former student's call for help. I quickly realized my role as teacher was not as his lecturer that evening. I am compensated to neither counsel nor talk with students who are under the influences of drugs, yet when he called and explained his predicament, the images in my head were inescapable. If that had been my child, I would have wanted someone to take the time to help.

In sharing these three personal examples I hope to demonstrate what many educational researchers are discovering about relationships between teachers and teenage students: Students saying they have relationships at school with their teachers is very different from saying that they know their teachers will go the extra mile for them. When a teacher shows profound concern, they necessarily touch the lives of their students beyond the classroom.[14] Doing so normally forms vital and unique relationships with parents, too.

Speaking with many teachers over the years and listening to their personal anecdotes affirms for me that students and families respond better to the school when appropriate relationships are a significant part of the education process for their teenagers. Education is a people profession. The parents of the suicidal young man who called me ended up being very glad a former teacher took the time to talk their son down from a drug-induced, escalated emotional crisis. Many teachers choose to involve themselves in similar crises because they have taken the time to form meaningful relationships with their students along the way. And many hurting students turn to teachers in the first place because of these nurturing, healthy relationships.

Let's Get Real

Teachers' roles have changed over the years. Even so, you won't hear much discussion about this coming from our universities' lecture halls. Strategies to develop and nurture vital and appropriate relationships with teenagers are lacking in secondary methods and psychology courses.[15] Philosophy-of-education courses should include the application of philosophy to the building of relationships. And so I recommend that courses for teachers-in-training include discussions of the relational philosophies of education and the philosophy of public service. This book could be used as a starting point.

Teachers enjoy normal, healthy relationships across many domains outside of the regular parameters of their employment. They just don't talk about them. Everyone in education is tacitly aware that each relationship means wearing a different hat, depending on the context. But where do teachers form these relationships outside of class?

Teachers may foster relationships with their students and their families by

- attending church where students and families attend;
- coaching a sport or a competitive academic team;
- offering online support for issues outside the scope of understanding of parents, through a website developed for a particular class or school program;
- sending regular digital communications about student progress;
- and phoning parents when kids are doing well so that the parents can also do well in hearing the teenager's progress.

Relationships are nurtured by regular communication. Students appreciate those teachers who go out of their way to show they care. In fact, research indicates that students work harder for teachers who genuinely care about them beyond the classroom and have a significant relationship with them than they work for those teachers who don't seem to care as much.[16] Students are not motivated to have an interpersonal relationship with academic content. Therefore, regular communication between teachers and parents and between teachers and students is essential to healthy teacher-student relationships. Without communication a relationship falters. And when unhealthy teacher-student relationships cross the line, there is inevitably more going on behind the scenes than is evident in the course of the regular school day.

THE GOOD-OLD-BOY NETWORK

Hiding controversial issues from media scrutiny or the general public has long been a part of our nation's cultural history, and the good-old-boy network survives today, with vestiges of it still visible in schools. This is in evidence in school districts where political power, size of faculty associations and unions, and money are in play. This network also subsists in places that cover up for administrators who've had sexual affairs with faculty. And this network exists where a teacher is to be removed from duty for wrongdoing only to wind up transferred to a new place of employment.

Transferring a teacher with a history of sexual complaints only shuffles the problem to a new location where it will affect more people. The same problems will emerge over time, because nothing has actually been solved—the same problem still exists. Switching a predatory teacher's environment merely provides new opportunities for conquests. The good old boys are selectively secretive, and they look out for each other. But this is not in the best interests of students and families, and so this culture must change—especially during this age of sex and social media.

There is a stark, legal difference between the adult on a campus who seeks to make a sexual conquest of another adult and the adult on campus who seeks to make a sexual conquest of a teenager. An adult with a predatory mind-set sees victimizing adults sexually as a conquest to tally; this adult should never work with teenagers. This person's moral compass is so differently calibrated than that of the type of person we hope to guide our students. Even though this kind of predator's sexual conquest may be legal, that doesn't mean it's moral or right. This is especially important for a person intending to mold young lives. Appropriate relationships consider morality as well as legality.

TOUGH TALK TO EDUCATION PROFESSIONALS

Educators ought to challenge themselves with the following:

1. Educators and all adults have a responsibility to consistently model the very morality they expect of their teenage students. If they do not model it, then they cannot expect students to live it.
2. On your campus do teachers actually enforce district and school rules by stepping in to halt students' public displays of physical affection and sexuality?
3. Teachers, administrators, and coaches should never be alone with other members of the school in rooms that are out of the way, where the doors are locked, or with the lights out. Administrators who only make themselves privately or inordinately available to one or two select faculty members are using work time to forge relationships that are likely inappropriate.

Here is a simple test to determine whether or not an administrator's on-campus relationship is appropriate:

- How often are the two together on campus, in private?
- Is there a sense of exclusivity between the two that appears to be part of the campus culture among administrators?
- Have there been any compromising or repeated questionable incidents witnessed by others on campus?

Across this nation, administrators and teachers have been hooking up in greater and greater numbers. How can a school expect to operate with moral purpose, staying focused on its mission, when the leader of the school is having an affair with the spouse of another faculty member or when teachers are sexually involved with each other? Invariably, students will see things that the adults did not intend for them to see. And since this models inappropriate behavior for students, people with power and authority should never behave this way.

School personnel engaging in workplace relationships may be inappropriate. The relationships eventually affect families, students, teachers, and the larger school community. This type of conflict of interest is not healthy.

When it comes to personal lives, we need to step back and remember what we stated earlier in this chapter: teachers are never off duty to students or members of the community, to the media, or to families. This same truth applies to administrators, coaches, and counselors. Like teachers, school administrators are in a similar position to influence the students in their care. And though every school district has its share of "personnel issues" unable to be disclosed by law, we have to acknowledge that we have a national problem on our hands and that it does not only involve teachers and students.

FIVE SUGGESTIONS FOR BUILDING RELATIONSHIPS THAT PRODUCE A HEALTHY SCHOOL CULTURE

The following are five very practical suggestions for developing a healthy school culture. They might sound simple at the outset, but as you consider each suggestion, ask yourself, To what extent does this assist in changing the culture of our school while promoting appropriate relationships on our campus?

Regular School Assemblies

Organize and promote school assemblies set up to define and promote healthy and good relationships across the school campus. Schools tend to focus on more immediate issues, such as bullying, back-burnering the larger issues associated with changing school culture in developing relationships. At these assemblies, experts in the district could define what appropriate relationships are and how to identify them.

At these assemblies discuss the dangers of inappropriate relationships, and bring people in to contrast the two. Unless students see and understand appropriate behavior modeled for them at school, they will default to emulating the culture outside of school. At that point, student relationships will have devolved into the inappropriate and will have to be addressed punitively.

Shaping Classroom Environments

Schools should follow up the assemblies by distributing posters for classrooms. Class discussions should take place immediately after the assembly and in continual dialogue in classes. Teenagers are highly sensory. Focusing on appropriate and wholesome relationships will yield positive results. One poster suggestion for the reader might include, "Keeping it friendly, wholesome, and professional."

Parent Opt-In and Opt-Out Forms

Schools should provide an opt-out form for parents and students so that their students may be exempt from social contact from their teachers after school hours. If parents do not want teachers talking, chatting, texting, or e-mailing their children, they should have the right to maintain this privacy. Administrators must cover this policy in detail prior to the start of a school year.

Developing and Posting Codes of Professional Conduct

Parents should be able to identify the location of the code of professional conduct. Classrooms should have these codes posted in plain view, as well. Teacher-parent capital is enhanced by forming joint committees to develop codes of conduct for the school. Educators have nothing to be ashamed of in holding themselves to higher standards. When teachers make every effort to live by a professional code, even in their private lives, their students will notice and will then look to these teachers as mentors. We are educating students for the present and the future.

Informative Faculty Meetings

Are there any meetings with teachers that warn of the dangers of inappropriate relationships with students and with each other? These do affect education and the campus. School communities that hold each other accountable are less likely to have to deal with allegations that will tear apart a community. Administrators should take the lead for the sake of all involved.

SUMMARY

Schools and local communities cannot escape the cultural reality of the twenty-first century: They are judged harshly, and the stakes are high. Test scores speak volumes about the perceived success of a school and are calling cards for families, students, and even athletes. The media publishes test scores, and these publications draw immediate comparisons, as well as criticisms. Families that are committed to schools have the right to expect much in return.

School culture operates best when there are guidelines to follow and when people know where they fit into the academic culture. In terms of teachers and students, three basic tiers address appropriate relationships between individuals and groups within the academic culture: (1) intra-school academic relationships, (2) intraschool extracurricular relation-ships, and (3) interpersonal non-school-related relationships. Teachers are never really off duty, even after their daily contractual hours end. In many ways, everyone associated with the school is an extension of the school.

There are two education models addressed in this chapter: (1) the student centered–education model and (2) the student focused–education model. The former puts students at the center of every decision made at the high school. The latter, on the other hand, addresses school mission and student-to-school relationships, incorporating collaborators and vested professionals who seek the best for students.

Every school has a schedule unique to its community and district. Most high school teachers in the nation only technically work an average of seven to eight hours a day directly with students, though the time they put in preparing and fostering a healthy educational environment is much greater.

Teachers and students spending more time together benefits both, as long as boundaries are established and the relationships are appropriate to the roles and tasks at hand.

Families rely on relationships with teachers, counselors, and coaches at the high school level for everything from emotional support to advice on rearing their teens. Teachers' roles have changed over the years. There is not much discussion about this change from educational theorists at the university level. In secondary methods and psychology courses there is a dearth of strategies for developing and nurturing vital and appropri-ate relationships with teenagers. Philosophy-of-education courses should include the application of philosophy in the building of relationships.

Five very practical suggestions to assist schools in building relation-ships that produce a healthy school culture include (1) convening regular school assemblies, (2) shaping the classroom environment, (3) offering parent opt-in and opt-out forms, (4) developing and posting codes of professional conduct, and (5) holding informative faculty meetings.

DISCUSSION QUESTIONS

1. In what ways are teachers, parents, and students overloaded to-day?
2. How does a school's culture and daily schedule assist in the devel-opment of relationships between teachers, students, and parents?
3. Why is it important that people and relationships be given a high priority in high schools?

4. What tiers of involvement exist between teachers and students that result in the formation of relationships?

5. What are some of the ways teachers can build and maintain relationships with students in the classroom?

6. What are some of the characteristics of teacher-student relationships?

7. What are some of the differences between student-centered and student-focused philosophies of education?

8. How can teachers and students spend time thinking about and discussing the roles of relationships at the school?

9. What is a "good" teacher, in terms of both classroom interactions and outside-of-class interactions with students?

10. Do you agree or disagree with the social roles taken on by the school, in terms of assisting families and students?

11. What are some excuses teachers might give for not developing relationships with students outside the high school classroom?

12. How would you describe a teacher who demonstrates an appropriate relationship with a teenage student? What are the characteristics of this relationship?

NOTES

1. Michael Fullan, *Change Forces* (New York: The Falmer Press, 1993), 10.

2. Deborah Stipek, "Relationships Matter," *Educational Leadership* 64, no. 1 (March 2006): 46–49.

3. I. Korkmaz, "Teachers' Opinions about the Responsibilities of Parents, Schools, and Teachers in Enhancing Student Learning," *Education* 127, no. 3 (2007): 389–99.

4. In *Teaching Makes a Difference* (Edmonds, Wash.: Teaching Incorporated, 1990, 1996), 13.

5. Nel Noddings, *The Challenge to Caring in Schools: An Alternative Approach to Education* (New York: Teachers College Press, 2005).

6. Jorge Barrientos, "Major Changes in Math, English Instruction Coming Soon," *Bakersfield Californian*, July 21, 2012, accessed July 21, 2012, www.bakersfieldcalifornian.com/local/x475201303/Major-changes-in-math-English-instruction-coming-soon.

7. D. L. Schussler and A. Collins, "An Empirical Exploration of the Who, What, and How of School Care," *Teachers College Record* 108, no. 7 (2006): 1460–95.

8. Stipek, "Relationships Matter."

9. K. Shultz, *Listening: A Framework for Teaching across Differences* (New York: Teachers College Press, 2003), 104.

10. D. V. Herman and M. Marlowe, "Modeling Meaning in Life: The Teacher as Servant Leader," *Reclaiming Children and Youth* 14, no. 3 (2005): 175–78.

11. V. Ruus et al., "Students' Well-Being, Coping, Academic Success, and School Climate," *School Behavior and Personality* 35, no. 7 (2007): 919–36. See also Edward F. DeRoche and Mary M. Williams, *Character Education: A Guide for School Administrators* (Lanham, Md.: Scarecrow Press, 2001), 51–58.

12. Stipek, "Relationships Matter."

13. Courtenay Edelhart, "Shrinking Pool of Future Teachers Worries State," *Bakersfield Californian*, September 22, 2012, accessed September 22, 2012, www.bakersfieldcalifornian.com/local/x485099342/Shrinking-pool-of-future-teachers-wor

ries-state.

14. R. Antrop-Gonzales and A. de Jesus, "Toward a Theory of Critical Care in Urban Small School Reform," *Education* 19, no. 4 (2006): 409–33. See also L. K. Brendto, M. Brokenleg, and S. Van Bokern, *Reclaiming Youth at Risk: Our Hope for the Future* (Bloomington, Ind.: Solution Tree, 2002); Stipek, "Relationships Matter"; Nel Noddings, *The Challenge to Caring in Schools: An Alternative Approach to Education* (New York: Teachers College Press, 2005).

15. R. Miller and J. Pedro, "Creating Respectful Classroom Environments," *Early Childhood Education* 33, no. 5 (2006): 293–99.

16. J. A. Hall-Lande, M. E. Eisenberg, S. L. Christenson, and D. Neumark-Sztainer, "Social Isolation, Psychological Health, and Protective Factors in Adolescence," *Adolescence* 42, no. 166 (2006): 265–86.

SEVEN

Education Policy: Morality, Purpose, and Common Sense

AT A GLANCE

The ten major sections in this chapter include (1) definition of moral purpose, (2) scratching the surface, (3) immoral purpose, (4) informing teachers about professional conduct, (5) interviewing teacher candidates, (6) teacher candidate interview questions and rationales, (7) teachers' rights versus student protection, (8) states' policies on communication technologies and social media, (9) appropriate uses of cell phones in high school, and (10) seven educational reasons to allow cell phone usage in high school classrooms. The chapter closes with a summary and discussion questions.

DEFINITION OF MORAL PURPOSE

Moral purpose is defined as a sense of commitment toward people with (1) clearly defined objective civic and character goals, (2) well-marked academic objectives and standards-aligned assessments to measure achievement, and (3) joint commitments comprised of the families, schools, and communities-at-large—all coauthorities involved in the process. Essentially, moral purpose is larger than self.[1]

Michael Fullan views the teacher as the moral agent. "The building block is the moral purpose of the individual teacher. Scratch a good teacher and you will find moral purpose."[2] Two decades have passed since Fullan penned those words. Twenty years ago, not every pocket contained a cell phone. In fact, most primitive cell phones were bulky devices that were usually plugged in to automobiles cigarette-lighter ports. Cell phones were so user-unfriendly and expensive that pay phones were still the vanguard of on-the-road communications.

If we were to scratch a good teacher today, might we find things to be as Fullan expected, would we find someone else entirely? Aside from the above-mentioned technological changes we've weathered, our nation has recently undergone some very trying times. And battered by these trying times is our national morality. Today in scratching a good teacher we might find that we've broken open a scab and in the process revealed old wounds.

But what is a good teacher anyway? Even the word *good* has taken on new meaning in American culture. Old wounds in the professional sense could be the result of the past two decades of educational experiments and changes in the profession. Or perhaps it references past personal issues of deep concern, only now manifesting themselves in those who now teach at the front of our classrooms. Whatever the case, we are a different nation today in many ways than the one we were twenty years ago.

Moral purpose still exists. But if a teacher's moral purpose is obscured by unresolved issues, how effective will that teacher be in the classroom? Does a person's past block the present? We must pose this question because more and more people are using their troubled pasts to justify their present troubles. And unfortunately teachers are no exception.

SCRATCHING THE SURFACE

Teachers born in 1990 have entered classrooms all over the nation. By the year 2022 most new teachers will not have any personal connection to the twentieth century. I began my teaching career at the age of twenty-two, directly out of college, as many American teachers have and continue to do. Districts hire many younger teachers to replace the veterans among us. Soon, many teachers of the baby-boomer generation will no longer be in the classroom. Education does follow the natural order of life.

What does this mean for the transition in the education profession? What do we know about the younger hires of today and those who will be hired over the next few years? What can we know about the teachers yet to come over the next decade? Will their training be sufficient? What will characterize them, and can we visualize how they are likely to view relationships with students and others?

One thing is certain: Many newer teachers will have no recollection of a time before cell phones and computers. They will never have seen a monochrome monitor, and they will use the Clinton administration as their starting point as a frame of reference in the world. Even as culture has changed and continues, one question persists: where is a teacher's moral center and purpose with respect to relationships and emerging technologies?

IMMORAL PURPOSE

If we adopt Fullan's definition of a good teacher, we cannot help but wonder whether scratching a bad teacher would reveal an immoral purpose. Today there is much evidence to conclude that some good teachers have gone bad. Teachers once considered good, once assumed to have moral purposes for teaching and leading young people, somehow crossed over to the other side. Something went wrong within their moral centers, their choices, or both. Schools suffer today from a lack of corporate character, falsely implying to adults and children that separation of personal lives from public lives is culturally acceptable.

Since the impeachment trial of President Clinton, it has become far too commonplace for people to separate who they are in the public eye from what they do in private. Today teenagers do not view certain sexual acts as "sex" and compartmentalize public and private actions. John Dewey's concerns of 1909 are quite relevant for today:

> The psychological side of education sums itself up, of course, in a consideration of character. It is a commonplace to say that the development of character is the end of all schoolwork. The difficulty lies in the execution of the idea. In addition, an underlying difficulty in this execution is the lack of a clear conception of what character means. . . .
>
> In our moral books and lectures we may lay the stress upon good intentions, etc. But we know practically that the kind of character we hope to build up through our education is one that not only has good intentions but that insists upon carrying them out. Any other character is wishy-washy; it is goody, not good. The individual must have the power to stand up and count for something in the actual conflicts of life. He must have initiative, insistence, persistence, courage, and industry. He must, in a word, have all that goes under the name *"force* of character."[3]

John Goodlad places Dewey in a more modern context when he says that, "yes, teachers require training, but they also need education, in the very best sense of the word. . . . Without this modeling, teachers of teachers run the danger of conveying that tiresome image, 'Do as I say; not as I do.'"[4] Hopefully faculties of teacher-education institutions are paying close attention.

"Teachers Can't Control Themselves"

Teachers cross the line to begin inappropriate relationships with students for many reasons. Certainly impulsivity can be a reason. The development of long-term relationships between teachers and students, including repeated and regular sexual acts, does not imply mere impulsivity. Teenagers are supposed to be impulsive. Adults usually ascribe a higher level of choice to their actions.

The word *relationship* implies something much more elaborate than a choice or act. If we are to conclude that teachers are in desperate need of counseling for past problems, and therefore have no control over what they do, then we face a national emergency. The interview process, and veteran-teacher evaluation, had better include professionals other than educators.

School districts are acutely aware of the times in which we live. The hypersexual environment of hormones and teenagers and preteens is something many teachers seem to understand. Yet with this understanding comes an illogical softening of morality, resulting, for some, in an eventual yielding to temptation. Consider the following recent cases of teacher predation, and ask yourself (1) what can districts do differently or do better at the interview stage to discover a person's underlying motivation to teach, (2) how can we pinpoint the nuances of candidates' different worldviews, and (3) how might we plant ideas of consequences of inappropriate teacher-student relationships to gather responses?

- A thirty-six-year-old Strongsville High School teacher offered herself as a date in the school's Win a Date with the Teacher contest. A seventeen-year-old student won the date, and over time a sexual relationship developed between the two. The teacher was eventually found out, arrested, and fired and later pled guilty.[5] A thirty-one-year-old South Central High School teacher was convicted of taking indecent liberties with a student. The teacher was unable to explain why her cell phone records indicated that she had talked extensively to her seventeen-year-old lover an estimated 130 times in a two-month period.[6] A thirty-four-year-old Culver City music teacher was charged with attempting to perform lewd acts on an eleven-year-old girl. He was arrested after he sent the girl inappropriate photographs and e-mail messages on a cell phone that he had given her for their private use.[7]
- A thirty-six-year-old lesbian teacher and coach at Lecanto High School was arrested for having a sexual relationship with a fifteen-year-old female student.[8] A thirty-one-year-old Buena Vista High School band teacher turned herself in to police after a warrant was issued for her arrest on child molestation charges. The charges included four counts of unlawful sexual intercourse with a seventeen-year-old student.[9]

Heightened States

We live in a very sensually heightened and sexually explicit society. Younger teachers do not really recall when pornography, Web cams, cell phones, chat, and texting were not readily available. Veteran teachers have points of reference that newer teachers lack. Are we now at the point in interviews where administrators must ask tough questions about candidate views on sexuality, sexual relationships, use of technology, and moral practices?

Veteran teachers might well disagree with any action that even hints at the notion of disclosure of private information. However, we live at a time when predators are using this very privacy to their advantage with students. Years in the profession are no guarantee of safety. Current laws confirm the interview questions legal to ask state- or public-level employees. The safety of our students requires the reformation of this process.

One of the downsides of cultural sexual empowerment is that it may eventually open candidates to interview questions they would rather not answer publically. Some issue-oriented groups want to be free to proclaim their sexuality but forbid anyone from asking about the way it would play out with teenagers in relationships. Consider a hypothetical male who is quite brazen in his lifestyle, flirts with female students in class and from home, using technology, even posting shirtless for photos he sends them. How can we say his actions wouldn't affect his relationships with his students? Does the school district have a right to know about his predispositions, use of technology, or whether he is seeking his first teaching job or is a veteran teacher?

A recent conversation I had with several teenage girls revealed a situation they felt was getting out of control. The situation involved a single, young male teacher, whom the girls said made them feel uncomfortable because he "look[ed] down our tops" when he walked around the room and "stare[d] at our legs" when he was in front of the class. "It makes us feel creepy," they all agreed.

The school's response was quite generic, placing some of the responsibility onto the students while noting and reporting their concerns exactly. The girls were then told, "Maybe if you wore clothes that didn't reveal so much cleavage or didn't wear your shorts so high, there wouldn't be a temptation to look." Were I their father, they would not have been allowed to dress like that.

Sometimes teenagers are not fully aware of the way their bodies appear to others. And sometimes they are fully aware. Regardless, any teacher who tends to be aroused by teenage displays of their bodies is responding inappropriately—regardless of what the students wear, their rippling muscles, how they smell, or how cute their smiles.

Teenagers who flaunt their bumps and curves must bear some responsibility. Most male teachers I know are quite uncomfortable with having to deal with teenagers' clothing issues, for obvious reasons. Yet how often is this issue ever addressed in teacher candidate interviews?

Perhaps it's time we considered a stricter dress code for our public schools. There is an easy solution to these types of temptations, and the solution is to cover up. Uniforms might be the best answer. No one knows how many inappropriate teacher-student sexual relationships began with repeated visual exposure. (And, really, no one is certain exactly how many students have taken the next steps with teachers sexually.)

There are reports, and there are estimates based on the reports.[10] Common sense allows us to draw general conclusions about the beginnings of abuse. Visual exposure to sexual images and movies online are sources of stimulation for the average person. Body-part exposure and attire have something to do with visual stimulation. Hence, students need to watch how they dress, and teachers need to avert their eyes and keep their passions in check. But this is insufficient to addressing the problem. We all know these things, yet we still face an epidemic of inappropriate teacher-student relationships.

The Immoral Teacher

Teachers from Boston to Chicago, Los Angeles to Dallas and San Francisco, have been fired when revelations of their sexual past have come to light—digital light, that is. These teachers appeared or even starred in adult films. In many cases, these porn stars–turned–teachers thought nothing of keeping their pasts hidden while accepting positions to work with teenagers. But word about their past profession eventually gets out, and tech-savvy teenagers hunt down the evidence on porn sites. On more than a few occasions teenagers have discovered more about their teachers than one could ever have expected. Aside from the prurient past of these teachers—in some cases, the very distant past—should not this discovery have been made during their application interviews?

Where there is great trust, there is often increased temptation. And where there is such great temptation, there must also be much greater accountability. As with most things in life, in the cases we discuss, choices are involved. Should the public forgive a teacher whose past recklessness might stir the raging hormones of teenagers? How many of us would think such a past would not be a distraction in classrooms? Taking the higher road means not allowing one's past to distract what occurs today. But some choices cannot simply be undone or overlooked.

Films showing a teacher naked, bound, and sexually used hardly provide the kinds of images teenagers need to start their days off right or around which to shape student morality. Teenagers' brains have difficulty enough focusing on the tasks of the classroom. Districts must consider not only the past of those they hire but also the applicant's moonlighting work when employed by the district.

Moral compromises can become common practice, and adults who choose to engage in morally compromising behavior do not set good examples for teenagers. The adult's compromise becomes the teenager's justification.[11] Though no one is perfect, a teacher who *practices* imperfection is no academic or moral role model.

Professional Development

Teachers are very busy. They show up at school extracurricular activities and sporting events, becoming parts of their students' lives and showing emotions in "real" ways. Are there any guidelines, aside from the criminal code, that assist teachers in setting appropriate boundaries for involvement with their students? There must be guidelines developed for the sake of the profession. Unfortunately, most districts use the "cross-the-fingers" approach, hoping that nothing will cause a community stir. This is no way to communicate excellence.

Rather, districts must provide teachers, coaches, and administrators qualitative professional development regarding the propriety and impropriety of teacher-student interactions and relationships. Two basic starting points to administer this training are (1) teacher-training institutions and (2) professional development. The concerns should be treated in the same way drug-abuse awareness is treated in schools.[12] As follow-up, schools could use the professional learning communities' model or develop accountability groups to address concerns.

Setnor-Byer and Salcedo maintain that much of the responsibility for appropriate relationships falls on the administrator, writing that

> teachers do not need to be taught that an intimate relationship with a minor is illegal or even inappropriate. Such knowledge is presumed. Rather, administrators need to adopt policy and training that
>
> - summarize the conduct that school administrators expect of all school personnel and the actions to be taken if suspicious behaviors are observed;
> - identify the behavioral signs that indicate a child is uncomfortable with a school employee's conduct;
> - characterize four types of behavioral triggers that create risks for school employees;
> - list general rules of behavior that help avoid claims of misconduct;
> - recognize personality traits and motivating factors that lead to inappropriate relationships;
> - analyze actions by asking peer-observation and self-policing questions that help detect potentially inappropriate behaviors; and
> - describe the criminal, civil, and ethical consequences of inappropriate behavior.[13]

Despite officially disregarding the above concerns, most faculty and teachers' unions fully comprehend the importance of the concerns. Rights to privacy are not taken lightly. However, there must be a balance of teacher candidate rights with the the students' right to the best education possible in a safe, protected environment. The possibility of sexual predators having access to teenage students does nothing to help the education profession.

INFORMING TEACHERS ABOUT PROFESSIONAL CONDUCT

States' Codes of Conduct

States develop education codes of ethics and professional principles of conduct for teachers. These codes apply both to veterans and new hires. Districts also are developing acceptable-use policies for teachers' use of technology. In many cases, the statements are "commandments" in the negative, specifying what teachers may *not* do.

Several states' policies have been analyzed in terms of professional codes of conduct and legal boundaries set forth for teachers. Various regions have also been analyzed, including specific states, which include California,[14] Florida,[15] Illinois,[16] New York,[17], Texas, and others. Tables 7.1, 7.2, and 7.3 provide excerpts of some of this data. As we begin, let us take note of a few common threads.

Summary of Data Analysis

Some of the common threads found in the states' codes include

- professionalism
- making certain to respect colleagues, students, and families
- and a focus on intellectual pursuits.

Some states that have published clear and concise professional codes of ethics for teachers have their documentation posted on their state's Department of Education websites. The codes we've reviewed indicate the directions many state codes are heading. Not all fifty states have such codes, but they should. States are seeing alarming increases in inappropriate teacher-student relationships, and this fact alone should prompt every state to move quickly.

For example, Kentucky saw a troublesome rise over one year in inappropriate teacher-student relationships. From 2010 to 2011, inappropriate sexual relationships between teachers and students rose from twenty-eight to forty-six. That is approximately one arrest for every two counties in Kentucky. Kentucky requires administrators and teachers to report the abuse of any student under the age of eighteen.[18] Between 2001 and 2005,

Table 7.1.   California Standards for the Teaching Profession

California Department of Education (Excerpt)

In California, under the state's Standards for the Teaching Profession, we find
California's state credentialed teachers . . .
6.7 Demonstrating professional responsibility, integrity, and ethical conduct
As teachers develop, they may ask, "How do I . . ." or "Why do I . . ."

- remain informed of, understand, and uphold the professional codes, ethical
  responsibilities, and legal requirements applicable to the profession?
- contribute to school and student success by being knowledgeable of learning
  goals, standards, and objectives established by relevant national, state, and local
  organizations and stakeholders?
- meet my professional obligations to implement school, district, state, and federal
  policies and guidelines?
- extend my knowledge about my professional and legal responsibilities for
  students' learning, behavior, and safety?
- maintain professional conduct and integrity in the classroom and school
  community?
- interact appropriately with students and families outside the classroom?
- demonstrate my professional obligations to students, colleagues, school, and the
  profession? . . .

Wisconsin saw forty-four public-school teachers lose their teaching li-
censes because of sexual misconduct.[19] The list goes on.

INTERVIEWING TEACHER CANDIDATES

Some states' professional codes of conduct and education policies are
drawing attention to some very serious contemporary issues. Other states
need to write their own codes or revise outdated policies and codes.
These policies must find their ways into the hiring process, either by
changes in law or by weaving creative questioning strategies into the
interview. After researching the state codes, reading case after case, and
having written a previous book about screening of child sexual perpetrators, several things have become abundantly clear to me, not the least of
which is the importance of the interview and screening process of teacher
applicants.

Changes in the Teacher-Candidate Interview Process

How does anyone recognize a bad teacher applicant in interview or
on paper—especially if the teacher applicant is new and has glowing
references from professors? Résumés are padded, references may be
biased, and yet we must somehow determine whether the person sitting
opposite us is qualified to work with students and not merely credentialed. Professional hiring determinations often occur after several per-

Table 7.2.   Florida Principles of Professional Conduct

Florida Department of Education (Excerpt)

In Florida, under the state's Code of Ethics for Education, 6B-1.006 Principles of Professional Conduct for the Education Profession, we find that Florida state–credentialed teachers . . .

- Shall make reasonable effort to protect the student from conditions harmful to learning and/or to the student's mental and/or physical health and/or safety.
- Shall not intentionally expose a student to unnecessary embarrassment or disparagement.
- Shall not intentionally violate or deny a student's legal rights.
- Shall not harass or discriminate against any student on the basis of race, color, religion, sex, age, national or ethnic origin, political beliefs, marital status, handicapping condition, sexual orientation, or social and family background and shall make reasonable effort to assure that each student is protected from harassment or discrimination.
- Shall not exploit a relationship with a student for personal gain or advantage . . .

sonal interviews. Does anyone clearly know whether someone is at greater risk for engaging in inappropriate relationships with teenagers? Consider this question in the contexts of the principles of professional codes of conduct from the states of Florida, Illinois, and others.

With the ubiquity of communication technologies, the prevalence of sexual explicitness in our culture, and the rapid rise of teacher sex crimes against students, being a willing participant in today's culture requires us to ask interviewees questions of a different sort. Many states are operating under laws that are not proactive in protecting children within the current culture.

The pressure to fill vacant teaching positions is real, and as a result teacher placement is sometimes quick and risky. The rationale is that having credentialed adults in classrooms is preferred over not having them. Some larger districts assume the risks of placing "warm, breathing bodies" in rooms with teenagers without having gone through a protective series of checks. But schools that have difficulty finding teachers are less apt to spend the requisite time in the interview process.

Reform must occur in the interviewing process of teacher candidates. Questions about moral purpose and moral practice should be raised during the interview. Laws must change to better protect students and families. Presently, predators and those who might desire sex with our teenagers are using the process to victimize many students. Crossing of our fingers that an after-the-fact discovery might not occur is not acceptable policy. Schools must hire teachers with a clear moral purpose and must ask candidates to define this purpose, both in words and potential actions in the classroom.

Barbara Murray and Kenneth Murray, offer advice for teachers, old and new: (1) Remember who the adult is, and do not blur this line. (2) Be

Table 7.3.   Illinois Code of Ethics for Educators

Illinois Department of Education (Excerpt)

In Illinois, under the state's Code of Ethics for Education, Part 22, we find that Illinois state–credentialed teachers fulfill the following:

Responsibility to Students

- The Illinois educator is committed to creating, promoting, and implementing a learning environment that is accessible to each student, enables students to achieve the highest academic potential, and maximizes their ability to succeed in academic and employment settings as a responsible member of society.
- Respect the inherent dignity and worth of each student by assuring that the learning environment is characterized by respect and equal opportunity for each student, regardless of race, color, national origin, sex, sexual orientation, disability, religion, language or socioeconomic status.
- Maintain a professional relationship with students at all times.
- Foster in each student the development of attributes that will enhance skills and knowledge necessary to be a contributing member of society.

Responsibility to Self

Illinois educators are committed to establishing high professional standards for their practice and striving to meet these standards through their performance . . .

---

careful about touching. The less touching, the better. (3) If there is an off-campus meeting, a party, or a get-together for students and the younger teacher is invited, it is best to decline. (4) When performing school-related activities when the teacher can anticipate being alone with one or more students, other adults should be invited into the activity. This accountability is very important and protects everyone involved. (5) Take extra care to guard one's private life away from school, which means taking extra precautions when posting on social-media websites and when interacting personally with colleagues, students, and parents.[20]

A Rationale for Change

Should school districts shift interview tactics, given news headlines? How important is knowledge of an interviewee's sexual identity? Are there restrictions to asking questions about an applicant's open sexual lifestyle? Moreover, should districts query teacher applicants regarding their uses of technology? Are teachers' past online postings, and whether they belong to any organizations or websites that promote deleterious behaviors, a legitimate part of today's information collection? Districts do have the obligation to determine whether the teachers they hire may sully the reputation of the district. There are so many questions, and the answers to these questions are as varied as there are school districts.

Issues stemming from teachers' unions, violations of personal and state privacy laws, and fears of resource-draining lawsuits might very well keep districts from asking the tough questions. However, I would argue that we live at a time when sex and social media are in the cultural mainstream and that this reality has changed many cultural rules of the past. This is why I say that a new approach is required. We live in a new age of sexuality that has not been kind to the educational moral purpose of the past and is wreaking havoc in communities all across the nation.

Furthermore, the time is right for school districts to bring lawyers into the interview process, along with experts on child abuse and adolescent psychologists. Their input would be valuable in the interview process.

And district applicants ought to open their social-media postings to the interviewers. Online behaviors are sometimes very different from one's regular, daily life. What an interviewee might have intended to keep secret could find its way onto a public forum, causing serious issues for many. Opening personal websites should become part of a background check, just like fingerprinting, for transferring teachers and teacher candidates seeking to work with teenagers.

The Teacher Candidate's Interview

The following list of seven questions comprises what some teachers and potential teachers might consider a bit more personal than necessary. However, after checking with local law enforcement, consulting personal and professional opinions of attorney friends, and reading interview procedures from other professions, on this issue I am squarely in the camp of protecting students over outcries of privacy invasions.

The teacher interview questions suggested would only be used for new hires to districts, whether these are veteran educators new to the district, or newly credentialed. The list includes select questions that should be part of the oral or written interview stages for new hires. Directly following each question is a rationale for each query.

The questions and the rationale are relevant and important. All I ask is that you consider the safest and most secure set of hiring practices for our students, their parents, and our profession. After all, veteran teachers currently on the job do not have to sit for interviews or be subject to these questions. Switching districts means that new hires then may have to submit to the new-hire question format.

TEACHER CANDIDATE INTERVIEW QUESTIONS AND RATIONALES

Interview Question #1: Divorce

"We notice that you have checked that you are divorced. Have you been divorced more than once, and how recent is/are the divorce(s)?

Would you mind providing a few details as to whether any form of abuse was involved?"

Rationale for Asking Question #1

Teacher applicants check the box indicating marital status, and this is on state and federal tax returns and on social-security and salary-deduction paperwork. Asking about divorce is appropriate, especially if the interviewee's significant recent relationships with adults have been violent or abusive, as that might affect the classroom or student learning. Students will ask about teacher's relationships. Divorce is commonplace today, but the reasons for the divorce could limit the classroom adversely, as well as the relationships with the faculty, particularly among close friends.

Interview Question #2: Drugs

"What is your view about recreational drug use and the legalization of drugs, such as marijuana?"

Rationale for Asking Question #2

Districts that have policies about tobacco and alcohol use on campus often do not have a policy about a teacher who might have elevated amounts of illegal drugs within his or her body because of recreational use away from school. Teachers' views about legalizing illegal substances affect the mind-sets of teenagers, especially those seeking support for alternate or untraditional cultural perspectives and practices. Districts risk much by placing a teacher when the candidate is known to use marijuana or other illegal substances recreationally.

Interview Question #3: Tattoos and Piercings

"Do you have any tattoos or piercings that are uncovered throughout the course of the regular school day?"

Rationale for Asking Question #3

The shift in culture has seen a marked increase of people adorning themselves with body art or tattoos. If a teacher has an offensive tattoo and there is any chance teenagers will see it, then the district could be liable. For example, if during the interview process a teacher withheld past or present gang affiliation, or if a students later saw a Nazi symbol tatooed on the teacher, the community would be very angry. Self-mutilation, earplugging, brow piercing, tongue studs, and cheek and nose piercings are fast becoming cultural norms. Districts must consider the extent these adornments or quasi-mutilations affect the educational process or distract from learning. Teenagers might not understand how self-mutilation and employment acquisition do not work together in their favor when applying for jobs.

Interview Question #4: Adult-Film Industry

"Is there anything in your past or present that connects you to (1) the adult film industry, (2) the adult sex-toy industry, (3) online pornography (either the appearance in or purchase or sale of these materials), (4) hosting or maintaining an adult or erotic website, or (5) the signing of any past or present contract to associate you in any way with the adult sex industry?"

Rationale for Asking Question #4

Stating the obvious is sometimes necessary. The philosophy and practice of what applicants do on their own time is a philosophy that does not belong in high school classrooms. Teenagers require good mentoring as their bodies and minds mature. Sexuality remains something that is deeply personal and should not be flaunted, made light of, or impersonalized as recreation.

Teenagers preparing for relationships as adults need exposure to good choices, including information that counters the philosophy that casual sex is inconsequential. Teenagers having sex *is* consequential. For further discussion, refer to the previous section The Immoral Teacher, found earlier in this chapter.

Interview Question #5: Sexual Abuse

"What is your personal opinion about (1) the impacts of child sexual abuse committed by adults who were abused as children and (2) would you speak to the effectiveness and professional ability of these adults to teach teenagers effectively?"

Rationale for Asking Question #5

Teachers who are arrested for sex crimes with their students often claim their past child sexual abuse as part of the reason for their crimes. Given that statistics and testimony indicate that there is a greater likelihood that adults who commit sexual crimes with students have suffered child sexual abuse themselves, it would be prudent during the interview process to discover whether psychologically impacting crimes were committed against the teacher candidate. We must ask ourselves where the balance exists between rights, legality, and student safety. Districts must consider whether to accept the risk and take chances or ask applicants for information so that the risk reduces significantly.

Interview Question #6: Addictions

"Are you aware of any addictions you have to legal or illegal substances, the Internet, or behaviors, and are you aware of any predispositions or moral weaknesses you might have toward addictions?"

Rationale for Asking Question #6

Smoking is addictive and harmful. Districts have policies and states have laws about purchasing smoking materials. Districts should know the daily vices of the candidates they intend to hire. Alcohol problems, drug addictions, smoking, and other vices are problems today for adults and children. It is fair to ask hypothetical questions about how a smoker would deal with a district's smoke-free environment. Everyone accepts that smokers must extinguish their cigarettes from the moment they step foot on campus. It is equally fair to ask in what ways certain addictions might inhibit a person's ability to be effective in the classroom: (1) daily use of prescribed pain medications, (2) habitual use of chewing tobacco, and things like (3) pornography.

Interview Question #7: Online Media

"What is your current use of online social-media sites, and what are some examples of private sites to which you subscribe? Would you have any problem disabling or deleting these sites before any offer to hire you, or allowing a neutral party to view your page(s) as a prerequisite to this hiring?"

Rationale for Asking Question #7

Teachers must be extra careful about what they post online. This is addressed in previous chapters. However, being careful and being accountable are somewhat different expectations. The former relies on the honor system, where the district would accept the word of the teacher. The latter would be more along the lines of the example provided by many law-enforcement agencies and political agencies that vet those whom they seek to hire.

The vetting process requires that candidates open their social-media pages for their potential employers to view, much like a background check and fingerprinting. Do we dare go there with prospective educational hires? In order to answer that question, we must first ask ourselves exactly how concerned we are with protecting our teenagers.

TEACHERS' RIGHTS VERSUS STUDENT PROTECTION

In California, the state legislature voted down SB1530, a bill written by a state Democratic senator that would have made it easier for school districts to fire teachers accused of gross misconduct. The bill emerged partly in reaction to a Miramonte Elementary School teacher who was accused of lewd acts with his students, including spoon-feeding his semen to students and lacing vanilla cookies with the same.[21]

Hundreds of cell phone photos were seized after the arrest of sixty-one-year-old third-grade teacher Mark Berndt. Along with another teacher at the school, Berndt was accused of committing lewd acts upon children. Berndt pleaded not guilty to twenty-three counts of lewdness on a child. Over ninety combined teachers and school administrators at the elementary school were released from their jobs and all new staffing hired after news of the scandal broke.

The California legislation was voted down in large part because the California Teachers' Association and other unions that weighed-in, fearing that the legislation would harm teachers' due-process rights were districts more easily allowed to outright fire faculty for gross misconduct. The bill did not even make it out of the California Education Committee of the state assembly.[22]

The term *gross misconduct* could have been refined clearly and carefully and the bill passed without unduly impacting teachers' rights. However, the CTA chose to defend its members' due-process rights over the children and families it serves. As a standing member of this association, I am in serious disagreement with their position. Yet part of the reason I am personally associated with the union is my ability to speak freely from inside the organization. That said, the decision of the CTA is an example of what is wrong within the current American education system.

Consider the story of former teacher Brittni Colleps, age twenty-eight, who allegedly had group sex with five male students. One of the students videotaped one of the sexual encounters, which was played in court to convict the former English teacher and mother of three small children. Police examined cell phone records of one of the students and found that Colleps wrote him hundreds of text messages. On several occasions she had texted that she craved the young male and that he "had something she wanted."[23]

How many teachers will be allowed to commit multiple crimes before a common-sense approach to reform addresses teacher hiring and firing practices? Do we have to continue to wait until more children are hurt, or can we catch some of these predispositions before they show up in the classroom?

STATES' POLICIES ON COMMUNICATION TECHNOLOGIES AND SOCIAL MEDIA

It is simply not practical to stay abreast of all the technology policies pending or drafted to date by states, districts, and schools. School districts in all fifty states either have policies or are in the process of writing policies.

The majority of districts with plans have not addressed teachers and students communicating with one another on their own time, after the school day ends. There are many hurdles to leap in seeking to "mandate or legislate" teacher behaviors that occur on their own time and in private. These hurdles pertain to elementary schools, middle and junior-high schools, and high schools.

State departments of education have general policy statements that address technology. For example, I have selected several states' policies to illustrate the movement that is currently taking place in the development of communication-technology and social-media policy. The latest research indicates schools are scrambling to catch up with the advances in communication technology.

For example, New York City public schools are in the process of developing a district-wide set of acceptable-use policies. New York City is the largest public-school district in the nation and is wrestling with the place social media occupies in the lives of students and teachers, both at school and at home.

Since 2009 districts and parishes in the states of Florida and Louisiana have been proactive in restricting teacher-student social interaction online, via Facebook, Twitter, and other private social-media sites. The policy of Pinellas County, Florida, states that "such communication could cause the appearance of inappropriate association with students."[24] The Terrebonne and Lafourche parishes in Louisiana approved policies "forbidding teachers from making any kind of electronic contact with students—unless they have express permission from a principal or other administrator.[25] That includes not just Facebook but texts and e-mails."[26]

Furthermore, the Nashua Board of Education in New Hampshire has developed policies that are more open-ended.[27] The board's policies allow for online communication between teachers and students on social-media sites, as long as the communication is for professional purposes and all students who desire such communication could access the teacher in the same transparent fashion.[28]

In March 2012, Nashua adopted the following policy:

> As long as they behave themselves at the keyboard and their parents are made aware of what is written, Nashua schoolchildren can now communicate on Facebook and other online social media while in school. . . .

There are many ways technology can be used these days. It seems silly to try and stop it. . . . A zero-tolerance policy on in-school social media would seem counterproductive to the goal of providing and supporting quality education. . . . All online interaction, including . . . Facebook, must pass the "TAP" test—that the communication is transparent, accessible, and professional. Facebook use is now allowed, as long as the communication meets the established standards.[29]

New York City

In the spring of 2012, the New York City Department of Education adopted a very detailed set of policies concerning the use of social media by teachers and students.[30] In these policies, the board considered nearly every aspect of communication between employees, teachers, and students. The document is several pages in length.

New York City newspapers recently covered the story of a female Bronx principal who posted a sexually suggestive photograph on her Facebook page. Before she was aware of what had happened, some students, parents, or faculty had accessed her social-media page and captured the image. It turns out that this same risqué photograph began to appear throughout the hallways of her school. The principal was extremely embarrassed, and the board was extremely concerned.[31] Despite the nature of the principal's photograph, the posting of it in the school hallways could have been considered "bullying and harassment," which raises a host of newer legal issues should faculty members ever be implicated in such actions.

States are moving in the right direction with their technology policies, though. That said, cell phone technology is a lightning-rod issue in many districts. Many consider cell phones to be social tools rather than tools for education. I think they can be both. What will it take for districts to allow cell phones to be used as learning tools, brought out from the dark corners to the head of the classroom?

APPROPRIATE USES OF CELL PHONES IN HIGH SCHOOL

Is there such a thing as a teenager using a cell phone at school appropriately? How many cell phone–captured videos of teachers have been posted online? In some instances, the teachers have become viral pariahs. Students seem to take pride in "snagging" their teachers' personal and private lives for their own sense of empowerment. They have no problem uploading videos recorded in class to the Internet. Photos also capture many funny and embarrassing teacher moments during the school day—as do stealth audio recordings. Many powerful tools are in the hands of any teenager who owns a smartphone.

Student use of cell phones in class ought to be restricted to academic applications pertinent to the class they are in, and the cell usage must not violate the norms established for that class. Technology boundaries are set at the district level. Exceptions exist for educational purposes at the school level, often granted after a mere request. Smartphones are calculators for math classes, GPS devices for geography, spellcheck for compositions, weather reports for school activities, timers for speeches, cameras for art classes, and on and on. Were students allowed to use their smartphones in smart, educational ways, then communication would not be the only thing on their minds in class.

As a side note, I believe that students who are absent from class ought to be allowed to photograph a PowerPoint slide that details the homework they missed. This would enable a teacher to print out only one copy and tape it to the board, saving a great deal of paper and keeping absentees in the loop. Students needing to catch up on the information could snap a quick picture of the slideshow printout for later study. They could also text or e-mail the photo to those with excused absences. Teachers can also post their entire PowerPoint lessons online to professional pages for the review of absentee students studying from home.

In the beginning when cell phone novelty was more an annoyance for teachers and a disruption to student learning, most teachers were quite authoritarian about usage in the classroom. But with newer teachers entering the ranks used to working with smartphone technology, and with much of the novelty-hype having been moderated, it is probably best to reexamine cell phone policies for the classroom. Meg Ormiston says that "regardless of your school's cell phone policy, the reality in most schools is that students have phones in their pockets, purses, or hoodies. Why not get these tools out in plain sight and use them for good and not evil?" [32]

District administrators and school-site principals should consider this section carefully. Take note of the many ways today's smartphones can be used in classrooms to enhance learning. But prior to examining the list, let us deal with one objection that is certain to arise. It pertains to fairness, because "Not all of our students have access to cell phones or have them at school." This is correct. However, the same applies to automobiles, computers, $300 athletic shoes, Advanced-Placement classes, and library computers. If we do not stop focusing on what students do not have and start focusing on what they *do* have, we will miss out on exploiting valuable tools and classroom incentives. Students are more than happy to share their mini-computers with partners in class. And, frankly, I'm convinced that is more myth than reality that "not all students have access to cell phones."

A 2011 study conducted by Stephen Blumberg at the National Center for Health Statistics examined cell phone ownership by state and concluded that [nearly] 40 percent of all adults living in poverty use only cellphones, compared with about 21 percent of adults with higher incomes. There appear to be many reasons for this. Cellular phones have become more affordable. The barrier to owning one is lower with pay-as-you-go plans. Some states allow subsidies for low-income residents to be applied to wireless bills . . . increasingly; those who cannot afford both types of phones choose their cellular phone. [33]

Realistically, it is not an access issue. In fact, it is quite easy to foresee a time in the near future when school districts provide cell phones for use in the classroom for all students, given that they are inexpensive, and great tools. Besides, high school students can now prepare for their SATs and other tests by using applications that tie their cell phones directly to approved websites. [34]

Concerns about disabling texting and buffering Internet websites for classroom use are alleviated by district-purchased dedicated phones linked to a school wireless network. These phones would have only Internet search and no texting plans. The time has come to take advantage of this marvelous medium and use cell phones in the classroom.

In closing, I offer a list of seven educational reasons to allow cell phone usage in high school classrooms.

SEVEN EDUCATIONAL REASONS TO ALLOW CELL PHONE USAGE IN HIGH SCHOOL CLASSROOMS

Educational Reason #1: Cost-Effectiveness

Using cell phones is a cost-effective measure in a time of budget crisis. Purchasing cell phones for all students to use in classes where Internet research is required is much cheaper than purchasing laptop computers. Cell phones are mini-computers, usable for far more than communications and photography.

Educational Reason #2: Improvement in Student Learning

This educational reason might scare a few teachers into teaching differently. Nevertheless, why are we not allowing students to record some of the lessons we teach? Cell phones in the classroom could improve classroom instruction. Students often need a second go at the day's lesson. Parents, teachers, administrators, and students could come to an agreement about limiting recording time and eventual usage of the recordings. Honestly, students upload things to sites every day—and sometimes right at the moment teachers are doing things other than instructing—so why not let them use recording technologies to improve their learning?

Educational Reason #3: Issue and Opinion Polling

Teachers could keep track of students' opinions and have them vote on issues. Sites like www.polleverywhere.com are good tools for classes where instant feedback about class opinion is valued. In order for students to access a school site, or a site set up by the teacher, students could scan a QR Code (quick-response code) or send a text to verify their identity.[35] Students love surveys, and students shy about responding to certain issues in front of a classroom of peers might find it much easier to participate in virtual surveys using cell phones, increasing overall class participation.

Educational Reason #4: Media Portfolios

Teachers could set up websites on the school server or on an unfiltered safe public site so that students could post messages right from class. Students could develop online academic and social-media portfolios. For example, students learning about John Locke and natural-rights philosophy could access the site from class, posting tweets or Facebook updates. Some districts, such as the Kern High School District, the largest high school district in California, have reexamined their policies covering social media and have decided to move forward with using them for educational purposes to enhance student learning and communication.[36]

Educational Reason #5: Applications Are Quick Sources of Information

Today's smartphones have a multitude of applications that could enhance communication and learning. There are far too many to put on a single list. However, smartphone applications exist for music, art, weather, sports, social media, food, and so on. Imagine for a second that a teacher sends out a text message to students in his classroom right from his smartphone or computer. Think about students plugging in earbuds and listening to a selection of music sent by the teacher—better engaging a student's work affect during work time. The possibilities are endless and the learning continuous.[37]

Educational Reason #6: Teaching Responsibility through Incentive

If students use their "personal" communication-only tools for educational purposes, the sneakiness diminishes, and the power of learning new things increases. Sneakiness is almost nonexistent with the use of district-dedicated cell phones. Teenagers best obey when they are given choices, and cell phone use gives them another opportunity to develop honest characters. Therefore, the creation of an incentive program for students to research, stay abreast of headlines, etc., while working keeps them focused on earning the privilege.

Educational Reason #7: Promote Good Character

Cell phone usage in the classroom could cut down on sexting, bullying, and other technology-related concerns. Students using technology for positive educational and uplifting reasons begin to turn the secretive aspects of the medium into opportunities to learn both tact and diplomacy, necessary skills for mature, healthy adults in today's society. Students using cell phones in the classroom must offer their number to the teacher, making any message posted from that phone trackable to a student, which alone would cause them to think first before posting any inappropriate messages.

Anonymity is reduced by involving cell phones as learning tools in the classroom. Instruction in academic and productive uses of cell phones and proper communication removes many of the secrecy elements. Such emphases also instruct in proper technology etiquette. Using cell phones in the classroom could also reduce the level of inappropriate relationships between teachers and students.[38]

SUMMARY

Moral purpose is born of (1) clearly defined objective civic and character goals, (2) well-marked academic objectives and standards-aligned assessments to measure achievement, and (3) joint commitments by the families, communities, and schools. Essentially, moral purpose is larger than self.

Many newer teachers will have no recollection of a time before cell phones and computers were commonly used. Many have never seen a monochrome monitor, and the Clinton administration was the first presidency they lived through. We live in a very sensually heightened and sexually explicit society. Younger teachers do not really recall when pornography and Web cams, cell phones, chat, and texting were not readily available.

In the teacher-candidate stage of the interview process, districts should begin to incorporate questions about the candidate's views on sexuality, sexual relationships, and uses of technology. The interview process needs to be reformed. Many teachers need current, qualitative professional-development advice regarding ways to interact and relate to teenagers. Administrators should receive training on how to create moral accountability for faculty and staff. This training could occur at two levels: (1) teacher-training institutions and (2) regular professional development.

States are developing education codes of ethics and professional principles of conduct for teachers. These codes apply to both veterans and new hires. Districts are also developing acceptable technology-use policies for teachers and students. This chapter includes states' professional codes of conduct and legal boundaries set forth between teachers and students. Some of the common threads found in the five states' codes for teacher conduct presented include (1) professionalism, (2) making certain to respect colleagues, students, and families, and (3) focusing on intellectual pursuits.

The probing of a teacher's background or views on particular personal issues is a sensitive subject. Application and personal interview questions are suggested, along with rationales for asking them.

This chapter makes seven arguments for the educational usage of cell phones in high school classrooms, asserting that their use will (1) be cost effectiveness, (2) improve classroom instruction, (3) keep track of student opinions and ideas on topics, (4) allow for the development of online academic and social-media portfolios, (5) allow for the use of smartphone technology and search-engine capability and applications, (6) create a class incentive for students to read headlines, listen to music, or do research with school-provided phones in class, and (7) instruct students in the healthy and productive academic uses of cell phones and their proper communication, which will then remove the aura of secrecy presently relegated to classroom cell phone use, all while teaching proper technology etiquette.

DISCUSSION QUESTIONS

1. How would you define *moral purpose*? Explain the extent to which it is important in education, using both general and specific terms.
2. What factors contribute to teachers and students becoming involved in inappropriate sexual relationships?
3. How would you identify the similarities and differences between states' professional codes of conduct?
4. Should administrators have more latitude to ask personal, probing questions at the teacher candidate interview? Why, or why not?
5. Do you see any reason to change veteran teacher–evaluation processes? In light of the arrests of teachers accused of sex crimes with teenage students, would you add anything to the interviewing or evaluative process for the sake of student security? If so, what would you suggest?
6. In terms of the issues addressed in this chapter, what is your opinion on the balance between teachers' rights in unions and students' rights for safety and protection?
7. How much responsibility do you think seventeen- or eighteen-year-old students should bear if they become involved in sexual relationships with any of their teachers?

8. Is there a need for professional development for teachers or a need for parent-information evenings for families in order to review laws and policies such as

   - general communication technologies
   - district and school communications acceptable-use policies
   - and the appropriate boundaries between teachers and students?

9. If so, what do you suggest should be included in the presentations to the employees and education stakeholders?
10. What three reasons could you provide to a board of education if it were to ask you for your best argument for including cell phones as learning tools in high school classrooms? What are some of the negatives about allowing cell phone usage in the classrooms?
11. In your opinion, why are state-level bureaucrats so slow in responding to changes in technology?

NOTES

1. Ernest J. Zarra III, "Character Education: An Analysis of State History–, Social Science–, and English Language Arts–Curriculum Frameworks and Content Standards" (doctoral dissertation, University of Southern California, 1999), 59. See also Ernest J. Zarra III, "Pinning Down Character Education," *Kappa Delta Pi Record* (Summer 2000): 154–57.

2. Fullan, *Change Forces*.

3. In "The Psychological Aspect of Moral Education," *Moral Principles in Education* (New York: Houghton Mifflin, 1909), accessed June 6, 2012, www.gutenberg.org/files/25172/25172-h/25172-h.htm.

4. John I. Goodlad, *Educational Renewal* (San Francisco: Jossey-Bass Publishers, 1994), 11.

5. Christine Scarlett, "Her Boy Toy and Their Boy," *Today in the USA*, May 14, 2007, accessed June 6, 2012, http://todayintheusa.com/page/115/?s=f%C3%A2.

6. Erin Rickert, "Jurors Decide against Teacher," *The Daily Reflector*, June 24, 2006, accessed June 6, 2012, www.williamslawonline.com/Press-Room/Teacher_Found_Not_Guilty_of_Sex_Offense_January_24-_2006.pdf.

7. "Music Teacher Accused of Trying to Arrange Sex Date with Girl," *Los Angeles Times*, September 19, 2011, accessed June 6, 2012, http://latimesblogs.latimes.com/lanow/2011/09/music-teacher-arrested-for-attempted-lewd-act-on-child.html.

8. "Lesbian Teacher Rapist Off Hook—No Jail Time," *World Net Daily*, January 20, 2006, accessed June 6, 2012, www.wnd.com/2006/01/34415/.

9. "The Big List: Female Teachers with Students," Anti Misandry, n.d., accessed July 4, 2012, http://antimisandry.com/female-pedophiles/big-list-female-predator-teachers-students-3668.html.

10. Brian Palmer, "How Many Kids Are Sexually Abused by Their Teachers? Probably Millions," Slate.com, February 8, 2012, accessed April 18, 2012, www.slate.com/articles/news_and_politics/explainer/2012/02/is_sexual_abuse_in_schools_very_common_.html.

11. "Teacher Fired after Students Spot Her as 'Tiffany' in Porn Flick," *Laist*, April 20, 2012, accessed May 15, 2012, http://laist.com/2012/04/19/teacher_fired_after_students_spot_her.php. See also "Oxnard Teacher Fired over Past Role in Adult Film Planning to Appeal Decision," KCLU, April 23, 2012, accessed May 15, 2012, www.kclu.org/

2012/04/23/oxnard-teacher-fired-over-past-role-in-adult-film-planning-to-appeal-decision/; Kip Michalak, "St. Louis Teacher Fired for Her Adult Films," WTSP News, March 9, 2011, accessed June 7, 2012, www.wtsp.com/news/article/179894/0/St-Louis-teacher-fired-for-her-adult-films; "Oxnard Teacher Fired for Doing Adult Films," KTLA News, n.d., accessed June 7, 2012, www.ktla.com/videogallery/69472886/News/VIDEO-Oxnard-Teacher-Fired-For-Working-In-Adult-Film-David-Begnaud-reports; Antoine Scroggins, "Adult Film Worker Turned Substitute Teacher Fired," *Your Black World*, August 25, 2011, accessed September 4, 2011, www.yourblackworld.com/2011/08/25/adult-film-worker-turned-substitute-teacher-fired/.

12. Child and Family Services of New Hampshire, "ParentLine," accessed August 2, 2012, http://cfsnh.org/pages/programs/parentline/studentteacher.html.

13. Anita Setnor Byer and Martin Salcedo, "Student-Teacher Relationships: Where to Draw the Lines," *Human Equation*, May 18, 2007, accessed May 29, 2011, www.thehumanequation.com/en/news_rss/articles/2007/05_18_Teacher_Student_Relationships.aspx.

14. Commission on Teacher Credentialing, "California Standards for the Teaching Profession (CSTP)," October 2009, accessed July 19, 2012, www.ctc.ca.gov/educator-prep/standards/CSTP-2009.pdf. See also Bridie Smith, "Teacher Code Tackles Student Relationships," TheAge.com.au, April 18, 2007, accessed July 19, 2012, www.theage.com.au/news/national/teacher-code-tackles-student-relationships/2007/04/17/1176696837268.html.

15. Florida Department of Education, "Code of Ethics: Education Profession," accessed July 19, 2012, www.fldoe.org/edstandards/code_of_ethics.asp.

16. ISBE, "Code of Ethics for Illinois Educators," accessed July 19, 2012, www.isbe.net/rules/archive/pdfs/22ARK.pdf.

17. New York State Professional Standards and Practices Board for Teaching, "New York State Code of Ethics for Educators," accessed July 19, 2012, www.highered.nysed.gov/tcert/pdf/codeofethics.pdf; See also David W. Chen, "Social Media Rules Limit New York Student-Teacher Contact," *New York Times*, May 1, 2012, accessed July 19, 2012, www.nytimes.com/2012/05/02/nyregion/social-media-rules-for-nyc-school-staff-limits-contact-with-students.html?_r=1&pagewanted=all.

18. Madelyn Coldiron, "Kentucky Schools See 'Huge' Increase in Inappropriate Student-Teacher Relationships," Kentucky School Boards Association, n.d., accessed August 28, 2012, www.ksba.org/Inappropriaterelationships.aspx.

19. Martha Irvine and Robert Tanner, "Sex Abuse a Shadow over U.S. Schools," *Education Week*, October 24, 2007, accessed September 2, 2012, www.edweek.org/ew/articles/2007/10/24/09ap-abuse.h27.html.

20. Barbara Murray and Kenneth Murray, *Pitfalls and Potholes: A Checklist for Avoiding Common Mistakes of Beginning Teachers* (Washington, D.C.: National Education Association, 2004).

21. Mark Duell, "I'm 'Very Happy You're My Student': Chilling Letters Sent to Children by 'Pervert' Teacher at L.A. Sex Scandal School," *Daily Mail* online, February 10, 2012, accessed June 23, 2012, www.dailymail.co.uk/news/article-2098811/Shocking-photo-Mark-Berndt-posing-tights-Mickey-Mouse-ears.html#ixzz22G54YYXt.

22. "Bill Responding to LA-area Teacher Sex Case Fails in Assembly Panel," *Bakersfield Californian*, June 28, 2012, 45.

23. "Texas Jury Sees Video of Teacher Allegedly Having Sex with 4 Students," Fox News, August 15, 2012, accessed August 15, 2012, www.foxnews.com/us/2012/08/15/texas-jury-sees-video-teacher-allegedly-having-sex-with-4-students/#ixzz23iKTqrBS.

24. Tim Walker, "Schools Still Struggling with Social Media," *National Education Association*, Summer 2012, 13, accessed August 24, 2012, www.neatoday.org.

25. Terrebonne Parish School Board Policy Statement, "Electronic Communications between Employees and Students," October 2009, accessed August 24, 2012, www.tpsd.org/home/files/F-12_9a%20Electronic%20Communications%20Between%20Employees%20and%20Students.pdf.

26. Walker, "Schools Still Struggling."

27. Nashua Board of Education Policy, "Communicating Electronically with Students," March 12, 2012, accessed April 24, 2012, www.nashua.edu/district-documents/POPPS/New%20POPPS%20Policies/GBEBD-Communicating%20Electronically%20with%20Students%203-12-12.pdf.

28. Walker, "Schools Still Struggling."

29. Dean Shalhoup and Cam Kittle, "Nashua Board Approves Use of Social Media in School," *Nashua Telegraph*, March 13, 2012, accessed April 24, 2012, www.nashuatelegraph.com/news/953323-196/nashua-board-approves-use-of-social-media.html; see also www.facebook.com/TheTelegraph/posts/186477528134735.

30. New York City Department of Education, "New York City Department of Education Social Media Guidelines," accessed April June 17, 2012, http://schools.nyc.gov/NR/rdonlyres/BCF47CED-604B-4FDD-B752-DC2D81504478/0/DOESocialMediaGuidelines20120430.pdf.

31. Jennifer Preston, "Rules to Stop Pupil and Teacher from Getting Too Social Online," *New York Times*, December 17, 2011, accessed April 19, 2012, www.nytimes.com/2011/12/18/business/media/rules-to-limit-how-teachers-and-students-interact-online.html.

32. In "How to Use Cell Phones as Learning Tools," K–12 Teachers Alliance, TeachHub.com, accessed June 3, 2012, www.teachhub.com/how-use-cell-phones-learning-tool .

33. Sabrina Tavernise, "Youth, Mobility and Poverty Help Drive Cellphone-Only Status," *New York Times*, April 21, 2011, accessed June 6, 2011, www.nytimes.com/2011/04/21/us/21wireless.html.

34. David Raths, "Revisiting Cell Phone Bans in Schools," *The Journal*, March 28, 2012, accessed April 21, 2012, http://thejournal.com/articles/2012/03/28/revisiting-cell-phones-bans-in-schools.aspx.

35. Mashable.com , s.v. "Quick Response Codes," accessed August 22, 2012, http://mashable.com/follow/topics/qr-codes/.

36. Kern High School District, "Who We Are," n.d., accessed July 25, 2012, www.khsd.k12.ca.us/Footer/AboutUs.aspx; See also Kern High School District, "Technology Plan," July 2010–June 2013, accessed August 22, 2012, www.khsd.k12.ca.us/Business/PDF/KHSD%20-%20Technology%20Plan-10-13.pdf.

37. Graham Attwell, "25 Practical Ideas for Using Mobile Phones in the Classroom," *Ontydysgu Bridge to Learning*, November 20, 2009, accessed June 30, 2012, www.pontydysgu.org/2009/11/25-practical-ideas-for-using-mobile-phones-in-the-classroom/.

38. David Raths, "How Educators Can Use Cell Phones in the Classroom," *How to Learn*, April 5, 2012, accessed June 30, 2012, www.howtolearn.com/2012/04/how-educators-can-use-cell-phones-in-the-classroom.

EIGHT

Technology: Tools and Tactics

Do you realize if it weren't for Edison we'd be watching TV by candle-light?

—Al Boliska

AT A GLANCE

There are six major sections in this chapter, which include: (1) tools of today's sexual predators, (2) capitalizing on communication technologies and social media, (3) capitalizing on teenagers' general environment, (4) "it's not my fault," (5) students are not our soul mates, and (6) a little understanding goes a long way. The chapter closes with a summary and discussion questions.

TOOLS OF TODAY'S SEXUAL PREDATORS

Some of the tools used today by sexual predators are instruments that ease access to victims and potential victims. Whether face-to-face, or by means of technology, predators seek human connections. Digital communications can produce the first steps toward victimization.

Today's sexual predators focus their attention on two key areas: (1) communication technologies and social media and (2) the general environment of their victims. Curiously, these are the two key areas in which teachers also find themselves.

Communication Technologies

Today's sexual predators use Internet communications, social media, and texting and cell phone–communication technologies. Furthermore, some of the environments exploited by sexual predators are places that make it easier for manipulation to occur. We cover the reasons for this in the following.

Sexual predators are aware that schools don't have cohesive, well-enfored cell phone– and computer-use policies. They are aware that parents are often ignorant about teens and their social uses of technology. Sexual predators are also aware that most teenagers are somewhat impulsive and curious and that these traits can lead to emotional excitement.

The Teenage Environment

We have discussed in earlier chapters how teenagers' view of the world is centered on "self." Teenagers desire the power that comes from knowing things the instant they happen, and teens feel a sense of urgency to share this information. There is power in commanding the daily gossip or in having knowledge that others don't. Teenagers do not want to miss anything "juicy," and this reality plays directly into the sexual predator's strategy.

Sexual predators exploit environmental concerns to access their victims. Teens in the following situations may be more vulnerable to a predator: (1) there is only one parent in the household, and that parent is often working a frenetic schedule; (2) the teen is troubled and needs a friend; and (3) teens naturally desire trust.

Many companies, including Facebook, are instituting defensive measures in order to ensure the best and safest practices available for online users. Because of screening, pedophiles, convicted sexual predators, and registered sex offenders are decreasingly able to exploit these social networks. Companies are investing in expensive resources to assure their users' safety and security.

Other companies that make applications for smartphones are especially aware of safety risks and concerns. An application by the name of Skout allows strangers to flirt with other strangers in the areas in which they live or attend school. Recently, Skout had to close its section for teenagers when they learned that sexual predators were using their application to access potential victims. Skout's move stymied potential predators, but all a teenager had to do to continue enjoying the service was reregister as an adult, and they were back in action, flirting with strangers.

Other nations are also struggling with sexual predators and their use of communication technologies. The United Kingdom discovered that two sexual predators had been victimizing children on a site called Habbo Hotel. According to a Reuters report, "the National Center for Missing and Exploited Children processed 3,638 reports of online 'enticement' of children by adults [in 2011], down from 4,053 in 2010 and 5,759 in 2009."[1]

Stranger sexual abuse might be decreasing, since technology can flush out many of the predators who previously sought to hide in the shadows. However, another trend is just as alarming, and it is growing. According to the same Reuters report, victims now know their abusers much more personally than in the past, which means interpersonal sexual abuse is on the rise. This has serious implications for the education profession, since many cases reported in the last few years involve teachers and students.

A study commissioned by the American Association of University Women in 2000 concluded that an estimated 10 percent of students suffer some form of sexual abuse during their school years.[2] The study centered on eleventh graders, who filled out surveys full of personal questions. In addition to lewd comments, exposure to pornography, and being groped and viewed in locker rooms, the researchers discovered the students had been victimized in the following ways:

- One in ten students said they had been victimized by a school employee or teacher in a way mentioned in the survey.
- Two-thirds of those reported the incident involved physical contact.
- If the numbers are assumed nationwide, 4.5 million students currently in grades K–12 have suffered some form of sexual abuse by a teacher.
- More than three million K–12 students have experienced some form of sexual assault.
- The numbers would include both inappropriate, criminal relationships between teachers and students and actions associated with pedophilia.

As a professional educator, the thought had never crossed my mind that my colleagues would be the focal point in the chapter of my book on sexual predators and their tools. The thought that teachers are emerging as predators and committing crimes against teenagers draws looks of astonishment from people.

Sadly, though, sexual predators are in some of our schools. They lie dormant as leaders in our classrooms, administrative offices, and on the playing fields. What triggers someone to cross a moral boundary? Sufficient is the knowledge that the explosion of teacher arrests for sexual relationships signals that the teaching profession has entered a new era of moral collapse. Sexually predatory criminals have now tainted one of the last bastions of trust in a community, and the enemy is within!

Sexual abuse of students by trusted professionals has desperately hurt the profession loved by many. How could this have happened? The victimization occurs where children associate—our schools. Predators are allowed daily and direct access to our most precious resource: our children!

CAPITALIZING ON COMMUNICATION TECHNOLOGIES
AND SOCIAL MEDIA

Accessibility

Today's sexual predators utilize technology as a tactical tool and manipulate the moment to capitalize on impulsivity. Victims are quickly engaged through manipulation and empathy. The strategy of quick and immediate communications fits right in with the energy and persona of the teenager. One of the reasons technology is so effective is because there is the notion that "everyone" uses this means of communication. Many use cell phones as toys and playthings. The ubiquity of cell phones and computers enables sexual predators to blend in with others seamlessly, as they take advantage of the medium and the moment.

This advantage works in favor of the sexual predator and provides a false sense of security. A journalist for CNN Justice, Christy Oglesby, wrote an insightful article showing how a predator can access children through cell phones—especially when the predator is a teacher:

> Now, teachers have weeks, months, and years to secretly undermine a child's parents and get a student to go along with sexual contact. "The fact is a teacher can show absolutely zero outward signs of interest in a child, but because of technology, they can have an ongoing relationship and no one would know," said Ted Thompson, the executive director for the National Association to Prevent Sexual Abuse of Children. Parents know chat rooms are dangerous. They warn their kids about the risk, but they give cell phones a nod. A New York mom, who requested anonymity because her kids don't know about her surveillance, said she uses software to regularly check her children's e-mail and online activity on the home computer. But she also gave her kids cell phones that have texting and photographic capability. Asked why she doesn't scrutinize the phone the same way she snoops on the computer, she said, "I hadn't really thought about it much."[3]

The rise of the Internet and computers allows predators to enter the homes of many teenagers every day, where they can chip away at the teen's guard while at school, on weekends, and through their messages that accompany their cell phone ringtones throughout the day. There is sufficient access to gain trust and maintain curiosity, much of which appeals to the very nature of teenagers. The environment of the teenager is a natural breeding ground for sexual play.

Proximity and friendship are also used to the advantage of the sexual predator. Schools are not the only places where sexual predators like to hang out. Churches, camps, Boy Scouts, Girl Scouts, and anywhere the trust of children can be gained are sought to be infiltrated by predators. Friendship is the aim of most initial connections of predators, and proximity helps create the environment for friendship. Furthermore, the Internet informs sexual predators where to meet up with their next victims. But luckily, some communities are beginning to take action.

Changing Tide

States legislatures have been battling political interest groups over the passage of the Jessica Lunsford Act in an effort to eradicate child sexual abuse. Jessica's Law, as the legislation is informally known, was named for Jessica Lunsford, who was abducted, sexually assaulted, and then murdered. Passed in Florida in 2005, Jessica's Law is pending or passed in all but six states.[4]

Jessica's Law mandates a minimum sentence of twenty-five years and a maximum of life in prison for first-time child sex offenders. This legislation is buttressed by Megan's Law, passed in 1996, which keeps tabs on the whereabouts of known sex offenders by requiring them to register in their places of residence. Megan's Law was named after Megan Kanka, who was also sexually abused and murdered. Under Megan's Law, "The privacy interests of persons convicted of sex offenses are subordinate to the government's interest in public safety."[5]

States have laws against and mete out punishments for teachers having sexual relationships with students. However, there is no current national database specifically aimed at teacher criminals, who are arrested or convicted of sexual relationships with students.[6] If convicted, along with losing their state teaching license, many teachers have as part of their punishment the requirement to register as sex offenders. However, the uniqueness of state laws brings with each as many qualifiers and definitions of crimes as there are states. Punishments for these crimes also vary, given the addition of federal offenses.

The Federal Bureau of Investigation operates a national sex offender–registry website, which includes links to all fifty states, U.S. territories, and American Indian tribes. Some teachers appear on this site. States also have their own sex-offender registries, under Megan's Law legislation, and many of these link to the federal registry.[7] Convicted teachers become part of this larger database.

The state legislature of Louisiana recently passed a new piece of legislation requiring all convicted and registered sex offenders and child predators to identify themselves as such and to reveal their status on any social-media site on which they surf and post—like Facebook. Failure to comply could result in arrest. While no law is perfect, Louisiana's is a start. Most states have sex-offender registration for convictions for sex crimes, and there is anticipation that other states will adopt similar laws in the near future.[8]

CAPITALIZING ON TEENAGERS' GENERAL ENVIRONMENT

Predators and Manipulation

A prime example of manipulation is the case of a forty-one-year-old California teacher, James Hooker, whom you'll recall from our discussion in chapter 4. Hooker began an emotional affair with Jordan Powers, one of his students, when she was a freshman in a business class he taught at a Modesto high school. While they claimed their relationship became physical only after Powers turned eighteen, they'd clearly developed a close relationship over the course of four years, using phones and computers, amassing over eight thousand personal messages to each other.[9] The teacher's proximity to his student throughout the day at school, coupled with the evening communications he exchanged with her, created circumstances in which a predator could thrive.

Hooker ended up leaving his wife and family for Powers, moving into an apartment with her. Ironically, Hooker's daughter also attended the school, and, when Hooker left the family, she dropped out.

The school put Hooker on administrative leave, but he subsequently quit his teaching job entirely. Authorities reported that he and Powers had exchanged thousands of text messages and that alleged hotel receipts were under investigation. If, as the case progresses, it turns out that Hooker had sex with Powers before she turned eighteen, he will be arrested as a sexual predator for child sexual abuse, among other charges.

Hooker had gone on record stating that he'd wanted to start a family with Powers and that the two of them should just follow their hearts, regardless of who had been hurt by their decision. However, early in 2012, Hooker was arrested and charged with the sexual abuse of another girl, dating back to 1998, when the girl was seventeen.

Upon learning this, Powers's mother, Tammie, swooped in and flew her daughter to Ohio. New allegations concerning yet another teenager then came to light, implicating Hooker. Tammie Powers, has since helped introduce and is still fighting to advance legislation that would criminalize teacher-student sex at any age. Other states are watching these proceedings very closely.

However, the story does not end there. In April 2012, Powers moved back in with Hooker in California. As of this writing, Hooker is out on bail awaiting trial. According to Tammie Powers, Hooker is "relentless . . . he's very manipulative . . . he's not going to quit."[10]

So, what is it that allowed both Hooker and Powers to engage in a four-year affair during high school? What enabled a teenage girl to leave her home at all hours and rendezvous with a teacher? What attraction existed that would cause a man over forty years of age to walk away from his wife and children? One answer to the questions suggests digital communication cultivated their relationship. What allows teachers to maintain contact with students after hours, if not cell phones and computers?

The teacher phoning the student's family number every night would have been too risky for Hooker. Certainly he would not have shown up at the house unannounced for business-class tutoring sessions, especially for a fourteen- or fifteen-year-old. Throwing rocks at Jordan Powers's window at night would have been out of the question. So, it truly is the ability to stay in contact secretly at most any time of day or night that fuels the passions of predators like Hooker—especially with younger females whose notions of romance and love are idealistic. Powers's teenage fancy melded with an actual authority figure in her life and at the right moment enabled Hooker to seize upon a new conquest. And Hooker manipulated her throughout each stage of their relationship.

Communication technologies often lull a predator into thinking that there is a diminished risk of discovery, since continual communication is the norm for today's teenager. And often the risk truly *is* diminished. One message slips in well with dozens—if not hundreds—of others from friends and family. How did teachers victimize their students before the age of immediate communications?

Recall our chapter 2 discussion of Mary Kay Letourneu's low-tech predation of a grade schooler. Her abuse was discovered when her penned love notes were discovered.

It Takes Time

Teachers and coaches arrested for crimes against students did not act in the course of a few minutes or in a vacuum. Circumstances often set things in motion that enabled their eventual predation long before the actual crime was committed, because the predator needs to know about the environment of the teenager before taking action. And there is no better way to get to know a future victim than to spend time with him or her in their teenage environment.

Actions are products of choices. And the choices leading to predation produce a gradual slippage from what is appropriate between teachers and students to the inappropriate. (Recall our discussion of chapter 4.) Add to this the fact that more and more adults are being diagnosed with bipolar disorder—while some of these adults are teachers claiming this disorder as a defense—and things become even more complicated. One must question the placement of bipolar teachers with continuous, shifting emotions into classrooms of teenagers.

Society tends to focus so very much on students with emotional and behavioral disorders and the creation of the best environment in which they could learn. There are excellent reasons for this, as "teachers spend great amounts of time over the years in a variety of relationships with students. This places teachers in a unique and powerful position to influence how students perceive life dilemmas and the behavioral life choices they make."[11] Without the care and concern of significant adult mentors, the lives of teenagers would be troublesome and often aimless. Teenagers look to their peers for modeling if there are no significant adults available for guidance.[12]

Think about the implications of these statements: If the adults have devious motives or are seeking something other than the students' best interests educationally, what then? Where are the mechanisms to weed out the adults who have no business influencing teenage lives in any fashion? Has anyone stopped to consider whether the teenage environment is good for the *teacher*?

"IT'S NOT MY FAULT"

Teachers arrested for sex crimes against students often blame their actions on emotional and psychological illnesses. Ought, then, personal medical history enter into the interview process before a teacher is hired? If it is used as a reason a crime was committed, why not use it while screening? It is a shame when students are damaged by teachers yet the laws protect the teachers until someone gets hurt. Teachers need help before something goes awry. Reforming the screening process would catch some of the applicants in need of assistance. (Revisit our discussion in chapter 7.)

Hypersexuality

Chair of the psychiatry department at Mt. Sinai Hospital in New York, Eric Hollander writes that "when women become hypersexual, the number one disorder that seems to drive that hypersexuality in women is bipolar disorder."[13] This opens the door to asking whether future employers should know about a prospective teacher candidate's bipolarity, which could very well become a major issue when working with students. The hypersexuality of some predators and the hyperemotional states of average teenagers make for a potentially dangerous combination. Why take the risk?

One of the better-known cases to involve the hypersexual bipolar defense is that of Debra LaFave. As a twenty-three-year old teacher, she began a sexual affair with a fourteen-year-old male on her school campus. The affair began with the two spending time together, communicating at and away from school; she would drive the youth to activities, and they would regularly flirt while on campus. Her *Dateline* NBC interview with Matt Lauer of September 2006 was quite telling:

LAUER: So how did we go from this kind of innocent Sea World trip, field trip, with your husband right there and the student there, to something more? Connect the dots for me.

LAFAVE: That's what I want to know. That's why things are so bizarre in my mind, because it did go from something so innocent to "bam."

LAUER: Well, let me stop you for a second. You should know more than he would know, I imagine, how these dots got connected. So, what was it? I mean, what created this bond between the two of you?

LAFAVE: I think he just became very flirtatious, and you gotta remember that at that period in my time—or in my life—I didn't feel like an adult. I was crashing fast.

LAUER: I would imagine there are parents watching right now, Debbie, and—

LAFAVE: Yeah.

LAUER: —they're saying, "Wait a minute. She just said that he became very flirtatious."

LAFAVE: Well, it's a difference. I don't know if it's a big difference. You know, a fourteen-year-old ten years ago is different than a fourteen-year-old today.

LAUER: Not in the eyes of the law.

LAFAVE: Right. Not in the eyes of the law. He consented, but I should have been the one to say, "Look. You are a kid. And this is not a good idea, whether you want it or not."

LAUER: You should have said it on a number of occasions.

LAFAVE: Oh, yeah.

LAUER: You should have said it when you first started flirting with him.

LAFAVE: Yeah.

LAUER: And you clearly should have said it before you had sex with this young man.

LAFAVE: Clearly. I think he's gonna have a hard time trusting women one day. I'm sure he has to be living with the guilt of "ratting me out."[14]

Gaining Trust

Teachers are placed into their students highly affecting, high-stakes, and enormously emotional learning environments. Imagine someone who thrives on being around teenagers and whose motives are not pure. Placing such a person in direct contact with teenagers means the predator can select his victims methodically and strategically. Let me reiterate: sexual predators that are full-time employees around minors find it much easier to sway their prey, breaking down their wills with affirmation and confidence building, all under the guise of adult mentoring.

Gaining the trust of teenagers and their parents and then encouraging teenagers to make important decisions based on emotions are two tactics used to win the affections of potential victims. Once there is an emotional connection between a would-be predator and victim, the connection only strengthens with private communications. The following two examples illustrate these points.

Example 1: Coach M

"Mr. M" is a physical-education teacher with tenure. He is also the varsity girls' soccer coach at a local high school. He is thirty-three years old and single and enjoys his work. He is thought to be personable and fun. Some of the players on Coach M's team live in rural areas. So, after practice—and after some evening games—the coach routinely transports a small number of players to their homes.

During the course of a season, Coach M is accused by some players of playing favorites and paying special attention to one player in particular. Girls complain off the field and on their social-media pages. Rumors abound among the players, eventually escalating among students on campus. One of the allegations made is that the teacher/coach is having an affair with one of his players. The administration checks into the rumors and downplays them.

All seems settled, until after one game, when Coach M is transporting one of his sixteen-year-old players to her home. While in transit, and driving a district van, the coach stops at a liquor store to purchase condoms. The female clerk notices the teenage female sitting in the van's passenger seat, the district logo on the van, and the age differential between the man and the teenager. This raises her suspicions. She calls authorities, and the school district is contacted the next day. Coach M is arrested and is awaiting trial on a variety of sexual molestation charges, including sending many inappropriate cell phone text messages and images after hours, which is now known as *sexting*.

Example 2: Mrs. J

"Mrs. J" is a newer addition to the high school. Her smile and personality are engaging. Her accomplishments as an athlete are storied, and her reputation as a coach at the school and in the community is now beginning to take hold. One high school sophomore girl begins spending extra time with Coach J after practices. The well-meaning coach drives her home on occasion.

Over the course of a season, the two chat online some evenings, texting and photo messaging increases, and a different sort of relationship forms between the female player and female coach. One day, the player and coach begin kissing and fondling each other in the coach's car, while parked in a dimly lit area of the school parking lot. They are caught. The coach is dismissed from her job and subsequently arrested for sexual assault.

Are states one day going to require teachers to check a box on their applications stating whether or not they are bipolar or have medical disorders or conditions that place them at a higher risk when working with students? There is no assumption that every female teacher arrested for sex with teenagers is bipolar or has some sort of emotional illness. And to what extent are men dealing with the same medical issue? However, if such a condition affects only a modest number of teachers who act out with their students, then something must definitely be brought to the attention of a wider audience. I envision a day when psychological screenings of teacher candidates are as commonplace as finger printing.

Unions must come to understand that we can no longer wait for a crime to be committed before we act; proactivity must become status quo, as it is the safest professional approach to creating a safe environment for students. The bottom line is this: bipolarity or mental illness are neither reasons nor excuses for having sex with teenagers. As we have written in several places in this book, relationships with teenagers do not happen in one or two meetings.

STUDENTS ARE NOT OUR SOUL MATES

Always remember that teaching students is not matchmaking and that it is not a process of discovering one's soul mate. Convicted rapists and sexual predators like Mary Kay Letourneau, despite their claims, are not lifetime partners of fourteen-year-olds. Finding romance with students who are young enough to still have braces and wear training bras is not right, regardless of any adult rationalization. Furthermore, even if a teen appears emotionally and physically mature, this must never imply such persons exist for the taking.

Great Responsibility

Teachers are entrusted with great responsibility granted by the parents, the community, and the state. We have the responsibility to remain focused on education and on mentoring young people. In a perfect world, all newer teachers should be asked, Would you like your fifteen-year-old son or daughter to have their first sexual relationship with an adult? These actions are illegal and an abuse of power. Add to this the level of authority accorded teachers, coaches, and administrators, and the disgust levels rise with it. Where is the teacher's sense of responsibility the first time her thirty-five-year-old mouth meets a fourteen-year-old's mouth for their first sensual kiss?

Questions, Choices, and Consequences

Seven questions are essential for teachers, administrators, coaches, and parents to consider. Faculty at schools and universities must cover these questions in their teacher-education programs, because teachers need tools to enhance their professionalism. Today's world requires that those working with teenagers in school settings take nothing for granted.

Taken together, the following questions force educators to take a hard look at school culture and the risks involved in crossing moral boundaries with students. Let us examine these questions in detail.

1. Is a teenager ever considered as a soul mate and sex partner for a teacher?
2. Is it all right for teachers to flirt with students?
3. Should teachers allow students to contact them at home?
4. What are the risks should teachers text message socially, chat on the cell phone, or send photos to students off hours?
5. What happens if a teenager falsely accuses a teacher of a sexual relationship?
6. Should teachers "friend" any of their current students on social-media sites?
7. Is there anything on the Internet that could implicate a teacher in a sex scandal?

Is a Teenager Ever to Be Considered a Soul Mate and Sex Partner for a Teacher?

The clear and unequivocal answer to this question is No! As we have learned in earlier chapters, teenagers are not yet emotionally mature enough to handle "adult-like" emotions and commitments. Their emotions and their brains are not ready, and adults should never conclude that physical maturity and sexual attraction are substitutes for relationships. Therefore, a student is never to be a teacher's soul mate or sex partner.

Some states, such as Arkansas, are decriminalizing sexual relationships between teachers and teenage students. However, based on the authority disparity, teachers may be liable for taking advantage of that disparity for sexual gratification. If teachers have sexual relationships with students, there is very high probability that the relationship will be discovered, the teacher will be arrested, charges will be filed, and conviction will result. Upon conviction for a sex crime, the former teacher will never again work in a school and will most likely have to register as a sex offender. These are some of the likely and probable losses suffered upon arrest and conviction:

- Loss of family
- Loss of teaching license and career
- Loss of freedom for prison time
- Loss of income
- Loss of reputation and respect
- Registration as sex offender

Is It All Right for Teachers to Flirt with Students?

Teasing is different from flirting, but the reality is that few of us know the difference. Both can be troublesome, but flirtation to allure, enamor, capture sensual attention, or to throw one's sexuality toward another is never to occur between teachers and students. Teenagers are not mature enough to catch the nuances that are intrapersonal between them and their teachers. They might misconstrue flirtation to be interpersonal attempts at relationships.

Flirting has sensual and sexual connotations and sends connectors to attempt to attract the person for more than professional discourse. This kind of flirtation often leads to emotional curiosity, leading to choices that are not in the student's best interest. Teachers and students are to avoid flirtation at all costs. Especially be on guard when the age differential is only a few years between teacher and teenagers.

Should Teachers Allow Students to Contact Them at Home?

First, few students seek to remain in contact with their teachers away from school, and for good reason. States like New York are implementing policies that recommend teachers not contact students at home for social purposes.[15] When teachers remain connected to students from home, it reminds students too much of school and work. Second, students often seek access to school information from home but not necessarily the teacher that comes along with the information. Athletics and academic events often require home communication. However, as a rule academics ought to occur entirely at school.

In April 2012, twenty-five-year-old Pennsylvania teacher Timothy Moll was accused of sending text messages to one of his students, a sixteen-year-old female, offering her decent grades in exchange for her indecent photographs.[16] In March of that same year substitute teacher Michael Zack allegedly sent four teenage female students over four thousand text messages, with several inappropriate photographs attached to some of the texts. He and the students were also found to be communicating during school hours via Facebook and text messaging.[17]

In another incident, thirty-three-year-old Erica DePalo—the 2011 Essex County, New Jersey, Teacher of the Year—was accused of having a sexual relationship with a fifteen-year-old student. She allegedly began the affair with her West Orange High School English honors' student on June 15, 2012, and ended the affair on August 28, 2012, the week prior to the beginning of a new academic school year.

DePalo was arrested and charged with several sex crimes with a minor. There is little doubt that when the facts of this case finally emerge they will show that technology played a role in keeping the romance alive throughout the summer of 2012.[18] What purpose, other than a sexual purpose, could a teacher have during summer to stay in close contact with and repeatedly privately meet a teenage student?

Generally, student contact at home should not be permitted. As often as possible, teachers or coaches who are talking with students or athletes while at home need to inform parents of the conversations and contexts, which makes this regular contact less risky. It is a good rule to involve parents in as much of the communication with their teenagers as possible. A good general rule to follow is that home contact should not be viewed as strictly social.

What Are the Risks Should Teachers Text Message Socially, Chat on the cell Phone, or Send Photos to Students Off Hours?

The closer a teacher comes to sociable, "friend-like" relationships with his or her students, the greater the risk of something—a word, photograph, or action—being misconstrued. The farther something drifts away from its contextual mooring, the closer it gets to misinterpretation—especially with teenagers whose contexts are short-lived, due to short-term memory issues. Teachers need to be wise and prudent and never forget they are working with someone's children.

What Happens If a Teenager Falsely Accuses a Teacher of a Sexual Relationship?

Unfortunately, this happens. False accusations are made against teachers by students and by parents. The old adage that where there is smoke, there is fire applies in cases where sexual allegations emerge. There is a rush to judgment, due to the emotions created by sexual allegations.

Is it possible that a teacher or coach has been misunderstood? Certainly. We are dealing with teenagers, after all—and they are dealing with us. However, we must ask ourselves whether our approach opened the door for anyone to conclude even the mere possibility of such an occurrence. This is reminiscent of a local trial that took place several years ago. The trial involved a male high school teacher arrested for a sexual crime committed against a sixteen-year-old female student.

The teacher's lawyers argued that the allegations were false, which was later proven to be the case. The teenage girl made up the allegations and eventually confessed to the falsehoods. The teacher was later exonerated at the trial. The teenage girl's reason for the allegations was the classroom strictness of the teacher. The teacher's reputation in the community was sorely tarnished, and he and his young family had to move elsewhere.

If there are false allegations of sexual relationships—or even if sexual-harassment charges are brought against a teacher—it is incumbent upon the accused to be as transparent and honest as possible. The truth will come out eventually. Seek district representation and legal advice on how to fight the allegations. What one person thinks is a false accusation might actually prove upon investigation to be a legal offense. However, seeking or retaining legal counsel is the appropriate thing to do.

Taking the high road as educators equates to holding ourselves to a higher standard than the one our students hold us to. It also means that if a student crosses a line toward us, we must report that occurrence. Reporting the occurrence is a first step to protecting both the teacher and the student. Therefore, report all suspicious words and actions by the teenager to administration and counselors.

Should Teachers "Friend" Any of Their Current Students on Social-Media Sites?

It all depends on the social-media site. If it is an open-to-all school site, academic- or activity-only-focused site, then it might very well be appropriate. Again, we must ask ourselves a serious question: aside from academics and athletics, what could an adult possibly gain from socializing as a peer with teenagers?

Having a photograph on a social site is quite different from actually socializing. However, if a student watches the ways in which adults socialize with his or her adult friends, teachers must always consider teenagers' exposure to anything of an adult nature that might be misconstrued or used against the teacher in any way. Also consider the following: (1) Do the parents know that their teenager is friends with teachers?

(2) Would the parents have granted permission for an online teacher-student relationship if asked beforehand?

Sharing information on social sites or private Web pages sites is not recommended. Private communications and private friendships between teachers and students are just not wise. Teachers, beware of invitations to private pages set up by students. There is wisdom in politely declining all such invitations. However, to the chagrin of the teenager, teachers ought to inform the parents of their child's access to any sites where they are friends with teachers.

Is There Anything on the Internet that Could Implicate a Teacher in a Sex Scandal?

The number of college students participating in adult films, recording homemade sex tapes, and compromising themselves at fraternity and sorority parties is astounding. Colleges do not consider themselves moral police, and young people's reputations are tarnished long before they expect to have to rely on them in a profession.

There are teachers who appeared in adult films both before and during their tenures as teachers. As we read in chapter 7, several teachers were fired for their past involvement in the adult-film industry. Some teachers, particularly women, have been released for moonlighting as strippers or for earning money as private sex escorts or prostitutes. Men have also been released for appearing in adult videos. No one knows how the teachers' pasts were discovered, but the teachers seemed to think that there was nothing wrong with making extra money in the sex-trade business as long as their teaching job was kept separate.

A LITTLE UNDERSTANDING GOES A LONG WAY

A recent local newspaper ran a series of photographs of a high school classroom during an afternoon class on fashion. [19] Several photographs were images of students who were modeling a clothing line. Other images were of the rest of the students with their cell phones out, taking photographs of the models and the clothes.

At first glance, the photo essay was quite interesting: students were engaged and celebrating the designs and the runway show. However, the district policy for cell phone use during school is clear: no cell phone is to be on during the day, while on campus, and this includes while classes are in session. The pictures revealed a clear violation of district policy. Yet though the infraction was there for the entire community to see, administrators included, no one said a word.

When teachers and students disregard a policy, the policy has no chance of working. The policy might as well be changed or the teacher disciplined—or both. Students uploading data to their social-media sites is not unimaginable, which calls to mind other violations of privacy and using class time to access social media.

The point here is not the use of cell phones in the classroom. In chapter 5 I already explained how I think they can be used responsibly in a learning environment. Rather, the issue is the example being set by a teacher who allows students to violate district policy. For the sake of charity, we'll assume the teacher in question was granted permission from the district.

However, in a broad sense as teachers, are our actions sending the wrong message? Or are we simply impatient as educators, understating the value of the instantaneous gratification born of capturing reality?

An Instantaneous World

Today's world offers instant gratification. Online programs and websites attract users with claims of their speed. Teenagers are now taking full advantage of instantaneous photography. One company even calls itself "Instagram," allowing users to post their cell phone pictures directly to a Web page.

As we discussed in chapter 5, real-time access to students' academic portfolios only adds to the already considerable pressure students feel, and teachers' work days don't end with the last bell now that parents and students can text them about a poor grade at virtually any hour.

The pace of our lives seems to be quickening with each passing year. Technology in the hands of those with good and decent motives, balanced by a fair-minded acceptable-use policy, can thwart the secrecy element that currently shrouds the hidden world of teenage communication. Policies on technology can be proactive and, in so doing, could serve to mentor proper usage of this wonderful twenty-first-century technology. Training teenagers on proper usage of digital technologies, practicing that proper use, and removing its use from the shadows might begin to encourage the setting of healthy personal boundaries out in the open.

Off-Limits!

Teachers seeking to capitalize on the natural social environment of students do not have their students' best interest at heart. Rather, such a teacher is manipulating the student's hyperemotionality—which seems so very real to the teen. Unless caught early on, relationships can catch fire and then usually lead to a more physical or sexual relationship. The initial connection is a setup. So any relationally romantic talk between teachers and students must stop immediately. This is basic but it is another reason why teachers must remember a very simple command: students are off-limits to teachers.

Efficaciousness

In this student-centered world, teachers are realizing that injecting their lessons with their personal lives brings a sense of genuineness to their instruction. Students enjoy viewing their teacher as "real," and this is apparently as important for teachers as it is for their students. There is both a sense of efficacy and even vicariousness on behalf of the teachers, often indirectly connected to students. There is nothing inherently wrong with connecting with students.

Studies show that efficaciousness and connecting with students provide excellent points of departure for extended learning, bringing with it the possibility of raising test scores.[20] Some of the newest research literature posits that real education connects with students' emotions and can be accomplished through appropriate relationships established between teacher and students and through positive mentoring, all of which has significant impact on teens' brains.[21] Positive, healthy, professional relationships are so very important.

Seizing the moment in education is a teacher's duty. Shunning moments that compromise moral integrity, harm students, or diminish learning opportunities is also important. The education world has all of us at the center, and everything we do is in focus somewhere. The use of technology as an educational centerpiece will help in overall relationship development. However, teachers must remain accountable in the process of educating students—an accountability that extends to the uses of technology.

We must all strive for the appropriate and avoid the inappropriate. Technology is a wonderful tool for learning. The very thing that gives us freedom provides opportunity for license to others. So as to avoid the latter—and for the sake of the futures of our teenagers and children—we must all be on guard. On behalf of the former, may our passion and moral purpose lead us ever forward.

SUMMARY

Tools used by sexual predators are instruments that ease access to victims and potential victims. Today's sexual predators focus their attention on two key areas: (1) communication technologies and social media and (2) the general environment of their victims. Victims now know their abusers much more personally than in the past, which means interpersonal sexual abuse is on the rise.

Proximity and friendship are also used to the advantage of the sexual predator. Schools are not the only places where sexual predators like to hang out. Churches, camps, Boy Scouts, Girl Scouts, and anywhere trust can be gained are places predators seek to infiltrate. Friendship is the aim of most initial connections of predators, and proximity helps create the environment for friendship.

The arrests of teachers and coaches for crimes against students indicate that the crimes were not the result of mere impulses. Relationships that involve sex with a teenager do not somehow happen within the course of a few minutes. These things have often been set in motion long before the point of action, which is why the predator needs to know about the environment of the teenager.

Teachers charged for sex crimes with students are resorting to emotional and psychological illnesses as rationales. So we must consider whether we ought to bring up personal medical histories in the interview process before a teacher is hired.

Teaching students is not matchmaking, and it is not a process of discovering one's soul mate. Teachers and students have nothing romantically in common. Teachers are entrusted with great responsibility. Teachers have the responsibility to remain focused on the tasks at hand—the education and mentoring of young people.

Seven questions are essential for teachers, administrators, coaches, and parents in order to take a hard look at school culture and the risks involved in crossing moral boundaries with students: (1) Is a teenager ever to be considered a soul mate and sex partner for a teacher? (2) Is it all right for teachers to flirt with teenage students? (3) Should teachers allow students to contact them at home? (4) What are the risks should teachers text message socially, chat on the cell phone, or send photos to students off hours? (5) What happens if a teenager falsely accuses a teacher of a sexual relationship? (6) Should teachers "friend" any of their current students on social-media sites? (7) Is there anything on the Internet that could implicate a teacher in a sex scandal?

Today's world offers instant gratification. Working in a highly charged environment of teenage hormones and youthful unpredictability can take a toll on even the most seasoned of professionals.

DISCUSSION QUESTIONS

1. How have communication technologies, and the environments of teenagers, enhanced sexual predators' accessibility to today's teenagers?
2. What are your feelings about changes in states' laws that decriminalize sexual relationships between teachers and students at, or above, the state age of consent?
3. What are some of the causes and effects of teachers and students choosing to enter into inappropriate relationships?
4. Why do you think so many female teachers are having sexual relationships with their teenage students?

5. What are some moral lines that teachers or persons of authority should never compromise in the development of relationships with teenage students?
6. What signs exist that indicate a teacher is getting too close to a student?
7. What would happen if false accusations were made against a teacher, coach, administrator, or counselor? How would you handle allegations that a colleague had an apparently inappropriate relationship with a student? Would things change if the colleague were eventually arrested for a sex crime though maintaining all the while that nothing inappropriate had occurred?
8. How would you evaluate the risks and the benefits of communicating with students outside of school hours by text and by posts on social-media sites?
9. What are some practical lessons learned after reading about some of the controversial relationships in this chapter?
10. To what extent are communication technologies tools for learning for teenagers and teachers, both inside the classroom and outside of the school day?

NOTES

1. Joseph Menn, "Social Networks Scan for Sexual Predators with Uneven Results," Reuters, July 12, 2012, accessed July 15, 2012, www.reuters.com/article/2012/07/12/us-usa-internet-predators-idUSBRE86B05G20120712.

2. Brian Palmer, "How Many Kids Are Sexually Abused by Their Teachers? Probably Millions," Slate.com, February 8, 2012, accessed December 2012, www.slate.com/articles/news_and_politics/explainer/2012/02/is_sexual_abuse_in_schools_very_common_.html.

3. "Cells, Texting Give Secret Path to Kids," CNN Justice, January 11, 2008, accessed July 17, 2011, http://articles.cnn.com/2008-01-11/justice/teachers.charged_1_cell-phones-texting-counts-of-sexual-abuse?_s=PM:CRIME.

4. Bill O'Reilly, "Jessica's Law," accessed July 28, 2012, www.billoreilly.com/jessicaslaw.

5. USLegal.com, s.v. "Megan's Law," accessed August 2, 2012, http://definitions.uslegal.com/m/megans-law/.

6. Jennifer Preston, "Rules to Stop Pupil and Teacher from Getting Too Social," *New York Times*, December 17, 2011, accessed August 10, 2012, www.nytimes.com/2011/12/18/business/media/rules-to-limit-how-teachers-and-students-interact-online.html?_r=1.

7. "Sex Offender Registry Websites," Federal Bureau of Investigation, accessed July 23, 2012, www.fbi.gov/scams-safety/registry/registry.

8. "Louisiana Forces Sex Offenders to Reveal Their Status on Facebook," Fox News, June 21, 2012, accessed June 22, 2012, www.foxnews.com/politics/2012/06/21/louisiana-forces-sex-offenders-to-reveal-their-status-on-facebook/.

9. Cecilia Vega and Kevin Dolak, "California Teen Moves in with Teacher," ABC News, March 2, 2012, accessed March 18, 2012, http://abcnews.go.com/US/california-teen-moves-teacher/story?id=15830971.

10. Gene Byrd, "Teacher Leaves Family for Student: 41-Year-Old James Hooker's Girlfriend Is 18-Year-Old Jordan Powers," *The National Ledger*, March 2, 2012, accessed

March 20, 2012, www.nationalledger.com/lifestyle-home-family/teacher-leaves-family-for-student-154061.shtml.

11. Stephanie Mihalas et al., "Cultivating Caring Relationships between Teachers and Secondary Students with Emotional and Behavioral Disorders," *Remedial and Special Education*, Hammill Institute of Disabilities, July 2, 2008, 4, accessed June 10, 2012, www.sagepub.com/scarlettstudy/articles/Mihalas.pdf.

12. M. K. Demaray and C. K. Malecki, "The Relationship between Perceived Social Support and Maladjustment for Students at Risk," *Psychology in the Schools* 39 (2002): 305–16.

13. Matt Lauer, "Crossing the Line: An Interview with Debra LaFave," *Dateline NBC*, September 13, 2006, accessed December 24, 2011, www.msnbc.msn.com/id/14499056/ns/dateline_nbc/t/crossing-line/. See also Douglas Holmes, "Charges Dropped in Teacher Sex Case," November 22, 2002, accessed July 2, 2012, www.dmholmeslaw.com/appiesboard/viewtopic.php?f=2&t=2237.

14. Lauer, "Crossing the Line."

15. New York City Department of Education, "New York City Department of Education Social Media Guidelines," accessed June 17, 2012, http://schools.nyc.gov/NR/rdonlyres/BCF47CED-604B-4FDD-B752-DC2D81504478/0/
DOESocialMediaGuidelines2012
0430.pdf.

16. Laura Hibbard, "Timothy Moll, Former Pennsylvania Teacher, Accused of Exchanging Good Grades for Student's Nude Photos," *Huffington Post*, April 5, 2012, accessed April 7, 2012, www.huffingtonpost.com/2012/04/05/timothy-moll-former-teacher-accused-of-exchanging-good-grades-for-nude-photos_n_1407026.html.

17. Nikki Krize, "Substitute Teacher Accused of Inappropriate Behavior," WNEP.com, March 16, 2012, accessed April 4, 2012, http://wnep.com/2012/03/16/substitute-teacher-accused-of-inappropriate-behavior-4/.

18. Mike D'Onofrio, "High School Female Teacher from Montclair Arrested for Sex with Student," *Montclair Patch*, September 3, 2012, accessed September 3, 2012, http://montclair.patch.com/articles/high-school-female-teacher-from-montclair-arrested-for-sex-with-student. See also "Erica DePalo, Former 'Teacher of the Year,' Allegedly Had Sexual Relationship with Student," *Huffington Post*, September 3, 2012, accessed September 3, 2012, www.huffingtonpost.com/2012/09/03/erica-depalo-teacher_n_1852369.html.

19. "All the News That Fits," *Bakersfield Californian*, September 1, 2012, A12.

20. Robert Marzano, Debra J. Pickering, and Jane E. Pollock, *Classroom Instruction that Works* (Alexandria, Va.: Association for Supervision and Curriculum Development, 2001), 89–90. See also W. James Popham, *Classroom Assessment: What Teachers Need to Know*, 6th ed. (San Francisco: Pearson Publishers, 2011), 233, 243.

21. Eric Jensen, *Enriching the Brain* (San Francisco: Jossey-Bass/Wiley Publishers, 2006), 24, 31.

Index

About the Author

Ernest J. Zarra III currently teaches advanced-placement and college-prep United States government and economics to seniors at the highly state-decorated and top-ranked Centennial High School in the Kern High School District. The Kern High School District is the largest high school district in California, with over thirty-seven thousand students and eighteen comprehensive high schools.

Zarra has also served nearly thirteen years as an adjunct instructor of education at California State University–Bakersfield, where he teaches in the secondary-credential and graduate departments. He has over thirty-three years of educational experience at all levels, both public and private.

Reared in Bloomfield, New Jersey, Zarra and his wife moved to California, where they have been teaching for three decades. Together they have two adult children who reside in southern California. He loves to hike mountains, lift weights, and cook.

Zarra has five earned degrees and holds a PhD in teaching and learning theory from the University of Southern California, with cognates in psychology and technology. He is an author, national conference presenter, district professional-development leader, and member of several national honor societies. He is honored in several *Who's Who* publications. Zarra is available to speak at conferences, district professional-development sessions, and teacher-education institutions.